The Rules of
Screenwriting and
Why You Should
Break Them

D1239374

ALSO BY BILL MESCE, JR.

*Inside the Rise of HBO: A Personal History
of the Company That Transformed Television*
(McFarland, 2015)

*Overkill: The Rise and Fall of
Thriller Cinema* (McFarland, 2007)

The Rules of Screenwriting and Why You Should Break Them

BILL MESCE, JR.

McFarland & Company, Inc., Publishers
Jefferson, North Carolina

Box office and budget figures come from
Box Office Mojo: www.boxofficemojo.com.

ISBN (print) 978-1-4766-6850-5
ISBN (ebook) 978-1-4766-2771-7

Library of Congress Cataloguing-in-Publication Data

British Library cataloguing data are available

Front cover image of movie show in cinema and seats
© 2017 razihusin/iStock

Printed in the United States of America

*McFarland & Company, Inc., Publishers
Box 611, Jefferson, North Carolina 28640
www.mcfarlandpub.com*

To Walter and Ellen, Tom and Renee,
who taught me what I wish I'd known at the beginning.

Acknowledgments

First and foremost, I need to thank Dave Beazley and the gang at website Shore Scripts. The seed of this book began with a series of articles for Shore Scripts on the six screenwriting myths, and it's safe to say this book would not have happened without that kick-start.

It also goes without saying that I am profoundly grateful to all those talents who contributed their thoughts and insights to this book. They speak from a higher vantage and deeper experience than I, and give this work a weight and breadth I could not have attained on my own.

Among them I have to make a special mention to those who have had a tremendous impact on my work over the years, but on me personally as well, so thank you "Pops" Persky, and Bernie Dunlap.

Another thanks to my research assistants who have always been there for me on this book as well as past ones: Madeline and Steven D'Alessio, Carol and Ron Kochel, and Bill Maass.

And, of course, as always, thanks to my family, whose forbearance warrants canonization.

Contents

*"Movies are like wars.
The guy who becomes an expert
is the guy who doesn't get killed."*
—Robert Towne,
The Craft of the Screenwriter

Introduction

I may not be recalling all the details quite correctly, but as I remember it, the story goes like this:

The research people at 20th Century Fox advised the studio *not* to go ahead with a project called *The War of the Roses*, an adaptation by veteran television writer Michael J. Leeson of a novel by Warren Adler. In the view of Fox's research wizards, the piece was saddled with too many off-putting elements to work commercially. It was a story about an increasingly bitter and nasty divorce, with the two main characters growing ever less sympathetic, even, at one point, killing each other's pets (this would later be softened to only *appearing* to kill each other's pets). Worse, it had a downbeat ending with both characters dying. Oh, yeah, I almost forgot; it was supposed to be a comedy.

For whatever reason, Fox chose to go ahead with the project. This 1989 movie that shouldn't be made went on to a domestic gross of $83.7 million, bringing it to #12 for the year in box office. Estimating the number of admissions based on the average ticket price of the time, that would translate into a present-day box office of somewhere between $160–170 million; more than 2015's *Mad Max: Fury Road*, almost as much as *The Revenant*, and putting it in the top 20 domestic earners of the year.

The point of the story being that trying to analytically approach the process of movie-making to guarantee success (or at least minimize failure) is nothing new. Also not new: nobody knows how to do that; they just *think* they do. It's like that scene in *Moneyball* (2011, screenplay by Steven Zaillian and Aaron Sorkin) between Oakland A's coach Billy Beane (Brad Pitt) and one of his scouts: "You don't have a crystal ball.... I've sat at those kitchen tables with you and listened to you tell those parents,

'When I know, I know, and when it comes to your son, I know.' And you don't. You don't."

A couple of generations ago, the movie industry ran, more or less, on gut instinct. There were no audience research departments. Nor were there film schools, or seminars on filmmaking or screenwriting. Nor was there an Internet to look any of this stuff up.

There was no "typical" screenwriter in those days. At one time in the early 1930s, the ranks of Movietown screenwriters boasted talent from across the writing spectrum: journalism (like one-time reporters Ben Hecht, Charles MacArthur, Nunnally Johnson, Orson Welles' *Citizen Kane* [1940] co-writer Herman J. Mankiewicz), theater (i.e., George S. Kaufman, Maxwell Anderson, Robert E. Sherwood), and literature (William Faulkner, Dorothy Parker among others) (Kael, 12).

And they forged their screenwriting careers without the benefit of going to a Robert McKee seminar or picking up a book by Syd Field or Blake Snyder. (Illustrative curio: Faulkner worked on *To Have and Have Not* [1944] when McKee was just three years old. So there!)

As for trying to figure out how to make a good movie good, well, that was as mystifying a process then as it is now.

Consider *The Big Sleep* (1946). It's long been considered something of a *noir* classic, although it's often also been said the plot doesn't completely make sense. Because it doesn't.

There's a story I've heard about the writing of the screenplay.... Actually, I've heard a couple of versions, but the gist is that while William Faulkner and Leigh Brackett were trying to adapt Raymond Chandler's novel (or, depending on the version of the tale you come across, while director Howard Hawks was shooting the movie), the parties involved became aware that Chandler hadn't accounted for one of his story's murders; there was a killing for which there was no killer. Chandler is called/telegraphed/somehow contacted by the concerned parties, says he's going to re-read the book, then comes back to the production saying something along the lines of, "Hell if I know."

Although reviewers at the time shook their heads over a plot which didn't add up, that plot hole never bothered audiences (or, for that matter, the generations of Chandler fans who've read the novel); not the ones who saw it in theaters, and not the later generations of audiences who saw the movie re-run countless times on TV, or in revival houses, or—as I did—in film classes. Nor has it bothered subsequent generations of critics and film academics who consider it a *noir* classic.

Why does it work?

Hell if I know. It just does.

The movies—like TV, music, publishing, any of the mass media—have always wanted to find a way to bottle and reproduce success, even back during the so-called Golden Age of Hollywood. "Hey, Humphrey Bogart, Mary Astor, Sidney Greenstreet, directed by John Huston—they made magic in *The Maltese Falcon* (1941)! Let's put them all together again in *Across the Pacific* (1942)!" (Huston, 98).

Anybody here remember *Across the Pacific?* Case closed.

But the motive is understandable; these are expensive endeavors, especially these days. A full 22-episode season of a half-hour network sit-com can cost upwards of $40 to $50 million to produce; a one-hour drama, $120 million or better, and the first-year failure rate for new shows among the four major broadcast nets is somewhere around three out of four (Stelter). The average cost of a studio movie, including marketing, is easily over $100 million (with break-even calculated at two to three times cost), and most studio releases flop at the box office. Yeah, if you were a network programmer, or a television producer, or a studio production exec, with those kinds of stats, if someone said to you, "I know how you can make a predictable success," wouldn't you jump at it?

The go-to strategy for Hollywood has been to turn out movies and television shows that look like earlier hit movies and television shows.

And so *Friends* begets a string of clones about young, pretty people trading one-liners in diners (*Union Square*) and bookstores (*Ellen*) instead of *Friends'* coffee shop. It's also why, at this writing, there are over 40 television series in development based on hit movies (Ratledge, 93). It's why *Die Hard* (1988) begets *Die Hard* on a battleship (*Under Siege*, 1992), *Die Hard* on a plane (*Passenger 57*, 1992; *Air Force One*, 1997), *Die Hard* on a train (*Under Siege 2: Dark Territory*, 1995).

It's not just Hollywood. New Kids on the Block hits and thereafter comes Backstreet Boys, Boyz II Men, 98 Degrees, O-Town, et al. Publishing is littered with the next *Twilight*, the next *Harry Potter*, and any number of Y/A action-adventures set in some future dystopia/post-apocalypse wasteland (i.e., *The Hunger Games* begets *The Maze Runner* and *Divergent*).

Some of these make money, some of them don't, a few of them are good, but a lot of them aren't, and they're almost never as good or as successful as the original because, at least in part, they're not, well, you know: *original.* When it comes to movies, it's hard, if you've reached a certain age, to sit through 20 minutes of trailers at the multiplex and not develop an oppressive feeling of Jesus-I've-seen-this-a-thousand-time-before. And that's just during the coming attractions.

Hollywood—like these other entertainment platforms—is afraid of originality. Originality has no track record to indicate the likelihood of success. That makes originality a risk, and at a $100 million (or better) a pop, Hollywood hates risks, too. *Entertainment Weekly* reporter Benjamin Svetkey, in the 1996 article, "Who Killed the Hollywood Screenplay?" writes:

> The studios play-it-safe attitude has given rise to a new form of high-cost, supposedly low-risk authorship: writing by committee. Before most major commercial movies start shooting, their scripts now go through a development process during which every word is massaged to assure maximum audience accessibility [36].

Hollywood is also afraid of that magical, mystical element often a part of success; that Unknown Factor which turns *The Big Sleep* into a classic, that takes out-of-nowhere little indies like *The Crying Game* (1992) and turns them into box office smashes (#20 for the year), or—like *The Usual Suspects* (1995)—into evergreen cult faves.

Hollywood is afraid of these things because whatever combustion has to occur to unify elements of these movies into a success is wholly, frighteningly uncontrollable, horrifyingly unidentifiable, and, therefore, chillingly unpredictable. And more than anything else Hollywood hates, Hollywood *really* hates unpredictability (Biskind, *Down and Dirty...*, 477).

Writer/director Paul Schrader put his finger on it in a 1981 interview in which he contended studio decision-makers avoid projects in which success depends on all the right elements—the right cast, the right director, the right script—coming together in just the right way. Instead, Schrader said, studio execs work defensively, looking for a property still capable of decent box office even if it "is done in a very ordinary way by mediocre people." The studio exec relying on movie-making magic "will be out of a job" (Brady, 281).

But, as I said, it wasn't always like this. Harry Cohn, the man who created one of the major studios—Columbia Pictures (which still exists under the Sony Entertainment banner)—used to claim he could tell during a screening if a movie was going to fly with the public or not. He used to say if his rear end started squirming in boredom, the movie was a dud (which led Herman Mankiewicz to say, "Imagine, the world wired to Harry Cohn's ass!," a comment which promptly got him fired from Columbia) (Blottner, 7).

But, to some degree, Cohn was right. Well, not about his particular ass, but that the old studio moguls had only their instincts to go by.

So, how did we get from Harry Cohn's ass to "development teams" generating reams of notes calling for an Act One "turn" on page 21?

In James Goldman's play and movie, *Lion in Winter* (1968), Eleanor of Aquitaine, reflecting on how her relationship with her once beloved husband, King Henry II, has degenerated into round after round of back-biting wheeling, dealing, backstabbing, and even war, asks, "How, from where we began, did we get to this?"

To which Henry grimly replies, "One step at a time."

* * *

By the 1960s, most of the major movie studios were dying. They had, in fact, been dying for some time. Weekly movie attendance had peaked in 1944 at 84 million (this in a country with a population of around 130 million), but had been declining ever since. By 1971, even though the country's population had swelled to 220 million, only 16 million people were going to the movies each week (Finler, *Hollywood...*, 288).

That ongoing bleeding-out had made the studios desperate, and out of that desperation came a perfect storm of circumstances which would make the 1960s–1970s probably the most creative period in American commercial filmmaking (Muller, 9).

By that time, the venerable old gentlemen who had been running the major studios for decades—think Louis Mayer at MGM, Jack Warner at Warner Bros., Harry Cohn, etc.—had either retired, died, been sidelined or pushed out, opening the door for a new generation of production chiefs. They were younger, hipper, in tune with the young audience that had been a main box office driver since the end of World War II; guys like Paramount's Robert Evans, Warners' John Calley, Fox's Richard Zanuck (Biskind, *Easy Riders...*, 21).

By the 1960s, the studios were dealing with an audience not only young, but cued into the movie scene. They had grown up watching the classic oldies on TV, and movies had become a part of youth pop culture, the same way rock music had (Biskind, *Easy Riders...*, 17). They put up posters of Humphrey Bogart and the Marx Brothers and W.C. Fields and King Kong in their dorm rooms, and, at the same time, they were plugged into the work of a new generation of filmmakers; young bloods, people of their generation sharing their sensibilities and priorities, directors like Martin Scorsese, Brian De Palma, Francis Ford Coppola.

With their studios financially hemorrhaging, with theater attendance plummeting, the new production chiefs were willing to gamble on these film school brats, and on exciting directors from overseas (i.e., Roman Polanski, Peter Yates, Nicholas Roeg, John Schlesinger), along with a breed of director who had learned their craft during the early years of television (i.e., John Frankenheimer, Sidney Lumet, Sam Peckinpah), and veteran directors who, under the new regimes, could make the kind of movies they hadn't been able to make under the old moguls (i.e., Don Siegel, Robert Aldrich).

Young production chiefs greenlighting projects for young filmmakers aimed for a young, cinematically literate audience looking for movies relatable to the world they lived in; in terms of creative adventurousness, it was, according to the influential French film journal *Cahier du Cinema*, "the furious springtime of world cinema" (Fine, 120).

But as the saying goes, all good things must come to an end. Ironically, what brought the good times to an end was that all this furious creativity managed to stop the bleeding.

*   *   *

By 1971, the attendance slide had bottomed out and weekly numbers began climbing. Although—with the exception of occasional blips up or down—attendance as a percentage of population hasn't improved much over the last 25 to 30 years, movie-going has been more or less stable.

At the same time the movie business was becoming comparatively less volatile, there were enormous changes going on on the business side. The maverick executives like Calley, the true movie-lovers like Zanuck and Evans, were gone. By the late 1960s, nearly every major studio had become part of a much larger media conglomerate (Balio, 330): Universal had been absorbed by talent agency MCA, Gulf and Western Industries had gobbled up Paramount, the hodgepodge of companies comprising the Kinney Group took over Warners, United Artists became targeted by financial services conglomerate TransAmerica Corporation (Bach, 53).

(Look up any of these brand names and it becomes quickly evident the cycle of buy-ups, sell-offs, and mergers didn't stop then. With the advent of new exhibition platforms—starting with the launch of Home Box Office in 1972 and the beginning of the modern cable TV era, and up through home video, direct satellite service, the Internet and downloadable services like Netflix—media companies have seen the necessity of owning content producers and developing strategies to cross-pollinate their various content and exhibition arms. And that's why today it's NBC Universal, and Paramount is part of Viacom, 20th Century Fox part of News Corp., Columbia—which had been bought by Coca-Cola in 1982— wound up part of Sony Pictures Entertainment in 1989, the Kinney Group—rechristened Warner Communications—merged with Time Inc. to form Time Warner.)

With that change, executives came into place with a mandate of serving the larger organization (Bart, 5). Their job wasn't just to find potential movie hits, but movies which could provide a platform feeding the various arms of the corporate machine, franchises capable of spinning off everything from television cartoons to action figures (Svetkey, 36). Example: When Warner Bros. landed the rights to the *Harry Potter* novels, two years before the first title in the franchise hit movie screens, various Warner division heads were already mapping marketing and ancillary strategies *ten years out* (Fierman, 27).

The big studios found a model for this kind of dynamic in the success of two landmark blockbusters: *Jaws* (1975) and *Star Wars* (1977, later rechristened *Star Wars: Episode IV—A New Hope*).

Jaws was the first movie to break the $100 million barrier in first run earnings—the first blockbuster. The success of *Star Wars* demonstrated that *Jaws'* success was no fluke; that that kind of money-making was repeatable (in fact, *Star Wars* out-earned *Jaws* $193.5 million in rentals *v.* $129 million) (McDonnell, 46).

The success of *Star Wars* was compounded by the blockbuster box office of its sequel, *The Empire Strikes Back* (1980). Sequels were nothing new to Hollywood, but the traditional concept had been a cheap quickie riding on the popularity of the original with the modest goal of a box office tally amounting to—hopefully—40 percent of the first flick's earnings (Dempsey, 31). But Lucas, instead, spent *more* on *Empire*—$23 million versus $9.5 million—and earned $134.2 million in rentals for his trouble. He upped the ante again for the third film in the original trilogy, *Return of the Jedi* (1983), spending $32.5 million, and running up, in return, rentals of $168 million—over 90 percent of what the first film had earned (Finler, *Hollywood...*, 277–278; Biskind, *Easy Riders...*, 380).

Lucas proved the way to consistent big money wasn't to *exploit* a hit with a cheapie sequel, but to *invest* in the franchise, nurturing it, making each installment bigger and more impressive (although only occasionally better).

And Lucas gave the industry another lesson as well. The moviemaker had shrewdly retained the merchandising rights to the franchise, and wound up earning more from merchandising than he would from the movies themselves (Harmetz, 26). By the 20th anniversary of the original *Star Wars'* release, Lucas had banked over $3 billion in licensing fees (Biskind, *Easy Riders...*, 341).

All of which explains the major studios' obsession with a bowling alley–narrow range of genres (Knauer, 143). Currently, animated movies and sci fi/fantasy are the two most profitable genres in the Hollywood arse-nal and not just at the box office. Disney's animated flick *Frozen* may have done a whopping $1.3 billion in ticket sales, but even bigger money came from ancillary revenue: *$6 billion* (Stock, 21).

Which explains Warners' 10-year plan for *Harry Potter,* and the Mar-vel big screen "multiverse" of crisscrossing superhero franchises, and why Warners and DC Comics (both owned by Time Warner) are trying to launch their own "multiverse" of DC characters with a 10-movie plan (Breznican, 32), and why New Line was willing to pad out the *Lord of the Rings* franchise by stretching Tolkien's slimmest book—the prequel *The Hobbit*—into three movies, and James Cameron's announcement at the 2016 CinemaCon in Las Vegas that he'll be turning out no less than *four* sequels to his 2009 smash hit, *Avatar* (Kaufman, 13). It's why *Spider-Man* is looking at its second reboot since the original's 2002 release, and why Warners has tried to reboot *Superman* and *Batman* twice each. It's why, in 2015, Hollywood released 29 sequels and reboots (Schager, 92).

Blaming *Jaws* director Steven Spielberg and *Star Wars* writer/director George Lucas for driving the movie business away from the creatively ambitious and topically relevant films of the 1960s/1970s into an era of big budget, pre-fab clones and rebottlings is as simplistic and plain wrong as blaming Syd Field and Robert McKee for what's happened in screen-writing. The dominance of franchises featuring intergalactic swashbuck-ling and/or masked avengers in tights is not a cause, but a symptom.

The movie business serves demands; it doesn't shape them. The movie-going demographic changed from the cinema literate, socially engaged college-and-up audience of the 1960s/1970s to a younger (Y/A and up), less engaged audience growing ever more immersed in a multi-media universe of over-the-top escapism on cable, in videogames, and later, on the internet. They were mediums which, combined, cultivated a kind of ADHD-visual sensibility demanding fast-paced, highly kinetic, escapist entertainment (Irvine, 24).

And what development staffs saw in Syd Field and Bob McKee and in the other just-follow-the-recipe evangelists was a way to bottle that kind of entertainment.

What they bought into, however, was not a proven formula, but a belief system. Most of these how-to concepts are an exercise in reverse engineering, looking for commonalities in successful movies. What they miss is the difference between good and bad movies that share those com-monalities; they overlook, or miscalculate, or simply forget the Unknown Factor which terrifies any movie company executive.

As it happens, as I was working on this book, I was reading an essay in *The Missouri Review* by John Nelson: "I Saw What I Said I Saw: Witnesses to Birds and Crimes." Nelson points out parallels between misidentifications by bird watchers and those made by witnesses to crimes. "(Perception) can't be separated from the perceiver's mind-set," writes Nelson, and quotes Jonathan Miller's *The Body in Question:* "What the mind sees is not what there is, but what it supposes there might be" (47). "Expectation," says Nelson, "conditions perception; perception confirms expectation. The possibility of self-deception is inherent in perception..." (39).

Or, to put it more simply, Hollywood *wants* to see in these formulae guarantees of success, so it does, because that's more comforting than the truth which is that making movies has always been and always will be a crapshoot.

In his book *Adventures in the Screen Trade: A Personal View of Hollywood and Screenwriting,* two-time Oscar winner William Goldman memorably cut through all the b.s. about who knows what about the movie business by famously writing, "NOBODY KNOWS ANYTHING [the caps are his]. Not one person in the entire motion picture field *knows* for a certainty what's going to work. Every time out it's a guess..." (39).

To make his point, Goldman then goes on to detail some historic goofs, like Universal passing on *Star Wars,* Columbia passing on *E.T.: The Extra-Terrestrial* (1982), and how *Raiders of the Lost Ark* (1981) had been turned down by every major studio in Hollywood before it landed at Paramount, even though it was a collaboration between George Lucas and Steven Spielberg, two of the most successful moviemakers of the day (40–41).

Talent and inspiration can't be bottled, and talent and inspiration is what turns a by-the-numbers genre flick (think *The Green Lantern,* 2011) into something which incorporates familiar tropes into a reconfiguration different enough to feel fresh and invigorated (Christopher Nolan's rebooting of the *Batman* franchise).

The how-to concept won: it was understandable, it made a superficial kind of sense, and you didn't have to be a writer or even understand good writing to exercise it. The idea that one could mass-manufacture creative success was less an idea borne out by box office numbers than it was a belief system; a faith, if you will, and out of that faith came commandments.

We're going to look at six of those commandments. There's more depending on who you talk to, but, in my view, these are the biggies. We'll also be treated to some commentary from a few industry pros I know, and, for whatever enlightenment, edification, and cautionary lessons they may offer, I'm going to share some of my most enlightening, edifying, and cautionary experiences with you to give you some idea of how these supposed rules play out/don't play out in the field.

This is not a how-to-write-a-screenplay book. What I hope it is is a how-to-*think*-about writing a screenplay book. I'm not telling you to arbitrarily break the commandments any more than I'm telling you to arbitrarily follow them. As I'll say repeatedly throughout this book, these are all useful tools, but they're lousy laws. You may find that, as tools, they work perfectly fine, sometimes even better in unconventional combinations, and even better when you can twist, bend, and invert the ways they're typically used.

As a storyteller, your obligation isn't to rules; it's to tell a good story as well as you can and use any tool you can lay your hands on to do so.

*   *   *

Having said all that, I'm obligated to address the sad truth that often creative executives—particularly those at the junior level—have trained themselves to look for a given work's adherence to the commandments rather than its overall quality. A good script can get passed over not because it's not good, but because it doesn't follow the rules (yeah, I know it sounds crazy, but welcome to the movie business).

They believe in these rules. They *have* to for one, big, fat, overriding reason:

They're not writers.

A lot of low level development people and junior agents like to say, "I'm not a writer myself, but I know good writing."

They're half right; they're not writers. But they *don't* know good writing. The rules give them something simple and understandable by which they can measure a screenplay.

You have to know this. The rules are their *lingua franca*, it's how they'll talk to you about your work, and how you're going to have to talk to them. It's how you'll explain and defend and try to protect your work, because once you get creative and imaginative and start going where no recent hit has gone, they're going to get nervous and twitchy.

As producer and studio exec Peter Guber once said about the movie business, "The only rule is there are no rules ... and you break them at your own risk" (Couturie).

The Programmer:
Dave Baldwin

I interviewed Dave Baldwin in the early '00s when he was still the Executive Vice President of Program Planning for Home Box Office. We primarily concentrated on the evolution of the thriller genre. While this piece may have some years on it, I find the observations of Baldwin—one of the smartest guys I've ever known when it comes to the changing tectonics of film and television—still relevant to our discussion here.

Dave Baldwin began at Home Box Office, the world's largest pay–TV service, in 1978 in audience analysis. Before leaving HBO in 2009 (Baldwin joined Starz Entertainment as Executive Vice President of Program Planning in 2012), he'd been the company's long-serving Executive Vice President of Program Planning, overseeing the programming and scheduling for the company's 15 HBO and Cinemax channels, digital products for both services, and helped develop the HBO Go and Cinemax Go streaming services. After over a quarter-century watching developments in the movie industry and dealing with their impact on pay–TV, Baldwin has developed a sense of the difference between what's good and what will play, and how those differences have come about. Speaking less like a researcher (which is how Baldwin began his HBO career) than a cultural historian, Baldwin outlines the sea changes in the movie industry which began over a half-century ago and moved the business toward its present state.

The major studios, he explains, were in trouble in the 1950s. Their first reaction to the threat of television was "overblown, overhyped musical extravaganzas. Television couldn't outdo the big screen in terms of size, sound, and colors, so then came an age of grand, oversized, color musicals."

But the late 1940s and the 1950s were also the era of a growing *film noir* sensibility; a vein of adult thrillers reflecting post–World War II unease in the atomic age.

Come the 1960s, the first wave of postwar baby-boomers brought with them a crop of filmmakers coming into the movie business influenced less by Hollywood classicism than by European filmmakers and their more character-based work. They were not afraid to tackle subjects provocative and downbeat, and they found an audience willing to share the experience with them. "In the early 1970s, we were coming through a dark period," Baldwin says. "This was the time of Watergate, the Vietnam War, we had assassinations. That *noir* sense was in full bloom."

The work of that new generation of moviemakers began to dominate American movies in the late 1960s and into the 1970s, but even the tyros had to deal with certain economic realities; the kind which could force decisions to get involved with projects like *The Godfather: Part II* (1974). The success of Francis Ford Coppola's sequel to his 1972 original presaged an emphasis on sequels in the 1970s unequalled at any other time in Hollywood's previous history.

If originality suffered from the hunger to repeat a success by turning a hit film into a franchise, so, too, did it suffer from a migration of writing talent from the movie industry to television. Baldwin sees a parallel in that shift to one in the 1930s when many a playwright "escaped" from Broadway to write for the movies. It was a way, he explains, of getting around the physical constraints of writing for the stage. And, it was more lucrative.

By the 1970s, television had become an enormously profitable industry giving it the money to siphon off writing talent from the big screen. In the 1980s, cable television's growing development of original programming put it in the position of throwing money at writers as well. The biggest financial lure to the screenwriter of television over the movies, according to Baldwin, were the rewards over the long-term trumping those of the "one-shot deal" of writing a movie where the stars and directors received the larger pay-outs and profit participation.

And, on the creative side, the frustrations were not as great. A legendary despair of movie writers is that of having their work constantly rewritten by everyone from a parade of follow-up re-writers to stars with the clout to get their way creatively.

The situation now is that the kinds of character-driven, gritty, realistic thrillers which made their mark in the 1960s/1970s struggle today. "*L.A. Confidential* (1997), *Insomnia* (2002), *The Usual Suspects* (1995) shared a darkness that almost foredoomed them to niche audiences," assesses Baldwin. "Modern *noir* is a hard sell. A lot of moviegoers don't want to spend their night that way." Baldwin points out that, "More people saw *The Usual Suspects* on pay–TV than in theaters."

Which, he says, explains so many of the movies that do get made. "Big pictures like *Titanic* (1997) and the *Star Wars* films thrive on repeat viewers; young hotties out on a date." These moviegoers want their pictures *big*. "Audiences want a different experience from watching TV, which, with the onset of big-screen TVs, must be *very* different."

Compounding the incentive to produce these kinds of big-budget box office monsters is the carryover business their box office success generates in ancillary markets. "The kinds of movies that work well in theaters generally worked well for (HBO)," Baldwin reports. "Comedies, action, caper films..."

Therewith the plight of the producer: he/she needs to deliver a movie which excites the public, that is perceived as fresh, and needs to gets its money back; no mean feat with average budgets of over $60 million (excluding marketing which easily pushes average price tags over $100 million). Ancillary sales to home video, pay–TV, basic and broadcast TV, etc., are all predicated on theatrical box office return. Baldwin knows there are moviemakers who hope a picture which underperformed in theaters will find salvation in a place like HBO, but, in general, that's a myth. "It's rare that a film that failed at the box office does well on HBO."

However, big box office or no, gearing a film for an adolescent audience is no guarantee of aftermarket success, either, where audiences tend to be older than the moviegoers for many major summer releases. "*Scooby-Doo* [2002, $153.3 million domestic box office; #13 for the year]," Baldwin says wryly, "did *not* do strong numbers (on HBO)."

Baldwin also points out box office numbers are not necessarily a true gauge of a picture's performance. There is, he says, a category of "mid-range" films which don't satisfy an audience but can still be propelled to a $60–80 million box office "through strong push and hype." He gives, as an example, *A.I.: Artificial Intelligence* (2001), Steven Spielberg's take on a Stanley Kubrick project, which received mixed reviews and left many viewers cold. Yet, thanks to the attachment of Spielberg's and Kubrick's name to a big budget sci fi tale, and a strong campaign from Warner Bros., *A.I.* managed a respectable $80 million domestic and $235 million worldwide.

Still, for all the money spent to produce and promote movies to a young audience interested in "thrill rides," Baldwin sees the industry as still capable of producing "evergreens" each year: movies which will be both successful, and whose appeal will stand up over time. The hunger for producers to find the next franchise, the next "something new" always gives hope for a future classic. "Every time you get that new vision, that new take on a subject, you have the possibility of an evergreen," is Baldwin's optimistic view. There have been enough summer event pictures with supposedly sure-fire elements failing to send the message to producers that "you can't go back and just rip off somebody else's idea and expect a hit."

There is also, he says, a healthy art house scene for smaller movies, though even the indie circuit is feeling pressure from what happens at the major studio level. "There's a middle level of film not getting made, pictures that are not commercial enough for Hollywood, but are too hard for an indie to get their money back on. It's the kind of picture that depends on a good idea, combined with good talent doing it well.... Fewer films like *The Usual Suspects* are getting made." Even once they're made, the struggle is not over. "Getting the film on screens is a problem; that's an art in itself." And, even if you can get the film made and into theaters, "even films made for that circuit—character-driven dramas, romances, quiet comedies—have a problem pulling an audience. They don't have muscle in the culture."

(*An addendum from Baldwin: The indie scene is enjoying a major explosion with more major talent getting involved in the kind of meaty, substantive projects that the big studios rarely undertake these days.*)

Which leaves most movie screens—at least in the summer months—overwhelmed with movies which are "balls-out fantasy; a juiced-up version of reality." Thirty-forty-odd years ago, Baldwin says, most audiences wanted to believe—had the *need* to believe—in some sense of reality onscreen. "Now, that need doesn't exist. Filmmakers no longer need to deal in exposition; just capture a collective sense or feeling. A short-hand has developed, like a set of key tones, that illicit a response. It doesn't have to be believable; the audience gets the reference."

Myth #1:
The Screenwriting Guru

Researching this piece, I went into Amazon and did a search for "books on screenwriting." I came up with 8,800 results.

Eight thousand, eight hundred. Eight-eight-zero-zero.

Wow.

Ok, take into account this total includes writing books not having anything to do with screenwriting slipping through Amazon's search algorithm (i.e., books on writing fiction, research papers, etc.), and let's discount narrowly focused works like Michael Rogan's *How to Write a Script with Dialogue That Doesn't Suck,* and William C. Martell's *Creating Strong Protagonists.* And, of course, there's a certain amount of duplication, some titles showing up repeatedly in the results. So, to be extra-safe, let's be brutal and say Amazon's stock holds "only" 1000 distinct titles on how to write a screenplay.

One thousand.

Wow.

Eighty-eight hundred or a thousand; either way, that's a hell of a lot of books, each bragging it offers an essential, unique strategy for turning out a saleable, effective script for a movie.

Now let's apply some logic to that math. Logic says that if all these books are correct in their assumption of offering a perfectly valid if distinctive strategy for writing a movie, then you're wasting your $5–20 (the range of prices I found excluding prices for used books) because if one strategy is just as good as another and there's a thousand of them out there, you'd do just as well blundering ahead without a book with a good probability of stumbling across one of these strategies on your own.

Or maybe they're all only partly right; that each one offers something worthwhile, but no one book offers a solid whole. If that's the case, and you only buy one book, then it's like having only one piece of a thousand-piece puzzle, and you're wasting your money again.

Or maybe they're all just saying the same thing but in different ways. You could run up quite a tab trying to find the one speaking in a voice which connects with you, or they all work for you in which case one is just as good as another.

Or maybe only one is right and the odds of you bumping into it are, well, a thousand (or 8,800) to one.

Or maybe they're all full of crap.

Or any combination of the above.

I used to be very dismissive of these how-to books. Then, a few years ago, I was in a writer's online chat room and one of the other participants—a veteran television writer (if he should come across this, I apologize for not remembering his name)—said something I've never forgotten. He said *all* these books are useful: "Anything that helps you put your ass in the chair is good." So, if one of these thousand (or 8,800) titles helps put your ass in the chair, than good for you and may God smile on your efforts.

Beyond that, my own personal, *highly* subjective opinion—and it's nothing more than that: an opinion—is that however helpful any of these books may be, beyond their initial assist of getting your ass in the chair to bang out a first draft, they're dangerous crap. Taken a step beyond that, in terms of what you deal with on a practical, professional level, they're useless.

Keep this thought in mind:

Screenwriting books are like books about how to get rich doing anything, like how to make a jillion dollars flipping houses. If all you had to do was follow the book, there'd be a kazillion people who'd read the book and became jillionaires flipping houses. That doesn't happen. What *does* happen is you often find out the guy becoming a jillionaire isn't the guy buying the book, but the guy selling books on how to become a jillionaire.

*   *   *

It's said that those who can't "do" teach, but that's often said as something of an insult and it shouldn't be. Albert Einstein managed to give us a pretty good idea of how the universe works without ever flying off into it.

Still...

There are some fields where you do look for—hell, *demand*—a certain level of experience-based credibility...

"Look, Doctor, I want to talk to you about this brain tumor I have—"

"Well, I'm not really a doctor."

"What?"

"But I've read a lot of books about neurosurgery."

"You're not a—"

"And I've watched a lot of brain operations from the gallery."

"You *watched*—"

"Jeez, I've read so many books about this stuff I could practically *build* you a brain. So what say you hop up on the ol' operating table and we crack open the ol' coconut, eh?"

"Ya know, I'm actually ok with the blinding headaches. See ya."

I tend to lean that way on screenwriting books. I see one of these titles and the first thing I do is go to the Internet Movie Data Base to see what this or that guru has actually done. William Martell, for example, who's written a fair number of books on various aspects of screenwriting, has quite a substantial filmography. Call me prejudiced, but with that in mind I'd be inclined to listen to him. On the other hand, Syd Field, author of what I consider the first modern-day screenwriting bible—*Screenplay: The Foundations of Screenwriting*—and that other patron saint of the how-to-write-a-movie church, Robert McKee, are surprisingly light in the credit department. IMDB, providing IMDB is anywhere near accurate, lists only a handful of television credits for McKee and nothing since 1993.

That lack of practical experience doesn't axiomatically mean somebody doesn't know what they're talking about or doesn't have some useful advice to offer ... but it does give one pause before taking that counsel and thinking one now has the key to the screenwriting universe.

There's also a historical perspective to consider.

*   *   *

The first movies were made around the beginning of the last decade of the 19th Century. There isn't much to them: only a few minutes long, they consist of scenes of the everyday, and stuff you could best describe as skits. But by the early 1900s, the movies were telling full, if short, stories (think Edwin S. Porter's *The Great Train Robbery* [1903] or Georges Méliès' *A Trip to the Moon* [1902]). While they did require someone to sketch out a scenario, they didn't need all that much in the way of a script, at least not as we know scripts. By the next decade, however, films were getting longer, their storytelling more complex; the movies were growing up (*a la* D.W. Griffith's *The Birth of a Nation* [1915]). And both in length, complexity, and maturity, so did writing for movies.

Come the 1920s, movies, although still silent and in black and white, kinda/sorta/pretty much looked like movies the way we think of movies in their shape and function. Their pace may be slower than those made today, silent movie acting a bit hammy by contemporary standards, but with a little bit of patience and tolerance, you'll find these movies every bit as entertaining as what's on present-day screens, and, even more clearly, see the ancestral lineage between them and contemporary big screen fare.

Then comes the early sound era and with it the head-spinning, machine gun-paced wordplay of screwball comedies (*Bringing Up Baby*, 1938), a line of tough guy urban crime dramas from Warner Brothers (*Angels with Dirty Faces*, 1938), the launch of the indelible Universal monster stable (*Dracula* and *Frankenstein*, both 1931). It's the era of the granddaddy of all monster movies, *King Kong* (1933), as well as the movie which perennially tops the list of greatest movies ever made; Orson Welles' *Citizen Kane*.

Then we have World War II and a parade of war movies ranging from flag-waving propaganda like *Desperate Journey* (1942), to thrilling action fare like *Objective, Burma!* (1945), to the grim battlefield poetry of *The Story of G.I. Joe* (1945) and *A Walk in the Sun* (1945).

After the war, the major studios enter into a long, slow, painful decline. Desperate to bring a faltering audience back to the movies, it was an era marked by incredibly expensive epics like *The Ten Commandments* (1956) and *The Bridge on the River Kwai* (1957), as well as big-scale, splashy musicals (*Singing in the Rain*, 1952). The studios chased after the burgeoning youth market with a flood of sci fi (*The War of the Worlds*, 1953), while postwar cynicism and disillusionment fueled a line of *film noirs* as varied as the existential gloom of *Out of the Past* (1947) and the hysterical paranoia of *Kiss Me Deadly* (1955).

With the 1960s–1970s, the studios are desperate; attendance is at an all-time low, and some of the majors seem on the verge of collapsing. A new, young generation of production executives comes into the business willing to give a new, young generation of filmmakers a shot at telling stories Hollywood had never told before in ways they hadn't been told before. Out of that caldron of new blood and commercial desperation comes the greatest creative explosion mainstream commercial cinema has ever seen. No period in American moviemaking ever turned out so many unforgettable, confrontational, provocative, remarkable films (Thomson, 90). This is the era of *2001: A Space Odyssey* (1968), *The Wild Bunch* (1969), *Planet of the Apes* (1968), *The Graduate* (1967), *Deliverance* (1972), *The French Connection* (1971), *Midnight Cowboy* (1969), *Cool Hand Luke* (1967), *Patton* (1970), *Rosemary's Baby* (1968), *Apocalypse Now* (1979), *Last Tango in Paris* (1972), *Nashville* (1975), *Chinatown* (1974), *Annie Hall* (1977), *Butch Cassidy and the Sundance Kid* (1969), *Sweet Sweetback's Baadasssss*

Song (1971), *Who's Afraid of Virginia Woolf?* (1966), *The Hustler* (1961), *Star Wars, Night of the Living Dead* (1968), *They Shoot Horses Don't They?* (1969), *Fail-Safe* (1964), *The Sand Pebbles* (1966), *Taxi Driver* (1976), *Dirty Harry* (1971), *A Clockwork Orange* (1971), *Blazing Saddles* (1974), *Jeremiah Johnson,* (1972), *Straw Dogs* (1971), *Jaws, Network* (1976), *Carrie* (1976), *All the President's Men* (1976), *Point Blank* (1967), *Bullitt* (1968), *Mean Streets* (1973), *The Godfather Parts 1 & 2, M*A*S*H* (1970), *Spartacus* (1960), *Dr. Strangelove or: How I Learned to Stop Worrying and Love the Bomb* (1964), *One Flew Over the Cuckoo's Nest* (1975) ... and, as the saying goes, the list goes on.

And as far as I know, nearly all of these movies ("nearly" being my Cover My Ass word because I'd be willing to put a little money on the table betting it should read "all") were written without their writers buying a screenwriting book or going to a seminar or writer's workshop.

My, my; however did they manage that?

*　*　*

Moviemakers had barely gotten the hang of how to make full-length movies before some in the business were trying to figure out a system for writing them. According to the Amazon notes for a 2015 reprint of *How to Write Photoplays* (originally published in 1915), by John Emerson and Anita Loos (one of the A-list movie writers of her day), there were already four books on film writing by 1913.

I haven't been able to find out how many followed in the decades after Loos' book, but I'm willing to bet there can't be more than a handful, at least in comparison to the present day. Oh, there were *other* forms of books about screenwriting; collections of interviews with veteran screenwriters like William Froug's *The Screenwriter Looks at the Screenwriter,* and John Brady's *The Craft of the Screenwriter* (the latter includes an interview with William Goldman, the concepts of which Goldman would expand on for his own *Adventures in Hollywood,* first published in 1983 and which I still consider the best book about the trade for reasons I'll get to in a second).

Strictly speaking, these are not how-to books. These are writers with heavy track records sharing their experiences, sometimes touching on elements of craft, but just as often talking about surviving in a horrifically competitive, unforgiving, unfair business. They offer no templates, no step-by-step processes. Writes Goldman, "You must cut the narrative string yourself, with what you emotionally feel is sound. No one can tell you how or when. Because there are no rules" (121).

But whether they're sharing an experience or some practical bit of know-how, it's all solidly based in on-the-job experiences. The contributors to *The Screenwriter Looks at the Screenwriter*, for instance, count among their credits movies like *M*A*S*H*, *The Magnificent Seven* (1960), *The Great Escape* (1963), *Some Like It Hot* (1958), *In the Heat of the Night* (1966), *The Graduate*, *Aliens* (1986), *The Dirty Dozen* (1967). Goldman's filmography alone includes home runs like *Harper* (1966), *Marathon Man* (1976), and *The Princess Bride* (1987), as well as Oscars for *Butch Cassidy and the Sundance Kid* and *All the President's Men*, both critically acclaimed as well as huge box office hits (Academy Awards, reviewers' huzzahs, and popular success—my friends, that's the Hollywood hat trick; you should listen to this guy).

I feel that mindset began changing in the 1980s, first with the 1982 publication of Syd Field's *Screenplay: The Foundations of Screenwriting*, then with Robert McKee's STORY seminars, which he began offering in 1983 and which evolved into his 1997 screenplay-writing bible, *Story: Substance, Structure, Style and the Principles of Screenwriting*.

Somewhere in there, the dam breaks and, *voila*, a thousand (or 8,800) books on screenwriting pour forth. And screenwriting, as a creative form, dies.

✳   ✳   ✳

I said before that these how-to books were dangerous. Here's how:

You have writers reading these books and going to these seminars and workshops, etc., and you have lower level development executives doing likewise, and having drunk the Kool-Aid, they are now convinced this is how movies are built; how they *have* to be built. So, with everybody on both the creative and development end reading the same books and speaking to the same reference points, screenplays tend to all feel alike.

Am I just being a grumpy old fart about this? Maybe, but when was the last time you saw a romantic comedy, a superhero movie, a maverick cop movie—*any* mainstream commercial flick—that you didn't know how it was going to play out after you'd sat through just the first few minutes? Hell, after you'd seen the *trailer!* When was the last time a major release *surprised* you?

That's what I thought.

And why should they? Most studio movies follow a set template, a recipe requiring "turns" at prescribed points, right down to the page number. They follow almost ritualistic formulae (a pair of total opposites meet cute, on the surface can't stand each other, but come to know each other better blah blah blah). Not only do you know *what's* going to happen, but pretty much *when* it's going to happen, and that, my friends, is the complete antithesis of dramatic suspense. That's not a satisfying home-cooked meal; that's drive-thru fast food.

What most of these books tend to do is tell you how to go forward by locking your eyes on the rearview mirror. They look at past successes (and, as a general rule, focusing primarily on relatively recent and major mainstream releases), pull out commonalities, and, out of that, form generic constructs of structure, plotting and character (Field, for example, according to the Introduction of *Screenplay: The Foundations of Screenwriting*, seems to base a lot of his concepts on the thousands of screenplays he read while working for location service Cinemobile Systems) (1–2). In other words, they shave off whatever was distinctive about those movies to find what's universal (Goldman, *Adventures...*, 49). The difference between, say, *The Dark Knight* (2008), *Iron Man* (2008), and *Ant-Man* (2015) isn't in their construction which, stripped down to their spines, aren't substantially different from each other; it's in the flavor of the execution of each (respectively: rich, tangy, bland) which no book can teach you.

*   *   *

In early 2016, editor/fiction writer Lincoln Michel, in his essay "The One Underlying Substance of All Story Structure Models: Bullshit," attacked this idea of guru-rendered narrative reductivism in prose for the same reasons I have a problem with it in screenwriting:

> writers I've known who've clutched the formula writing advice books closest to their chest always produced the stalest, most uninteresting work. They focused far too much on how their work could be similar to other work rather than how it could be different" [Michel].

What the gurus—in prose and screenwriting—are essentially saying is if you step back far enough and squint, Melville's *Moby Dick* and Peter Benchley's *Jaws* are kinda/sorta the same, without acknowledging the *differences* that make Melville's book a timeless piece of Western literature, and Benchley's novel... Well, do even fans of the movie remember there was a book?

Look, strip any corpse down to its skeleton, and all skeletons tend to look alike. It's not the skeletons that make us each look and sound and act different from everyone else, but what *does* distinguish us is unrepeatable. The myth of these books is that if you ape the construction of a *Jaws* (the movie) or *Men in Black* (1997) or *Batman Begins* (2005) or *The Hangover* (2009), you'll end up with a screenplay that works just as well.

Uh, no.

That's like saying if you learn how to paint using a color-by-numbers kit, you're going to be the next Da Vinci.

Uh, no.

You wind up with writers—a generation of them—writing to a formula rather than writing to what may be a uniquely flavorful, distinctive vision in a uniquely flavorful, distinctive voice which is uniquely, distinctively theirs.

Ok, that's the dangerous part. Here's where these materials become totally useless.

If you're lucky enough (or, unlucky enough, depending on how horrific your experience is) to place your material with a production company, every rule, guideline, construct, step process, etc., goes out the window. What many (if not all) of these books and seminars neglect to tell you is that once your stuff is optioned or bought, it doesn't belong to you, and, thereafter, your job is simply to do what you're told. You're not a creative element in the project anymore; you're a short order cook, and like any other hired hand, you can get fired at any time, even from work you originated (Brady, 38).

Some years ago I was hired to be a "ghost" on a television movie script. The original writer, whose name had gotten the production deal placed, was laid up in the hospital and the production company needed a draft in one–two weeks to keep the project alive. I had to step in and bang something out based on the original writer's treatment. I was working with a terrific development guy which, on a short date, is what you hope to have. But then I was also getting notes from several people in the production company's New York office, and notes from their Los Angeles office, and notes from the network, and notes from the original writer. None of these people were conferring with each other so the notes were often in conflict. My job was to get *something* of what each party was throwing at me so they could be happy seeing it in the script. In circumstances like that, you're not trying to write a good script; you're happy if you can make it coherent.

Which connects to an interview I partly remember with a veteran screenwriter (can't remember who). He said something to the effect that no one tells the production designer what to do because nobody else can do what he does, and no one tells the composer what to do because they can't compose music, but *everybody* knows the alphabet so they all feel entitled to tell the screenwriter how to write.

This is why I find Goldman's *Adventures in the Screen Trade* still so potent and educational (as well as the Froug and Brady books). In the stories these screenwriters tell, the only thing they all have in common is that each project is an exercise in problem-solving. Each story is different and presents different problems. Each set of circumstances (different production companies, directors, stars, etc.) is different and presents different problems, all ultimately having a direct or indirect impact on the material, and few of which have anything to do with making the material stronger, more distinctive, more flavorful. I wouldn't be the first person to argue that the development process, at least when it relates to mainstream commercial filmmaking, seems designed to take unique material and beat the hell out of it until it resembles all the other crap out there (Svetkey, 36). You're not going to get any help from Bob McKee or Syd Field in that process. More useful is a family-sized bottle of Maalox.

Now, having said all this, I'll repeat the advice I offered in the Introduction (with a bad taste in my mouth) which is to read some of these how-to books and sit through a seminar or two not because they'll serve you well, but because it's the language of the day, and you need to be able to talk to and understand the people speaking in this tongue. Just don't make the mistake of thinking it has anything to do with truly good writing ... and keep the Maalox handy.

The Director: Rick King

(When I asked Rick King for some biographical details, he began with, "Besides being extremely handsome and full of personality...." In the interest of maintaining a 20-year friendship, I've decided to let that part go unchallenged. The rest of his track record, however, is unquestioned. Over the course of a 40-year career, King has directed 13 feature films—including Road Ends *[1997] which we worked on together and which I'll talk about later—and also including two works which took him to the Sundance Film Festival. Of the 13, he's written or co-written the scripts for two of them. The 1991 Keanu Reeves/Patrick Swayze starrer* Point Break *originated with King. He has also written and directed more than 20 documentaries for PBS as well as the National Geographic, Smithsonian, and Discovery cable channels. His critically-acclaimed 2005 documentary feature* Voices in Wartime *played in theaters across the country.)*

The Helping-You-Write-Your-Script industry is all pervasive in the film world. In fact, reading this paragraph, you are part of it. Of course, Robert McKee and Syd Field are the Alpha dogs in this pack. But it is a hierarchy that we accept. The more we accept it, the more godlike their pronouncements become. Their rules become not guidelines, but commandments. And there seem to be more than ten.

I think we can gain insight into this situation from an unlikely source: pets.

Cats and dogs are creatures we feed and love. But the owner is meant to be superior in the hierarchy and set the rules. The pet (no matter how precious) is ultimately there for our convenience. But sometimes this natural order breaks down. And the pet rules the owner.

We all know people who search convenience stores at midnight to find the proper, organic cat food. Or whose Saint Bernard is allowed to sit on your lap, even if you don't want him to. Or who let their dog snap at you as they point out that the animal is actually friendly. Or who construct their daily life around their cat's needs.

Well, Robert McKee and Syd Field are our pets. Our money and respect feeds them and provides a perverse sort of love. But we should act like their owners (forget calling yourself the cat's "mommy" or "daddy"), not their slaves.

Their rules are guidelines and nothing more. Personally, I recommend reading their stuff *after* you write your script. That way you express your personal individuality. There may be aspects that are cringe-worthy, but at least it is yours. Now you can look at what you have with a more objective perspective.

Do McKee, Field, and company have any helpful ideas for making the script more compelling? Within their rules and regulations, are there any insights? At the same time, keep things in perspective. No question many of these writing gurus know a lot about scripts. But they don't seem to have written many actual movies.

The truth is there are no rules. Movies work because they touch a chord (or many chords) within us. That's it.

If a two-hour, stable, wide-shot of a hummingbird plays in a movie theater and the audience emerges thrilled and excited, then the script was great. Even if it broke all the rules.

Think of McKee and Field as your 14-year-old Siamese cat wandering around the apartment. Or maybe the squirrel you feed peanuts to in the park. Or your lovable German Shepherd that can't seem to refrain from chasing cars and skateboarders.

Because that's what they are.
Now, please get them off my lap.

The First Cut Is the Deepest: *Blow Out*

Here's how stupid I was about the movie business when I got out of college in 1977. I tried to get screenwriting work by sending out resumes.

Resumes.

Like it was any other kind of job.

Even stupider; it wasn't like my college resume contained anything all that braggable. The University of South Carolina wasn't noted for its film program then (or now). I'd had a few semesters of film production working with Super 8 cameras, and exactly one class—just one—on screenwriting.

Pretty stupid.

William Price Fox taught my screenwriting class. Fox was a southern writer of some literary standing, and had worked in Hollywood for a time although he received credits on only two films: a for–TV adaptation of his short story collection *Southern Fried* (1970), and as a collaborator with Norman Lear on the screen story for *Cold Turkey* (1971).

My understanding was Fox hadn't been teaching at Carolina very long when I landed in his class, and it showed. He wasn't very good at it. In the two semesters I spent with him (I also took a creative writing class with him), I doubt he ever put together anything resembling a lesson plan.

But he did know good writing, and what it was that made it good, whether it was on the page or the screen. If you kept your ears open and sifted through the meandering conversations which took up our class time, you could learn a hell of a lot.

Example I never forgot:

The television movie *Collision Course: Truman vs. MacArthur* (1976, teleplay by Ernest Kinoy) had just aired, and there was a scene in the movie Fox pointed to as a perfect example of how *not* to write for the screen. Henry Fonda is playing the egocentric general, and he's with one of his underlings, and the other guy is saying something like, "Remember, General, when you did such-and-such a thing?"

"Yes, I remember."

"And so on and so forth?"

"Yes, I remember."

Or something like that.

"That's not this guy talking to MacArthur," Fox told us. "Of course, MacArthur remembers that stuff! He was there! That's the writer talking to *us!*" What made it bad writing was that in order for the writer to get some exposition across to the audience, he had the underling talk to MacArthur like the general was senile.

Fox also provided some practical advice should our fortunes ever take us to Hollywood, like, "Your I.Q. drops 15 percent the minute you step off the plane in L.A. Don't worry about it; there's nothing you can do about it." And he also tried to tamp down our idealism a bit: "You get out there thinking you're going to change the system. Six months later, forget the system; it's all you can do to keep your family together."

What he never offered among all these gems was any practical advice on how to get started.

Which is why there I was after graduation, 22, living back home with my mom and brother in a cramped four-room apartment in a two-family house, bringing home a little less than $100 a week working for a company out in the Jersey swamps updating television listings for crappy little free TV guides given away in supermarkets, and sending out resumes to movie studios and production companies. (FYI: I must've sent out a couple of dozen resumes and only received one response; some paranoid wanting to know how I'd gotten his contact information.)

So, let me clue you in: don't do that. If possible, don't do *any* of that!

Second bit of counsel: Hollywood doesn't hire writers. What it does is it buys screenplays.

Ok, that's grossly inaccurate and oversimplified. If you're Akiva Goldsman or Aaron Sorkin, yeah, there'll be a conversation like, "You know who would be good for this? Sorkin is great with dialogue, he does those fun walk-and-talk scenes, let's reach out to him."

But if you're not Akiva Goldsman or Aaron Sorkin, if you're some anonymous lower-tier writer, or—more relevant to our discussion—you're a newbie with no track record at all, it's not you they want; it's what you wrote, providing you've written something they think is either worth making, or that they think is a strong enough calling card to try you out on something they have in mind.

Bottom line: you need to have written something. And I hadn't. I'd done some crappy student films, not the kind of things that get you into a short film festival and catch some agent or production exec's eye, and I hadn't written a screenplay. And even if I had, how the hell was I supposed to get it in front of anybody? You don't just say, "Boy, I'd like to have Warner Bros. make my movie. I'll send it to them!" Might just as well send them your resume while you're at it.

At the time, I was subscribing to a couple of film magazines including *Take One*, a cheaper, shabbier-looking *Film Comment* wannabe. Along came an issue with this bearded, balding guy on the cover, reaching out toward the camera to make a film frame with his hands: Brian De Palma. *Take One* was partnering with De Palma on a screenplay contest, the winner of which would get a contract with the filmmaker.

Today, if you're an aspiring screenwriter, you can go online to look for screenwriting competitions and drown in the search results: BlueCat, Austin Film Festival, Story Pros, PAGE International Screenwriting Awards, the Nicholl Fellowship, CineStory, Scriptapalooza... The list goes on and on (and I'm not counting websites like InkTip and the International Screenwriters Association which offer the opportunity to showcase your stuff for window shopping producers).

But in those pre-internet days, this kind of thing was rare, and it wasn't easy to stumble across them (it would be a dozen years before I would find another screenwriting contest). And even the ones you see now don't offer what this one was offering.

Today, a lot of them offer some money, maybe meetings with producers and agents, feedback, freebies to a film festival, etc. This one was offering a nice paycheck and a contract to write a movie for a hotshot, honest-to-God, major movie director.

De Palma was a rising star from among that generation of film school brats who'd come out of the top-of-the-line film schools like NYU and USC and had started filtering into the movie business in the 1960s/1970s; directors like Coppola, Scorsese, Lucas. And at that particular moment, De Palma was on a hot streak and getting hotter.

After some under-the-radar indie films, he'd started generating some buzz with the thriller *Sisters* (1973), then came the culty rock musical *Phantom of the Paradise* (1974), then he'd gotten buzzier with another thriller, *Obsession* (1976), and finally had a commercial breakout with the screen adaptation of Stephen King's first novel, *Carrie* (1976), following it up with another supernatural thriller, *The Fury* (1978). He was just coming off working on a return to the indie scene with *Home Movies* (which wouldn't be released until 1980) and was now looking to give a wannabe a break.

De Palma was a self-admitted "disciple of Hitchcock," and, if you liked him, his thrillers were homages to the Master of Suspense. If you didn't like him, they were empty knock-offs (Chute, 68). Either way, his biggest successes had been with oddball, bloody, (some would argue) over-the-top thrillers, and now he was making noise about turning to work a bit more real-world connected (69). That seemed to be where he was trying to go with the *Take One* contest.

De Palma had provided the magazine with a scene-by-scene outline of a project entitled "Personal Effects," a political thriller set in Canada. Each entrant was to select two scenes, script them out, the judges would pick the best of the two for each entrant, and, out of those, select five finalists. The finalists would then complete a full draft and the winner would get a contract with De Palma and a payday.

The story of "Personal Effects" ran like this:

Jack does sound effects for cheapie exploitation flicks. One night while he's out in the boonies recording natural sounds, he witnesses a car go off a bridge. He dives into the water, the guy in the car is dead, but there's a young girl whom Jack manages to save. At the hospital, he learns the dead guy was some big shot political figure, and, for the sake of the dead guy's family, Jack is advised to keep the business about the girl—who is not the decedent's wife—to himself. But then, after pictures of the accident surface in the press, Jack begins to suspect the accident was no accident, that maybe this had been a set-up. Turns out the girl—Sally—regularly worked with a cameraman—Manny—on blackmail cases, seducing married guys while Manny covertly took pictures. Jack gets Sally to help him figure out what the hell's going on, she manages to steal the film from Manny, and Jack tries to put it together with his recording of the incident as evidence of a set-up.

Meanwhile, a maverick agent working for a largely off-screen conspiracy has tagged Sally as a threat to whatever's been going on, and has been strangling girls who resemble Sally to get people thinking there's a serial killer on the loose. Jack's evidence gets stolen, Sally gets lured into a meeting with the killer which Jack tries to monitor electronically, the meet goes bad, Sally is murdered like the other girls, and an emotionally burned-out Jack uses his recording of her death screams in another cheesy slasher flick.

The story plugged into a strain of political conspiracy paranoia running heavily through the zeitgeist of the day. This was the late 1970s; the country was still trying to recover from the tragedy—and lies—of Vietnam, Watergate, the Church Committee's revelations of CIA hanky-panky. Out of that sense of suspicion and betrayal and powerlessness in the face of dark goings-on within the circles of power had come movies like *Executive Action* (1973), *The Parallax View* (1974), *The Conversation* (1974), *Three Days of the Condor* (1975), *Marathon Man,* and *All the President's Men.*

Problem for me was I wasn't a De Palma fan. I was one of those people who didn't think his flicks were Hitchcock homages, but Hitchcock knock-offs. I also thought he was a filmmaker more interested in eye candy than telling a good story.

De Palma described himself, in a 1984 interview, as "a visual stylist, a *visual stylist"* [his emphasis], more interested in the visual opportunities a piece promised than storytelling (Palley, 15). Film critic Gavin Smith gave, I thought, an on-point description of the De Palma style in a review of the director's 2002 neo-*noir, Femme Fatale,* ironically praising him for the very same stylistic tics cited by his detractors: "(De Palma) delights in taking liberties with suspension of disbelief in sequences of absurd, impossibly escalating jeopardy ... logic and believability aren't important ... (his movies are) adventures in cinematic form..." (28).

I also wasn't too comfortable with how the kick-off event in the story—the accident—echoed the true-life Chappaquiddick incident in 1969 which almost derailed the political career of Ted Kennedy and forever destroyed his presidential ambitions. I didn't like the idea of a knock at my door and some guy in a suit standing there handing me the blue-covered paperwork of a lawsuit courtesy of a Kennedy attorney.

So, on the one hand: not a fan, and creepy-crawly feel about the topic.

But, on the other: Living with mom, making less than $100 a week, entry into the circle of Hollywood pros with money in my pocket on the arm of a hot director.

Kind of hard not to see which way the see-saw was going to tip.

I picked my two scenes, wrote the hell out of them, sent them in. I don't remember how much time went by; in those situations it always feels like forever. Then I received a notification that I was one of the three finalists (what happened to five finalists? We'll come back to that). I now had to sit down and do something I'd never done before: write a full-length screenplay.

The first thing I did was change the title from "Personal Effects" to "I.P.S." standing for "inches per second"—the rate at which the speed of magnetic tape passing through old reel-to-reel recorders was measured. I thought my title was cooler, but, frankly, it was a pointless, stupid change, the kind of thing that can bring a reaction like, "You even changed my title?" I should've left that alone.

Bigger change: ditching the Canadian setting for New Jersey. In retrospect, I'm pretty sure the Canadian setting had less to do with De Palma's interest in politics north of the 49th parallel than something having to do with film financing. My reason for moving it was simple; I didn't know anything about Canadian politics, about Canadian geography, about Canadians, about Canada. I felt I could do a better job setting the story where I knew the ground and could take advantage of settings familiar to me.

I've since become a big believer in this. Whether it's prose or a screenplay, I try to set pieces where I've walked the ground. That's not always possible or even practical, but when I do, the advantage of being able to use unique and not overly familiar and trite settings can add a flavor to a piece that can't be accomplished purely in the text. Would *The French Connection* have been *The French Connection* if it had been set somewhere other than a New York cinematographer Owen Roizman brought to life in all its gritty glory? Same thing for *Midnight Cowboy* and *Mean Streets* (1973). Would *Bullitt* or *Dirty Harry* have worked as well if they hadn't been shot in San Francisco?

I thought De Palma might appreciate this since it was a tenet of Hitchcock himself. In a 1969 interview, the Master discussed "a particular approach I have to settings. I'm a great believer (that) if you have a setting, it should be dramatized, and be indigenous to the whole picture, not just a background" (Higham, 98). You can see it at work in the way Hitchcock used Mt. Rushmore and in the classic crop duster scene in *North by Northwest* (1959), or the way he used the small California town of Santa Rosa as the setting for one of my (and Hitchcock's) favorite Hitchcocks, *Shadow of a Doubt* (1943) (Humphries, 76).

In that same Hitchcockian frame of mind, and feeling I had a read on the kind of material De Palma would connect with—something where he could find opportunities to exercise his visual élan—I came up with a visual plan for the movie. I gave each of the four major characters—Jack, Sally, Manny, and the killer—a visual identity matching their character.

Jack I had as a burnout, socially disaffected, somebody who had retreated from the world and buried himself in his work. I slid in suggestions that something traumatic must've happened to him during the storm-tossed years of the late 1960s/early 1970s, implications someone close to him had died back then, but I liked the idea of it not being too specific; it seemed more haunting that way. I had him living in a converted storefront on a back road, the interior barely furnished but cluttered with recording equipment.

Sally was immature, a young woman with no particular skills, relying on her only tool—her sexuality—but who was, in many ways, still an innocent. Sally's small apartment was cluttered with stuffed animals and dolls, big girly pillows, and the like.

Manny I made a Latino; an ostracized outsider (a bit of racism sadly credible in the late 1970s). Like Jack, he didn't have much going for him either, and his place was cluttered with photographic equipment.

I wanted the killer to be an outsider, too. From De Palma's original Canadian setting I got the idea of the killer being French Canadian, only unlike Jack and Manny, he wasn't ostracized but observing from a remove, an alien who stood above the goings-on, a sociopathic commentator who played with assassination as if it was a game, and with the players like they were game pieces. His place, then, was a playground, a loft cluttered with games and toys.

I submitted my draft, and waited. And waited. And waited. During the wait, *Take One* folded which meant there'd be no public platform for the announcement of the results. I'm a little embarrassed to admit I'd been hoping to be trucking that issue around if I'd won; "Oh, I didn't tell you about this little contest? I just happen to have a copy of the magazine with me, you can read all about it. And I insist that you do."

I remember it was warm—spring or maybe summer—I was coming home from my job out in the swamps, had just parked my car when my mother stuck her head out the front door and yelled across the front yard, "You just missed him!"

"Him" was a phone call from The Man himself, De Palma, telling me I'd won.

There is nothing like a First Time. First car, first girlfriend (or boyfriend), first job, whatever. And when the first is the first of something like this?

For a brief moment, you see all your fantasies coming true. I was going to get a gig on a major motion picture. I was younger than Orson Welles when he'd done *Citizen Kane*, younger than Steven Spielberg when he'd gotten *Jaws*. Ok, I wasn't a director and this wasn't *Citizen Kane*, but I was still buzzing, still imagining talk show interviews (not yet knowing how disregarded screenwriters are, but I'll get to that).

But here's the biggie, at least it was for me. There are people who get into this kind of work with a huge, unshakeable ego. They have absolutely no doubts about their ability, even when there's a universal consensus their work sucks (their rationale being, "People just don't *get* me!" as if they're ahead of some cultural curve instead of just being bad at writing). Doesn't matter to them; they *know* they can do this.

I don't have that. I can talk a good game, but there's often—and still— a niggling doubt about whether I really know what I'm doing, whether I should be doing this or studying accounting instead. At least when it came to screenwriting, hearing I'd won put that particular demon to rest (for the moment; in my case, this happens to be a resilient demon).

Soon after, I received a letter from De Palma with my contract, and not long after I signed the paperwork and returned it, I got my check. I wrote to him asking, what was the next step? I knew there'd be rewrites, that was a given, I'd read enough about how the business worked to know that, and I couldn't wait to be working with him.

No answer.

I wrote a few more times.

No answer.

I suspected I might be bumped, and I understood that, too, but wondered if there'd be a novelization of the movie (back when people used to read for fun, novelizations of presumed big releases were common, and since I was angling to get published as much as produced, this seemed a way into print). So I wrote another letter.

No answer.

And then, finally, an answer: a curt, two–three sentence letter saying Mr. De Palma had no further need of my services.

I didn't know if this meant he'd pulled the plug on the project, or had just pulled the plug on me, but in either case, it meant as far as I was concerned it was over.

But then, not quite.

* * *

The episode was not without its consolations. My paycheck was enough to pay off an uncle who'd loaned me money to buy my first car, and helped bankroll my move out of my mom's place into my first apartment (a basement studio in Weehawken). And, it helped keep me fed because by 1980 I had a job in New York for what was then Elsevier-Dutton, a midsize New York book publisher (it's now E.P. Dutton, an imprint within the Penguin/Random House empire of imprints), and even though it was better money than I'd been making out in the swamps, it was still little more than subsistence pay.

One of the reasons I was happy to be at Dutton was I thought being inside a publishing house might help me get my own work published. I hadn't yet heard the old canard that everybody in publishing has a novel in their desk. I did soon learn, however, that that wasn't quite true; not everybody had a novel in their desk. But a *lot* of them did, and they'd been there a good deal longer than me and it hadn't helped them a damn in getting published.

In the company's library I came across a booklet simply titled "The Author-Publisher Handbook." It was a 95-page primer for the new author on the mechanics of the publishing business: how to submit, what happened to books after they'd been picked up, how to go about getting an agent, etc.

On this last point, a New York agent had written the chapter on agents and had included his name and address. I figured he wouldn't do that unless he was trawling for clients, so I wrote to him, told him about what had happened with "Personal Effects" and that I had a fiction manuscript I'd like to show him. He had me submit it, then called me in for a visit.

On the chance he's still alive and might see this and might not agree with my take on our relationship, let's call him something other than his real name. Let's call him Bombastic Bushkin (reference to an old Johnny Carson joke; kids, look him up).

Bushkin's office wasn't far from Dutton, so he had me meet with him one evening after work. The building didn't look like much on the outside; a three-story pre-war walk-up over a corner store, but Bushkin had turned his floor into a rather impressive suite of offices. His particular office, which looked out over the Avenue of the Americas, was set up not to look like an office: hardwood floors, arty bric-a-brac hanging on fashionably bare brick walls, Persian rug, Chinese-styled stone dragons guarding a cushy settee. Bushkin sat behind a small, almost petite desk in a corner. He was maybe in his early thirties, tanned, fit, shirtless, sock-and-shoeless, and munching on a bunch of grapes: "I'm trying to eat healthy these days."

We'll come back to Bushkin in a later chapter, but he has a relevant role here and also illustrates something about the reliability of agents.

I brought up "Personal Effects" saying I wasn't sure what had happened. For all I knew, the project was going forward; just without me.

"I had lunch a few days ago with somebody who works for De Palma," Bushkin said. "I asked him about it. He says they're not making the movie."

Sigh.

The summer I'd moved to Weehawken was the same summer De Palma's *Dressed to Kill* (1980) was released, maybe just a few weeks after my meeting with Bushkin. Even though I still wasn't a De Palma fan, I went to see it, curious, thinking maybe this was the movie he'd shot instead of "Personal Effects." As I passed through the lobby of the theater, there was a stand for a small, free movie magazine (the title escapes me). I had a while before the movie started, so I picked up a copy, and thumbed through it in my seat while waiting for the lights to go down.

There was an interview with cinematographer Vilmos Zsigmond in which he talked about having recently completed shooting a film in Philadelphia for Brian De Palma. It was about a guy who did sound effects for seedy low-budget movies, and he witnesses a car accident involving a political figure...

I could feel a sense of heat creeping up my neck into my face. The more I read... Yep, you know it: same story as "Personal Effects," only now it was called *Blow Out*, and, according to the story, it was written by Brian De Palma. And *only* Brian De Palma.

Part of me immediately thought I'd been screwed, while some small, reasonable part of me told me to hold off making a judgment. The story Zsigmond described sounded a lot like "Personal Effects," and it gave De Palma sole screenwriting credit, but in those days before there was an internet to poke around and see what any other source was saying, I figured I couldn't be sure until *Blow Out* came out.

July 1981, and you can bet your ass I was at the multiplex for *Blow Out*'s opening weekend.

Lights down, projector on, credits roll, up comes "Screenplay by Brian De Palma." Me sitting there going, "Oh, yeah? We'll see."

Was it "Personal Effects"?

Well yes ... and no.

Did I get screwed?

Not really.

The story was pretty much the same, but then it had been De Palma's story to begin with. It was now reset in Philadelphia probably for the same reasons it had originally been set in Canada; something to do with financing, tax breaks, that kind of thing. Jack (John Travolta) didn't have the same sense of disaffection I'd given him, but was now a guy who'd used to be a techie for the cops and had been responsible for an undercover agent's death when a wire he'd rigged on the agent shorted out and blew the agent's cover. Sally was played with a Betty Boop voice by De Palma's wife at the time, Nancy Allen. Instead of the outsider Latino, Manny was now a big-gutted slob played by Dennis Franz in a stained T-shirt, and my French Canadian commentator was now John Lithgow as a renegade agent speaking in that movie assassin lingo where killers say "terminate" and use a lot of other multisyllable words to not say what they're saying. And, as for that visual plan of mine: out the window. The usually high-style De Palma went with what was, for him, a more natural look.

There wasn't much left of my screenplay: a line here or there, an image or two. I'd had one of the stranglings take place lit only by the fireworks of an Italian street festival; De Palma has Sally murdered under the lights of fireworks over a political parade. The only thing close to resembling a whole scene of mine is a confrontation between Sally and Manny where she tries to get his film of the accident from him. If you add it all up, even with some generous interpretation, it probably doesn't come to more than five minutes, if that, out of the movie's 107.

I still felt burned, and for years I remained ticked off at De Palma. The goal of the contest had been to give an aspiring screenwriter a break, and if he was only going to keep a few shreds of my material, "Hey, Bri, give the kid a break, throw him a bone, give him some kind of screen credit, like an 'Additional Material by'" (me not knowing the Writers Guild had done away with that credit).

But the fact is that even under the standards of the WGA, De Palma had not kept enough of my material for me to warrant a screen credit. And as for throwing me some kind of bone? Welcome to Hollywood, kid.

Here's what you need to know. It's the screen credit that matters. The money's nice, but a screen credit is the currency of the realm. When you're starting out, that's what you want: your name on a movie that actually gets made. Your name on a movie that actually gets made and actually makes money is even better, but your name up there at all is what the next guy weighs when considering whether or not to hire you.

As for *Blow Out*, the movie was reviewed quite well (some think it's among De Palma's best, and I've heard Travolta say it's one of his personal favorites), but it cost $9 million to make, another $9 million to market, and its box office plateaued at $13.7 million. That's the kind of math typically defining what, in Hollywood parlance, is referred to as a flop. One theory for the film's failure I remember hearing was that De Palma's usual fans were disappointed by the movie's (comparatively) real-world grounding, and the viewers who might've liked it didn't go because they suspected it would be another bloody De Palma Hitchcock clone. The movie fell into the gap in between.

What do I think?

Does it matter?

If you cruise around on the internet, some places where the movie pops up do have my name listed either as a co-writer (not accurate) or an uncredited writer. I guess that's something. And I did get paid well, so while I can still be unhappy things didn't break my way, I really have no grounds to complain and have to—if begrudgingly—give Brian De Palma credit for giving me my professional start.

But don't go away; there's more.

* * *

Sometime after *Blow Out* was released, I received a letter from one of the other two finalists; the Third Place winner. Seems him and Mr. Second Place were considering suing De Palma.

It was their interpretation of the contest that in doing a full draft they were entitled to what the winner had gotten. It didn't matter the movie had died; like me, they saw this as a once-in-a-lifetime shot and felt they'd been screwed out of it. They felt he'd taken material from their scripts and incorporated it into *Blow Out*. Third Place wanted me to be a part of the suit.

It was an awkward position for me. It would be the height of ingratitude to say, "Well, Mr. De Palma, thank you for this opportunity and this very nice little pile of money, but now I'm going to help these guys beat the crap out of you in court." But I also didn't want to be one of those I-got-mine-to-hell-with-you types if these guys had a legitimate beef.

I read the contest rules and contract over a few dozen times and couldn't see in them what these two guys said they saw. I asked to see their scripts, and I shared mine with them.

Mr. Third Place had the weakest screenplay, so weak, in fact, I was surprised it had made the top three. It was no more than a filling-in of De Palma's outline, adding almost nothing in terms of plot or character, and filled with stilted dialogue.

Mr. Second Place, on the other hand, well, frankly, I was surprised he hadn't won. It was a beautifully written script and had only taken De Palma's inciting action—the accident—before going off on an entirely original path. The only reason I could think this guy hadn't won was because he'd departed so far from De Palma's story.

But I didn't see any incidences of theft.

We had all exchanged phone numbers and I called Mr. Second Place to get his take on this. In that conversation, I got the feeling he was more or less in the same boat as I was; he didn't quite buy Mr. Third Place had a case, but felt he'd be a bit of a schmuck if he was unsupportive. Neither of us thought this would come to anything.

I told Third Place I'd split the difference; I wouldn't be party to the suit because I had no grounds, but I'd answer any interrogatories frankly and honestly. He seemed satisfied with that, but then the whole affair seemed to evaporate. After that initial flurry of letters and calls, I never heard anything more about the suit.

Some of you might wonder why anybody would fight so hard to be associated with a box office loser. This goes back to what I said about screen credits being the currency of the realm. It's better to have your name associated with a produced flop than to have it attached to nothing.

* * *

Back in the days when I was still miffed at De Palma, I'd written to some entertainment magazine (can't remember which) about the whole affair, thinking I had this juicy expose to hand them, and they sent a guy to interview me. He gave me my first practical lesson in the position screenwriters hold in the movie business.

"The way you were treated is pretty typical."

Here's another thing you need to know: with some exceptions, and depending on the character of the people you deal with, by and large screenwriters are valued about as much as the tissues in a box of Kleenex, and may be used and discarded similarly.

Take *The Flintstones* (1994), a live-action version of the 1960s animated television series. According to various sources, anywhere from 32 to over 50 screenwriters worked on the project off and on over the several years it was in development. Only three got an on-screen credit, and the critical consensus is that all that cumulative talent produced was a brontosaurus-sized turd. *The Flintstones* may be an extreme case, but it's hardly a rarity (although I've heard more than three dozen writers were involved in screwing up *Catwoman* [2004]). It took seven writers to turn out the forgettable Arnold Schwarzenegger actioner *Eraser* (1996), and also seven to hammer together the hyperkinetic, nonsensical Michael Bay pyro-fest *The Rock* (1996) (Svetkey, 37). In his book, *The Gross: The Hits, The Flops—The Summer that Ate Hollywood,* one-time studio exec and *Variety* editor Peter Bart details the screenwriting process behind Michael Bay's *Armageddon* (1998) in which a procession of screenwriters were brought into the project sometimes to do something as specific as develop a particular scene or punch up dialogue for a given actor (88–89).

Even if I had been a veteran pro at the time I worked for De Palma, there's a reasonable possibility the scenario would've played out the same way; me being told my services were no longer needed, here's your check, and don't let the door hit you in the ass on the way out.

"Your first movie," says veteran screenwriter Robert Towne, "is terribly traumatic" (Brady, 398). I do wonder what's worse: the first time when you don't know what you're in for, or the times thereafter when you *do* know what you're in for.

*   *   *

There's a little coda to this story. A couple of years later, I was in New York City's Chinatown one night, going out to dinner with some friends, when I bumped into Sam Irvin, Jr. This is incredible it's-a-small-world stuff; Irvin (now a filmmaker himself) had been the grad assistant for my first film professor back in Carolina. Flukier still: as we chatted, he congratulated me on the De Palma win and that's when I learned he'd been working for the director at the time of the contest, and had actually been one of the people stuck with having to read the screenplays which had been submitted.

"Hey," I said, "there's something I always wondered about. When *Take One* first announced the contest, they said there was going to be five finalists, but you guys only picked three. What happened?"

Irvin smiled. "We couldn't find five good enough to be finalists. We had to stretch to find *three*."

The Producer: Gerald W. Abrams

(Abrams' four-decade career as a producer of films and miniseries for television includes Houdini, *the top-rated cable miniseries of 2014; Emmy-nominated Holocaust drama* Out of the Ashes *[2003]; true crime thriller* 44 Minutes: The North Hollywood Shoot-Out *[2003]; another true-life-inspired thriller in the Emmy-nominated* Family of Spies *[1990]; and* Nuremburg *[2000], nominated for four Emmys and one of the highest-rated miniseries made for cable.)*

Essentially a good script has to start with a good story and good characters. You don't have to read more than four or five pages of any script to sense if you're in the hands of a good writer. Whether it's the attention to detail or making the reader visualize what the writer sees, you know pretty quickly.

The most common fault among badly written screenplays is when the writer is writing about something he (or she) doesn't know anything about. It's like an actor failing at holding a foreign accent. It's just immediately apparent.

As for developing material, it's simply a process, like growing grapes for wine. And if it's changed over the years, I'm unaware of it.

And finally, as for the how-to seminars, I'm not a believer. I think it's like being a fast ball pitcher. You either are or you're not. Writing, like acting or directing (or pitching, I'd say) comes down to talent. Talent, whether it's in sports or entertainment, is what sets those special people apart. And when you have it, it's once again, apparent.

Myth #2:
Three-Act Structure

So, what's wrong with the three-act structure?

Nothing.

Absolutely nothing.

I'd go as far as to say the three-act structure may be the most writer-friendly form of narrative architecture there is. It's logical, common-sensical, it has a beautiful A-B-C elemental simplicity. Rom coms, sci fi, crime thriller ... the genre doesn't matter; it works. Writing for the big screen? Little screen? Stage, *Saturday Night Live* skits, radio dramas? The medium doesn't matter; it works.

It works because it's a natural way to tell a story. It's *so* basic a form that much of the blather about three-act structure used to fill out books on the topic can seem like just a lot of padding around this simple formula described herewith by Oscar-winning screenwriter Paddy Chayefsky in a 1981 interview: "You generally present a situation in Act I.... In Act II you solve that problem, producing a more intense problem.... In Act III you solve that problem..." (Brady, 51).

William Price Fox used to describe the structure to our screenwriting class, in those days before "three-act structure" became a screenwriting mantra, in even more simpler fashion: "You set up two guys around a tree stump; one guy chases the other guy around the tree stump for a while; the one guy catches the other guy, or he gives up."

So why is three-act structure on my screenwriting myth list?

Like the nice kid new to the neighborhood who starts running with the thug-types always hanging around the corner bar, it fell in with bad company. Over the last 20–30 years, three-act structure has gone from a writer-friendly tool into something carved deep into granite tablets as an inflexible, only-way-to-go commandment. The present-day concept of the model has become so rigid and restrictive that development execs will even specify at about what page each plot "turn" marking off the acts should take place: "Ok, Bill, around page 21 we have to move into our second act...."

Says who? Was there some research I'm unaware of reporting the human brain automatically loses interest if there's not a major plot turn twenty-odd minutes into a movie? If it comes earlier? Later?

I suspect one of the reasons script development people, agents, a young generation of screenwriters, etc., have glommed on to this as a commandment is "three-act structure" has the sound of a long, respectable pedigree, something reaching back to the earliest days of theater—the first form of script writing.

Well, it doesn't.

Elizabethan drama, for instance (think Shakespeare), has a five-act structure. Go back to the ancient Greeks who birthed this first form of mass entertainment, and their stage works don't have acts. Instead, they have 10–12 sections, alternating between performers carrying out the plot and a chorus providing the audience with commentary, character insights, back story and other odds and ends. Many, if not most, modern-day plays are written in two acts (although three-act sticklers would make the case the first act is really two acts jammed together). And I'm not even going to get into the category of one-act and experimental plays.

The point here being that if theater—which presumably gives us the concept of the three-act story—hardly holds any kind of blind allegiance to the structure, why should film?

What this dogmatic commitment to the concept has done is take this writer-friendly tool and twist it into a story-killer by infecting the form with the storyteller's worst enemy: predictability. By banging the structure into an inflexible form, anybody who has sat through just a few mainstream releases can already sense plot turns coming. In some forms already fighting an inherent form of predictability (like, say, rom coms and superhero flicks), the infection becomes lethal. Complained *Entertainment Weekly* reporter Benjamin Svetkey even back in 1996, "pretty much *all* of the big commercial films being released by major studios these days have a certain written-by-chimps-locked-in-a-room-with-a-laptop quality" (34).

Take one of summer 2015's contributions to the superhero category, *Ant-Man* (screenplay by Edgar Wright, Joe Cornish, Adam McKay and the movie's star, Paul Rudd). Structurally, there's not much difference between *Ant-Man* and *Iron Man* (2008, screenplay by Mark Fergus, Hawk Ostby, Art Marcum, Matt Holloway), the first *Spider-Man* (2002, screenplay by David Koepp), or even the first *Spider-Man* reboot, *The Amazing Spider-Man* (2012, screenplay by James Vanderbilt, Alvin Sargent, Steve Kloves). The execution gives them different flavors (Robert Downey, Jr.'s breezy, witty Tony Stark in *Iron Man;* the geeky charm of Tobey Maguire in *Spider-Man;* director Marc Webb bringing a sweet young-love awkwardness to *Amazing*), but if you strip all four of those movies down to a plot schematic (social oddball comes into possession of superpowers, wrestles with responsibility of having superpowers, assumes that responsibility and faces down nemesis who manages to put one of the hero's loved ones— Ant-Man's daughter, Tony Stark's secretary Pepper Potts, Spidey's crushes Mary Jane Watson and Gwen Stacey respectively—in danger), it's pretty much the same thing. The reason *Ant-Man* is so terminally bland is because it's so terminally bland; there's not enough flavor to distract you from the fact you've seen this story before. A lot. That you knew how it was going to play out when you saw the coming attractions.

For a storyteller, that's Death On Wheels.

I became aware of how fatal that kind of predictability (combined with familiarity) could be stuck on an airliner where the in-flight movie was the gooey 1996 romance *Bed of Roses* with writer/director Michael Goldenberg stirring in the goo. Christian Slater is a shy but talented florist, Mary Stuart Masterson a hard-driving career woman, and as mismatched as they are, they still click (non-surprise Number One), they have a misunderstanding and almost break up (Number Two), they overcome their misunderstanding and wind up living—you guessed it—happily ever after (Number Three). Maybe if you were a Martian (and a pretty oblivious Martian at that) who'd never seen an American romance flick made in the previous 20 years, any of these see-it-a-mile-away plot turns might've surprised you. Otherwise, instead of being pulled along by the story, you'd be ahead of it, glancing at your watch while you wait for the and-there-it-is moments you knew were coming. Storytelling Death.

Some screenwriters have gotten around that predictability by scrambling the chronology of their stories. A favorite of mine is (*500*) *Days of Summer* (2009, written by Scott Neustadter, Michael H. Weber). Neustadter/Weber reshuffle the 500 days of the relationship between greeting card writer Joseph Gordon-Levitt and free spirited Zooey Deschanel (the Summer of the title). For instance, the movie skips ahead to the day when Gordon-Levitt finally sleeps with Deschanel. Neustadter/Weber and director Marc Webb pull out all the stops to capture Gordon-Levitt's exhilaration. Not only is he singing and dancing his way through midtown Manhattan, but everybody from passers-by to a couple of animated birds join in to share the joy. Then we smash-cut to several hundred days in the future and see that same Gordon-Levitt standing in an elevator, disheveled, depressed, dejected, and whatever other de-fill-in-the-blank you can come up with. The conjunction of the two impressions—delirious joy/spiritual destruction—is funny as hell, but that gap of several hundred days creates mystery, suspense, questions. That's the definition of audience engagement. As the movie pinballs back and forth through the 500 days, the audience has to mentally assemble the chronology and emotional arcs, none of which are complete until the last pieces fall into place.

Betrayal (1983), Harold Pinter's screen adaptation of his play, tells the story of a marriage/friendship-destroying affair in reverse order. Christopher Nolan's screenplay for his thriller *Memento* (2000) tells his story of an amnesia-afflicted man trying to avenge the murder of his wife through two narratives: one moving forward in time, the other in reverse. Guillermo Arriago's screenplay for *21 Grams* (2003) bounces back and forth in time along three ultimately intersecting plotlines, while in his Oscar-nominated screenplay for *Babel* (2006, and directed, like *21 Grams*, by Alejandro Inarritu), he amps up the concept and caroms between four independent plotlines spinning off from a single incident. And then there's Quentin Tarantino's scrambled narrative for *Pulp Fiction* (1994).

Tarantino was actually borrowing a structure Stanley Kubrick used in one of his early features, the 1956 crime thriller *The Killing*. Kubrick regularly halts the forward narrative of his heist flick, then retells it from another character's perspective. If you were to break the movie up into its various narrative lines, you'd wind up with several mini-movies, each with its own three-act arc, but Kubrick's artful jumbling regularly has us witnessing what-the-hell-happened? moments, then answering them by rewinding the narrative and showing us that part of the story from another perspective. Like (*500*) *Days, Betrayal, Pulp Fiction*, etc., Kubrick pulls the audience in deeper by making viewers have to work out how all the pieces of the puzzle fit together.

These flicks are also a testament to the hardy nature of the three-act structure because, at heart, they don't violate the model as much as they stretch, twist, compound, and toy with it.

What they also show is there's no emphatic rule about when demarcating plot turns need to happen. If you want to look at one movie which puts a stake through the heart of that bit of arbitrary dogma, check out Frank Capra's Christmas classic, *It's a Wonderful Life* (1946, screenplay by Capra, Frances Goodrich, Albert Hackett, Jo Swerling, and an uncredited Michael Wilson).

For those of you who've managed to miss the annual holiday airing of this eye-dampener:

Prayers reach Heaven on behalf of George Bailey who, faced with financial ruin, is ready to throw himself off a bridge. His guardian angel is briefed on what put poor, forlorn George in such a spot. The movie then tells—at great length—George Bailey's story in a series of episodes ranging from boyhood to the present. Always someone of high ambitions and big dreams, George Bailey's life is one frustration after another, necessity and then the responsibilities of family dismantling piece by piece his once grand visions of his own future until George is left with a family he can barely support, a financial hole threatening to put him in jail, and a lifetime of lost and regretted opportunities.

Wonderful Life's first act takes up a little more than 75 percent of the story. You read that right: three quarters of the movie is the set-up. Act II—where George is granted his wish that he'd never been born and sees the crap-hole his hometown would've become without him—takes up about 15–20 percent. The quick dash that's Act III—George realizes he's been so focused on the negatives of his life that he's missed its golden positives and wishes the world be put back the way it was, including his financial problems—gets the rest.

As out of whack as this construction is by contemporary standards, *Wonderful Life* only works because of that meticulous construction of the life of George Bailey, the audience living George's mounting disappointments along with him. Imagine *It's a Wonderful Life* with the events of the first act compressed into the first 20–30 pages, and the second act padded out to about the same. Do that and what you *don't* wind up with is a movie which has damned near everybody watching it on TV reaching for the tissue box.

*   *   *

Wonderful Life's proportions may be off the modern-day scale, but it's still a classically-structured three-act story. There are, however, movies in which storytellers flat-out disregard the form.

The classic anti–Western, *The Wild Bunch* (screenplay by director Sam Peckinpah and Walon Green) begins its 145-minute run with an approximately 15-minute section in which the titular bunch—a group of ruthless outlaws—ride into a Texas border town disguised as soldiers to rob a railroad office, are ambushed by waiting bounty hunters, then fight their way out in what is still one of the most brutally violent scenes in mainstream cinema. However, the forward movement of the movie doesn't begin until sometime after this sequence (about 50-minutes in) when the robber band's survivors drift into a Mexican town and hook up with a local warlord. This prologue, like the irrelevant-to-the-main-plot Omaha Beach sequence in *Saving Private Ryan* (1998, screenplay by Robert Rodat), is about setting a tone, a sense of the mindset of the principals, a sense of dread now that we know what's possible in their universe, what these characters are capable of, what mental scars may mark them.

You could eliminate these sequences and the proper plot of each movie would still be intact; each would still have a beginning, middle, and end. Don't believe me? Try coming in after those sequences. You've still got a movie. Just not the classics we know.

The epic World War II biopic *Patton* (1970, screenplay by Francis Ford Coppola, Edmund H. North) takes the same concept—a structurally "unnecessary" prologue—still further. The opening scenes of *The Wild Bunch* and *Saving Private Ryan* may have little to do with their respective main plots, but they fit chronologically; they're still part of each story's timeline. Not so with *Patton*.

The movie opens with a pre-credit scene of the World War II commander (played by George C. Scott) standing in front of a screen-filling American flag and delivering a six-minute monologue to his off-screen troops (the oft-quoted "No bastard ever won a war by dying for his country" speech). The scene sits outside the chronology of the film; it doesn't fit anywhere, it doesn't drive the plot or directly connect to any of the events which follow. The prologue is its own, self-contained, wholly independent thing. What it does do is prime the audience with an in-your-face introduction to a man both frightening and inspiring, profane and romantic; a passionate, demanding, committed warrior with a big-caliber ego and a penchant for self-aggrandizing showmanship.

As with the *Ryan* and *Bunch* prologues, *Patton* doesn't *need* that opening scene. Yet it's one of the best-remembered and most-quoted scenes from the movie. Call it a rule-breaker, call it unconventional, but *Patton* took the Oscars for Best Picture and Best Adapted Screenplay, and was the tenth biggest box office hit in its year of release.

* * *

One structure three-act fanatics have labeled anathema/blasphemy/taboo is the "episodic" structure. You can see episodic films at work—and working quite splendidly, thank you—during the heyday of the Hollywood epic.

First, you've got to readjust your head a little. These days, when every summer weekend sees some new $200 million FX extravaganza roll into multiplexes, the idea of an "event" film might be meaningless. But there was a time in pre–CGI antiquity when blockbusters like *Gone with the Wind* (1939), *The 10 Commandments* (1956), *The Bridge on the River Kwai*, *Ben-Hur* (1959), *The Longest Day* (1962), *The Big Country* (1958), *The Sand Pebbles*, *Lawrence of Arabia* (1962), etc., were *huge* events if, for no other reason, in those days they were so damned hard to make. Maybe only a handful of these behemoths rolled into theaters in a year, playing, at first, in only the biggest movie houses in the biggest cities, complete with musical prologues, intermissions, and souvenir programs. Like I said: *huge!*

They were often based on equally mammoth books, and it was the intent of their makers to, in their film adaptations, try to capture the same texture and dramatic gravitas of their source novels. Big novels tend to be episodic, and so were these epics.

Three-act police, trying to force-fit their structure, will say the middle hunk of these films (and it was a big hunk; the running times of these gargantuas could run from 2½ to 3–4 hours) is actually a second act, and, in some cases, that's true. In a lot of cases, though, that's pure self-justifying crap.

Let's look at the 182-minute *The Sand Pebbles* (adapted from Richard McKenna's novel by Robert Anderson). The set-up is relatively simple and quickly laid out: Steve McQueen plays a U.S. sailor assigned to a river gunboat in 1920s China who is only interested in running his little engine room without interference. But over the course of the film, McQueen's character lives through a series of mini-arcs—episodes with their own three-act structure—that do *not* comprise a traditional second act. For instance, McQueen gets into a feud with the Chinese coolie in charge of the engine-room coolies, the Chinese dies in an accident, McQueen trains a new coolie with whom he develops a friendship, the coolie has to fight one of the biggest bullies on the gunboat to earn his place in the engine room, then later he's sent ashore by the ship's chief coolie in a demonstration of power resulting in McQueen's friend being captured and tortured by Chinese communists and in McQueen's having to mercy-kill his friend. At that point, the movie is far from over. There will be other incidents, some of which will overlap this arc (a friend of McQueen's marries a Chinese woman, dies from illness, his wife is murdered by the communists; there's a humiliating march through a Chinese city; and more).

The Sand Pebbles is not a plot-driven story. It's a character piece, and we can see how each of these episodes begins to alter the isolationist McQueen character into someone who ultimately has to take a rebellious stand. The length of the movie, the broad tapestry formed by these independent episodes immerses us in McQueen's world in a way shorter, more plot-driven films usually don't (and sometimes can't).

Or consider *The Godfather* (1972). The opening wedding scene has little to do with moving the film forward. Yes, it introduces us to the principal characters, but spends even more time in a static basking in a family extravaganza that, in itself, tells us something about these characters and the world they live in (outside in bright sunlight, a party celebrating life; inside in the paterfamilias's shadowy den, discussions of violence and moral corruption). Then follows the Johnny Fontaine episode—climaxing in the infamous horse's head scene—which also has nothing to do with the central plot of the movie. It is, in fact, a digression, but one showing us how grandfatherly Don Corleone (Marlon Brando) is capable of incredible brutality. The movie doesn't gain any true forward momentum until Corleone turns down an offer to get into the drug business. By that time, we're somewhere around a half-hour or better into the film.

And then there's *The Longest Day,* a sweeping recreation of the Normandy invasion during World War II. Like the Cornelius Ryan book on which it's based (adapted by Ryan, Romain Gary, James Jones, David Bursall, Jack Seddon), *Day* is less a story than a mosaic comprised of dozens of independent incidents and mini-arcs. *Day* is the definition of "episodic," and a perfect illustration of why "episodic" can work ... and work beautifully.

So is *Citizen Kane.* And *12 Angry Men* (1957). *Odd Man Out* (1947). *The Great Escape. Lawrence of Arabia. Midnight Cowboy. Apocalypse Now* (1979). *Goodfellas* (1990). Give me some time, I'll find you more, but next time you hear a development guy or agent or writing guru throw up his/her hands in dismay sighing, "This is too episodic," keep in mind this prestigious company.

As some of the titles above indicate, workable episodic storytelling is not the sole province of big, long epics, or artistically ambitious work. The 1950 Western *Winchester '73* (1950, screenplay by Borden Chase and Robert L. Richards) was the first, and most uniquely structured of a series of midrange oaters director Anthony Mann made throughout the '50s, most starring James Stewart. The plot hook here is a prized rifle, won by Stewart in the opening act, but which passes from one set of hands to another (stolen by his nemesis, bad guy Stephen McNally, then lost by McNally in a card game to a gun runner who loses it to a Sioux chief in a gun deal gone bad who loses it to a cavalry unit who awards it to a civilian who helped them fight off a Sioux war party and who loses it to a psycho gunman who has it taken from him by McNally ... well, you get the idea). Subplots spin off and cross and re-cross the main narrative line (Stewart's dogged pursuit of McNally), forming episodes and mini-arcs until they all intersect in the movie's action-packed climax. It's a wonderfully elegant waltz of a screenplay which pretty much craps all over the three-act concept.

*   *   *

Broad comedy has a particular tolerance for structural violations, and the broader the comedy, the greater the tolerance, even to the point of tolerating no structure at all.

The Marx Brothers movies of the 1930s–1940s, particularly their early films for MGM like *Animal Crackers* (1930), *Monkey Business* (1931), and probably their most insane effort, *Duck Soup* (1933), all have the same structure (or lack thereof); there's a perfunctory set-up at one end, an almost arbitrary close at the other, and where the second act should be is, instead, a rapid fire parade of jokes and set pieces which often have little connection to the main plot (such as it is) providing they have any connection to it at all.

You can see that same barely framed chaos at work in movies like *Blazing Saddles* (1974), the early Woody Allen movies *Take the Money and Run* (1969) and *Bananas* (1971), some of the films from the Monty Python comedy troupe, i.e., *Monty Python and the Holy Grail* (1975) and *Life of Brian* (1979), and the Pee-wee Herman movies. In all of them, the plot serves only as a who-cares platform for a run of jokes and gags. Three act structure? Do these scenes further the plot?

Seriously?

In his review for *Pee-wee's Big Holiday* (2016), syndicated film critic Stephen Whitty captures the aesthetic of all of these joke-fests:

When reviewers walked into the first screenings of *Pee-wee's Big Holiday,* they were handed a letter from its star ... begging them not to give away the plot... Wait. What plot? The strange appeal of a Pee-wee Herman movie is that there's not much story at all ... [23].

These plots may only serve as comedy platforms, but they're still plots (if barely). With his 1960 *The Bellboy,* slapstick king and writer/producer/director Jerry Lewis demonstrated that some comedies could get by with no plot at all. I mean, *none.*

Tasked by Paramount with having to quickly pump out a flick to fill a hole in their summer schedule, Lewis stitched together a series of stand-alone comic bits, their only connecting tie being they all featured Lewis as a bumbling bellboy working at Miami Beach's posh Fontainebleau Hotel. The movie's plotlessness was such a novelty that Lewis has the movie open with Jack Kruschen as a fictional Paramount exec adjusting audience expectations by explaining they're about to see a movie without a plot. Despite bad reviews and predictions of failure, Lewis's movie without a story was a hit (*The Bellboy*).

And he wasn't the only one. Woody Allen took a handful of topics from psychiatrist David Reuben's informational bestseller, *Everything You Always Wanted to Know About Sex* But Were Afraid to Ask,* and turned them into hooks for a series of mini-spoofs in the 1972 movie of the same name. *The Groove Tube* (1974) and *Kentucky Fried Movie* (1977) used the barely-there framework of a programming day at fictional television stations as show-cases for parodies of commercials, television shows, and movies. David Zucker, Jim Abrahams, and Jerry Zucker, who wrote *Kentucky,* pulled off something similar as the writers/directors of *Airplane!* (1980), *Top Secret!* (1984), and *The Naked Gun* movies, using a shred of plot only as a line on which to hang a cascade of parodies, jokes, slapstick gags, and visual puns.

You can see the concept still at work in the *Scary Movie* (and similar parody) flicks, and even, to some extent, in *This Is the End* (2013, written by Seth Rogen and Evan Goldberg,) and *The Hangover* (written by Jon Lucas, Scott Moore). Ok, yeah, these last two do have something of an honest-to-God plot: *This Is the End* has a posse of Hollywood celebs hole up in James Franco's house to sweat out The Rapture; while in *The Hangover,* a bunch of friends take a buddy on a Vegas spree before his wedding, and wake up the next morning having lost both their memories of what happened ... and their buddy. But the middle hunk of each movie is a series of nearly stand-alone, proudly profane comic set-pieces; less a developing Act II then a train of hey-you-know-what-would-be-really-funny/gross/funny-and-gross moments.

Although silly and chaotically structured, *This Is the End* did monster business with $101.5 million domestic, while *The Hangover* went stratospheric with $277.3 million domestic making it #6 at the 2009 box office ahead of *Star Trek, Sherlock Holmes, Fast and Furious 4,* and *Terminator Salvation.*

So much for structure.

* * *

You can't talk about three-act exemptions without talking about Stanley Kubrick, because no filmmaker working in the commercial mainstream pushed further outside movie-making conventions than Stan the Man. We've already mentioned *The Killing,* but that movie seems practically traditional in structure compared to *2001: A Space Odyssey* which Kubrick himself described as "(departing) about as much from the convention of the theater and the three-act play as possible" (Agel, 169).

One of my undergrad film teachers, the esteemed academic and one-time host of the PBS series, *The Cinematic Eye,* Dr. Benjamin Dunlap, said the way to understand *2001* was to look at it not as a story, but as a "tone poem" (not unlike composer Richard Strauss' "Also sprach Zarathustra," which became the film's signature piece of music). The movie (which Kubrick co-wrote with sci fi maven Arthur C. Clarke) is divided into four barely connected parts: "The Dawn of Mankind" taking place millions of years in prehistory; then the "present" concerning the discovery of a mysterious monolith on the moon; then 18 months hence and a space mission to Jupiter; and finally a psychedelic extravaganza representing a transition from human to "star child." While there is a direction to the story, the movie is, for all intents and purposes, close to plotless, lacks any substantive characters, and its sparse dialogue is, by design, forgettable. Kubrick wanted, in his own words, *2001* to be "...a non-verbal experience..." and it's not only non-verbal, but a non-traditional non-narrative experience as well (Nordern, 328).

Kubrick went for something similar in his 1987 Vietnam War epic *Full Metal Jacket* which is also comprised of barely-connected parts and has no particular narrative through-line or character arcs. According to Kubrick's *Full Metal* collaborator, Michael Herr, Kubrick was not interested in telling a war story as much as presenting an observation of the "phenomenon" of war (Harlan).

Even in some of his movies with more clearly defined narratives, i.e., *Barry Lyndon* (1975) and *The Shining* (1980), Kubrick was more interested in a poetic, immersive experience than the conventions of plot and character.

Perhaps the only filmmaker I can recall who could give Kubrick a run for the money in ignoring movie storytelling conventions was Robert Altman, particularly in his ensemble films, the best of which are *M*A*S*H* (screenplay by Ring Lardner, Jr.) and *Nashville* (1975, screenplay by Joan Tewkesbury).

The frame of an Altman film at its most Altmanesque is packed with information: bits of business happening at the periphery or background, some of it as important—sometimes more so—than what's front and center in the frame. Dialogue—much of it ad-libbed—is piled on overlapping layer upon layer, some of it mumbled, tossed off, weaving in and out of other conversations. The best Altman movies are not about story, or even characters, but are—not unlike Kubrick, but with a quite different, intentionally muddier style—an impressionistic take on some larger concept (Finler, *Directors...*, 180–181). Altman is about—and I'm going to steal a phrase award-winning author and essayist Thomas E. Kennedy used to describe the designed chaos of modernist literature—"artful artlessness" (Mesce, *No Rule...*, 25).

Altman wasn't looking to screenplays to provide a firm base for a story, but something like the I-beam skeleton of a high rise; a framework within which he could mix actors and free-flowing dialogue, stirring them with the aim of producing a unique kind of movie magic, and, indeed, Altman films—when they work (and they don't always, i.e., *Buffalo Bill and the Indians, or Sitting Bull's History Lesson* [1976], *Health* [1980], *Prêt-à-Porter* aka *Ready to Wear* [1994]), look and sound like no other.

M*A*S*H, for example, begins with the arrival of Army surgeon "Hawkeye" Pierce (Donald Sutherland) at a field hospital during the Korean War, and ends with his rotation home. Forget about three acts; there's not even a narrative line extending between those two points. Instead, like the Richard Hooker novel on which the movie is based, there is a series of episodes, mostly unrelated, combining to present a comic (and often darkly comic) portrait of life in the unit. Sometimes there are arcs which may extend for a few episodes (like Pierce's ongoing feud with a tight-assed colleague played by Robert Duvall), but most of the episodes are stand-alones.

And then the movie ends. Suddenly, abruptly. There's no resolution as there's nothing to resolve. No arc comes to its conclusion. It's this simple: Pierce's time of service is over.

At least *M*A*S*H*, while an ensemble piece, provided the hook of a few central characters (Pierce and his immediate cronies). *Nashville* has a bit more of a defined arc (the few days leading up to a political rally), but there is no center anchor among the more than a dozen main characters (and I'm not counting secondaries), each following their own narrative line, those lines running parallel, sometimes crisscrossing, sometimes bouncing off others, forming not a story but a tapestry of mid–1970s American tumult.

It's worth noting that despite Altman's "artful artlessness," Tewkesbury copped a Golden Globe nod for her *Nashville* screenplay, the film was nominated for a Best Picture Oscar, and its box office—calculated into today's ticket sales—would've placed the movie somewhere between 2015's *Spotlight* and *Brooklyn*.

*M*A*S*H* performed even better, being one of the landmark films of the 1960s/1970s. The film was Oscar-nominated for Best Picture, Lardner went home with an Oscar for Best Adapted Screenplay, and the film was the seventh best performing film of the decade (1961–1970), out-earning the likes of *Lawrence of Arabia, West Side Story* (1961), and *Goldfinger* (1964).

✻ ✻ ✻

If most of the titles referred to in this section are familiar to you, there's a reason. All of them were money-makers; quite a few of them among the biggest hits of their release years, some the biggest of their decades. Most of them have, over time, attained classic status, or are at least favorite oldies, the kind that can still pull an audience when they resurface on Turner Classic Movies.

And they *all* managed this without adhering to what is, in the end, only an arbitrary rule.

So, not to belabor the point any more than I already have, what I'm saying is not that there's anything wrong with three-act structure, but that it's not the only game in town. Three-act structure is a hardy, strong house; four stout walls holding up a tight roof. But as Frank Lloyd Wright so grandly taught us, that's not the only way to build a house.

The Author: Steve Szilagyi

(Graduating with honors from Columbia University, critic/journalist/illustrator/novelist Steve Szilagyi's brilliance on the page was evident even before his work saw print. His unpublished story collection,

The Night Sophia Loren's Dress Caught Fire in a Restaurant, earned him Columbia's Bennett Cerf Award for Fiction as well as the Pushcart Prize for Outstanding Writer. When Szilagyi's first novel, Photographing Fairies, *was published by Ballantine in 1991, it enjoyed the kind of success first novels rarely have: earning out its advance and actually throwing off royalties [first novels rarely earn back their advances]; critical acclaim ["mesmerizing..."—Publisher's Weekly; "an engaging mixture of fact and fiction..."—Library Journal], award recognition [short-listed for the World Fantasy Award]; and, the Big Tamale, the Brass Ring, the author's wet dream—a movie deal. Which is not always the dream authors dream it will be.)*

Now Let Me Die

I'm thrilled and honored that some very talented people, some of them American and some of the British, got together and decided to make a film out of my first novel, *Photographing Fairies*. I will always be grateful to producers Larry Greenberg, Wanda Snyder, and Michelle Carmada, and director Nick Willing for coming together on this project, and making a film that has earned a seven out of ten rating on IMDB, been seen and enjoyed around the world in theaters, video, and TV, and allowed me to hold my head a fraction of an inch higher than other minor novelists of my generation for having my work made into a movie. *Photographing Fairies* is a good film. It is well-directed, well-photographed, and Simon Boswell's music is insidiously and powerfully effective. I urge everyone to see and enjoy it.

Fighting for Their Lives

The film was made in Great Britain and released in 1996. I read somewhere on the internet that the screenplay went through multiple drafts, and there was some turmoil among the production team. I never got the full story, and when I attempted to stick my nose into the situation, had the door slammed on it (and deservedly so). By the time production was underway, my role in the picture was well in the past. The young people making the movie were past all interest in the author and his opinions. They were fighting for their lives against the whole array of economic, technical, and personal challenges that combine against any film production, and which make cinema the most difficult and desperate of all the arts.

As producer Larry Greenberg told me at the American film festival premiere of *Photographing Fairies*, "We shouldn't wonder that there aren't more good movies being made; we should be amazed that any movies get made at all."

Heart, Humor, Rich Characterizations—Forget It

The novel takes place in 1926, and tells the story of a London commercial photographer who makes his way to a small Cotswold-ish town to investigate reports that two little girls have captured still images of fairies on film. Originally intending to debunk the images, the photographer becomes convinced that the fairies are real. This belief overturns the photographer's moral universe, and he goes on to make rash choices that lead to his falsely being accused of murder, convicted, and placed in a cell on death-row.

Early on, I'd written my own screenplay for the movie, and submitted several drafts to the producers. They were rejected. I was fortunate to have once shared an office at HBO with Bill Mesce, a talented novelist, playwright, and keen student of film, and I asked if he'd like to take a shot at it. Bill came through with a solid, well-paced screenplay, full of heart, humor and rich characterizations. The producers passed on it and a subsequent revision.

The film that was ultimately released was written by Chris Harrald and the director, Nick Willing. It starred Toby Stephens, Edward Hardwicke, Frances Barber, and Academy Award–winning Best Actor (*Gandhi*) Ben Kingsley.

"I'm Sorry You Had to Sit Through That"

Film critic Joanna Conners from the *Cleveland Plain Dealer* newspaper accompanied me to my first viewing of the film at a private screening in March 1996. Here's what she wrote:

> On the screen, clouds scuttle in accelerated motion above a snowy peak in the Swiss Alps. Beethoven thunders ominously on the soundtrack. The titles roll, *Photographing Fairies*, followed by the names of actors, the cinematographer, the designers of the costumes and sets, the editor.
> And then it appears: "Based on the Book by Steve Szilagyi."
> In the dark theater, Steve Szilagyi leans over a seat, smiling. "Now, let me die," he whispers.
> After six years, 17 screenplay drafts, a fabulous trip to Hollywood and countless meetings and phone calls, his first novel has finally made it to a theater near him.

And, like almost every author before him who has sold his book to the movies—a process not unlike selling your soul to the devil—he has mixed feelings about the whole thing.

"I'm sorry you had to sit through that," he says, very somberly, after the final credits roll and the lights come up. When the two people at the screening with Szilagyi reassure him that the movie is delightful, he brightens and flushes. "Oh, well, in that case I don't feel so guilty."

On the Finality of Death

The screenwriters gave the main character a wife (who did not exist in the book) who dies at the beginning of the film, and whom the main character rejoins in death at the end.

I regret that I have to express strong emotion here, but the truth is I absolutely detest and avoid all plot contrivances involving life after death. It's my pop-cultural pet peeve. If you can't do a plot without resorting to people coming back from the dead, don't do the thing; that's what I say. Because the one immutable lesson we learn from nature is that death is death. That's it, brother. The story ends there. Unless your characters are named Jesus or Lazarus, they should abide by the rule that once dead, always dead.

Why? Because storytelling requires tension. Death is the ultimate constraint. Without death, there is no constraint, no tension, and no story. The permanence of death is what gives not only stories their meaning; it gives life its meaning.

I realize that arguing for the strictures of reality may sound odd, coming from someone who wrote a book about fairies. And let it be known that my objections to returns from the dead don't apply to ghosts in a ghost story. There is nothing in literature greater than the appearance of Marley's ghost in Charles Dickens' "A Christmas Carol." But, as you may recall, the first words of that story are, "Marley was dead: to begin with. There is no doubt whatever about that."

And a ghost is not a resurrection.

How Reviews Matter

How did I wind up getting a movie deal in the first place? The book was released by Ballantine Books in 1991. At that time, I was living in Cleveland, Ohio, and working in a hospital. Almost as soon as the book hit the stores, the smalltime agent who'd flukily gotten it published began receiving calls from Hollywood. The book had gotten positive reviews in *The Wall Street Journal*, *The Washington Post*, and—most importantly, I believe— *The Los Angeles Times*, which gave it almost a half-page. These reviews were read by movie people over their morning coffee and must have piqued their interest. So it was that producers called us; we didn't call them.

In 1994, I flew to Los Angeles with my now-wife, and we met with a half-dozen producers and directors who'd expressed a strong interest in the book. I'll never forget the thrill of driving up to the gates of the major film studios, giving my name to the guard, and being whisked through— just like in the movies. I had the chance to stroll around the lots, wander onto sets, and more or less indulge a film fan's fantasy. (A high point of the trip was a visit to the staircase where James Parrot directed Laurel and Hardy in their classic Oscar-winning short, "The Music Box" [1932]— a location now appropriately memorialized, but then obscure.)

After getting a solid offer from Paramount, we eventually sold the rights to a group of young producers from America and Great Britain who won us over with their enthusiasm and sympathetic literary tastes (and by matching Paramount's dollar proposal). Being made in England was part of the appeal of their proposal—I had visions of *Masterpiece Theater* and Merchant Ivory-style faithfulness to the book that never materialized.

Advice to the Young

From my dealings with producers and directors during this period, I gathered the impressions that informed what is now my sole advice to writers who hope to get into the movies. It is this:

Don't write a screenplay.

Write a novel.

Producers have no respect for screenplays, but they seem to have a deep and abiding respect for published novels and novelists. (They may be faking it, but fake is as good as real in Hollywood.)

Why is this? Stand-up comedian Jackie Mason once told me that the stand-ups of his generation were different from modern comics. "They were guys that didn't want to work." The same could be said of people who write screenplays. They'd like to be writers, but aren't up to the task of filling whole pages with prose. In an earlier age, they might have attempted poetry, but that's no longer an option (poets have zero status in today's society). So, they open a screenplay. They look it up and down. They flip through the pages and see lots of white space. They think, "White space. I can do that."

Producers have crates full of screenplays by these people who are able to fill page after page with white space. A novelist, however, simply by virtue of filling a goodly number of pages—both sides—with words, demonstrates a better than average work ethic, a quality that recommends you to any potential collaborator in or out of film. And while a screenwriter is just a screenwriter, a novelist is his or her own screenwriter, director, cameraperson, set dresser, casting agent, lighting director, and continuity person. The people who actually make movies appreciate this on some level. The novelist is a peer; the screenwriter is a peon.

Be Your Own Boss!

If your screenplay never gets produced, your manuscript is impotent. It will never be read or enjoyed in its own right. A novel, however, is a thing that is complete in itself. As the sole creator, you have the satisfaction of making every creative decision on your own. You have an unlimited budget, and comfortable access to any location, however remote, in the universe. If your novel is good enough, it might someday be made into a movie. This movie will very likely bear little resemblance to your original novel. But that's okay. The original novel will still be out there for people to read and enjoy—plus you'll have the personal prestige of having had your book made into a movie.

Every argument I've made here on behalf of novels applies to memoirs and other non-fiction as well. So, get busy. Write a book. Be your own boss! If Hollywood wants your work, that's all good and well. If not, they can go to blazes.

Crash Landing: *Free Flight*

There's a joke about agents which gives you an idea of what people in the business—including their clients—think about agents.

This agent and his wife are on a Caribbean cruise. They're out on the main deck one afternoon, watching the seas roll by, and the agent leans too far over the rail and falls overboard. His wife runs up to the bridge shouting about her husband. The captain looks very grave and says, "I have to be honest with you. It'll take a half-hour to get this ship turned around, and these are shark-infested waters. You have to prepare yourself for the worst."

A half-hour later, the ship has made its circle and there's the agent treading water, surrounded by sharks which keep circling him but make no move to attack.

The captain is amazed. "I've never seen anything like that!" he says. "It's a miracle!"

"No miracle," the agent's wife says. "Professional courtesy."

A red flag had gone up in my head on Bombastic Bushkin the day we first met when he was shirtlessly popping grapes in his office. It wasn't just the shirtless grape-eating. He'd been invited to a pre-release screening of *The Blues Brothers* (1980) that evening and asked me along. I guess he was showboating a bit. You know; "Look who I know!"

It was pretty piss-poor showboating. Since I was riding in on his coattails, there'd been no allowance made in the seating arrangements for me. The only seat open wasn't really a seat; some kind of projection control panel had been jammed into the same space as the last seat in the last row. Somehow I got myself squeezed into the chair, folding my feet inward because there was almost no floor space. By the time the movie was over, I'd lost feeling in my toes. The lights came up and I limped out after Bushkin, but when we got outside, he only walked a little ways down the block before stopping to look back, standing there like he was waiting for something.

There was a limo parked in front of the building, and Bushkin wanted to see who it was for. Out of the building came some gray-topped guy in a suit, the limo driver popped out and held the rear door for him. I don't know who he was; Bushkin did. Some honcho from Universal, I think (Universal had bankrolled the movie).

Bushkin said something hinting that that was what he wanted; *that* was his ambition—to be a guy limos were always waiting for. That's when I knew he didn't give a crap and a half about me.

*   *   *

Agents come in all flavors of good and all flavors of bad. Some bad agents are just inept; they couldn't sell a boat to Noah. But you have that kind of bad in any profession. Then there's another kind of bad that's distinct to agents: the kind of bad agent that goes cold on you ... without telling you.

They take you on, submit your work to a few contacts, but if it doesn't place quickly, they figure they gave you your shot and they're done with you. Only you don't know it. All you know is when you call, you never get your agent; maybe their voice mail, maybe a subordinate telling you they'll pass on the message and your agent'll call back. Only they don't call back. You write (or email), but you don't get an answer. And maybe somebody eventually 'fesses up that your stuff hasn't been getting sent out, but nobody'll tell you why. You've been dropped ... without being dropped.

Bombastic Bushkin was that kind of bad. And this was even after he'd built himself an escape hatch in case our relationship didn't work out; an agreement on paper stating he would only represent me for a year (I've never signed such an agreement with any of the seven other agents I've had in the over 35 years since I was with Bushkin). But our relationship headed south long before we were anywhere near a year along.

On one call just a few months after I'd signed with Bushkin to see what was happening with my novel, I was shuffled off to one of his junior associates, a pleasant young lady I'd met in his offices once. She didn't sound very pleasant, now; more angry and bitter. She admitted Bushkin hadn't read my manuscript, one of his juniors had, and he'd only submitted it to a single publisher where it had, evidently, struck out. She wasn't angry with me, but with Bushkin, so much so that—without going into specifics—she'd become fed up working for him and was quitting. She told me who would be handling me—another pleasant young lady—said she was sorry about how things had worked out, and wished me luck.

When I got to talk to the new pleasant young lady, she, too, had stopped being pleasant and was also clearly unhappy. She didn't know what was happening with my material, if anything, and she, too, thought Bushkin was something of a dick and was fed up working for him and was quitting.

I did not feel in a good place at that point. The temptation was there to tell the guy to kiss my ass and dump him, but dump him for what? I didn't know any other agents or even how to approach one. I could have an agent who didn't work for me, or no agent at all; a quintessential damned-if-you-do-etc., scenario.

I was working at Dutton as a secretary (this was before corporate America had taken to calling them "assistants") having gotten hired because of my ace typing skills (in those days before kids grew up with a computer keyboard in their cribs, typing was still a prized skill). Publishing didn't pay very well (at the time there was a survey saying it was one of the lowest-paying white collar professions), and my boss, seeing an opportunity for me to pick up a few extra bucks while doing a favor for a friend of his, hooked me up with, well, let's call her Little Ruthie.

Little Ruthie was about as big as my pinkie, looked and sounded and acted like a typical Yiddish mama, treating her clients more like her kids (well, grandkids) rather than business associates. But when it came to business, all those hugs and cheek pinches went out the window and she became the kind of operator the sharks would respect. What business was she in? Good question.

My after-hours job was to do some filing and type correspondence for her, and from what I could see she had her hands in a couple of things. She and my boss had known each other for years, and he had gotten her a contract with Dutton to see if she could milk any money out of the company's backlist; books no longer in circulation, but whose rights the house still controlled. Ruthie peddled domestic reprint rights, overseas rights, sometimes television or film rights. None of it was big money stuff, but cumulatively Ruthie could do well by tirelessly flogging Dutton's dusty old titles everywhere and anywhere.

One of Ruthie's other myriad businesses was agenting. She handled a number of Young Adult and children's authors, a couple of adult authors. Again, no big dollar clients as I recall, but, nevertheless, she was a working agent. I don't remember how it came up—probably me seeing her agent correspondence and doing a big, sad sigh to draw a what's-the-matter-booby from her so I could boo-hoo about my southbound relationship with Bombastic Bushkin. And, I also mentioned the De Palma gig which definitely piqued her interest since the bottom end of the WGA scale paid better than most of her clients were getting in advances (at the time, a typical advance from a major commercial publisher for a first-time adult author was $10,000, and if you were a "midlist" author—the non-headline writers who make up the bulk of a big house's list—you might only improve on that incrementally over time).

By nature, agents good and bad are opportunists which is a nice way of saying they're vultures (when they're not being sharks). Another agent's unhappy client who might be a money-maker, well, that's choice roadkill on the pavement just screaming to another agent, "Gobble me up!"

Ruthie asked to see my manuscript which Bushkin had stopped trying to place. A few weeks later, when I went down the hall to her office to do my after-hours typing for her, she showed me a reader's report on the novel. Ruthie herself hadn't read the novel, but she'd given it to a reader she trusted who's final assessment went something like this: "I don't normally like this kind of thing, but if I did, I'd probably like this."

For some reason beyond my understanding, Ruthie considered that a strong enough endorsement (well, that and the De Palma gig) to take me on. By this time, there were only two months left on my contract with Bushkin, but she wasn't going to wait. She helped me draft up a request to be released which detailed reasons for my dissatisfaction in somewhat pissy fashion. Bushkin didn't even bother with much of a response; he sent my letter back having typed across the top: "Sorry, but we are not pursuing your work, and yes, you do not have any obligation to this Agency. Best of luck."

Ruthie did hustle my manuscript around, but she wasn't much of a pitchman. I know because I typed the pitch letters. They were usually only a couple of sentences long, offered very little about the book or why she thought it would sell, but assured the recipient they'd like it and it would work well for their house.

What you get with an agent is access. Well, that's what you're *supposed* to get. Ruthie had a lot of access, but not to a lot of editors doing adult fiction, and she seemed to be counting on quite a few of them taking her at her word rather than her trying to exercise some salesmanship. She said—and I partly agree with this—that a pitch didn't matter; a manuscript sold itself. If the material sucked, nothing you said in the pitch was going to make up for that.

True enough, but on the other hand, editors have to plow through a lot of material. You have to give them a reason not to skim, not to ask their assistant to read it for them, to invest any time in it at all. No bait, no bites.

The rejections piled up.

All the time she was flogging my novel, she had an eye out for possible screenwriting gigs and that's how we hooked up with Homer (as you might have guessed, not his real name).

Homer was an immigration lawyer by trade, but wanted to be a ___. Well, I'm not sure. I think he wanted to be something, *anything* in the movie and television business; a big agent, a producer, something. To that end, he was always wheeling and dealing some property.

Ruthie dealt with him while peddling the rights on a series of mystery books for what, years later, would be referred to as the "tween" market; too young for children's books, not old enough for the Y/A market. The author had burned out, Homer wanted to see if he could perpetuate the series and was looking for someone to ghost for the author. He also had been looking at the possibility of selling the series as the basis for a television series.

Ruthie's ears picked up on all counts. Books, TV ... she smelled blood. She sent me to meet Homer.

He had an office uptown, in the 50s I think, couple floors up in a corner building. A very attractive woman, his assistant, led me into his office. Big, spacious, a polished wood floor. Homer had put his desk in the outside corner so the windows overlooking Avenue of the Americas on one side, the cross street on the other, radiated out from his desk. On the wall behind and over his desk was a gold sunburst clock.

He was a good-looking guy if a bit short, on the hyper side, and thought quite highly of himself. Ruthie had given me the lowdown on him: rich family, then he'd married rich, lived in a big house out on Long Island where the big houses cluster. He'd written a book on immigration law— "I'm a writer, too!" he'd tell you—and he thought that made him the kind of writer who knew good writing (he didn't).

He, Ruthie, and I agreed I'd give one of these kid mysteries a shot.

I did.

It sucked.

When I'd been a kid, my mother had thrown out my rather impressive stack of comic books saying they were giving me nightmares (they still give me nightmares when I think what they'd be worth today). My mom and dad were big readers; the house was filled with books, there were boxes of volumes in the basement. Bored without my comic books, I started reading *their* books. While other kids were reading the Hardy Boys mysteries, I was reading Alistair MacLean's *Ice Station Zebra* which was why when this opportunity came along I had absolutely no facility for it at all.

But at least now we had a link to Homer, and, according to Homer, he had links elsewhere. And because of that, I did a dishonorable thing.

Ruthie had decided we'd hit a wall on submitting my novel. I'd been working on another one, a cop thriller, and she thought that one might be more marketable. She started sending that around with just as much of a pitch to carry it as she'd given my first book. Unsurprisingly—at least to me—we got the same kind of response.

I don't know how it came up in a conversation with Homer, but he confided that he didn't think Ruthie was a very good agent and didn't know how to sell my stuff. That pushed the right button on me since I didn't disagree. He asked to look at the cop novel, actually read it (well, he *said* he'd read it) and swore he could place it.

I didn't want to break up with Ruthie; she may not exactly have been Mike Ovitz, but she was trying, and she had certainly taken more of a personal interest in me than Bombastic Bushkin. In fact, it had gotten personal.

Let me pause here for a second to share a cautionary thought with you. It's an agent's job to be likable. Successful agents have that quality, all of them work at it. Their function is to make you think of them as a friend.

Reliable, loyal, got your back—that's a friend. That's not an agent.

It may happen that you come across an agent who means well, but when you only get fifteen cents of every dollar your client gets, expediency will trump this not-really-a-friendship almost every time.

I didn't know this yet. My relationship with Ruthie was more like, well, I won't say motherly, but maybe aunt-ly. She'd had me up to her apartment for dinner with her family, said all the right, supportive things all the time. She may not have been the most effective of agents, but I think she really cared about my fledgling career, at least to a degree. Our connection tangled the professional and the personal; not always a good thing, since it confuses issues when it's time to make tactical decisions.

Like this one.

I hesitated over Homer's offer.

"Let me send it out," he prodded. "If somebody bites, we'll figure out something with Ruthie later."

That was enough of a rationalization for me to live with, so, like a dishonorable ass—a greedy, desperate, dishonorable ass—I said yes.

As soon as I said it I regretted it. There are times—especially in this business—where you do things you don't want to do out of some self-justifying pragmatism, or even for sheer survival. The state of your conscience and the measure of how lousy the things that you do are can be calculated by how well you can live with having done what you did. Like I said, I didn't disagree with Homer about Ruthie, but even as I was walking away from his office I felt like no amount of scalding hot water was going to make me feel clean about it. I'd read plenty of horror stories about double-dealing in Hollywood; I didn't want to be one of *those* people.

I managed to choke it down for a few days, but then I called up Homer. "Wherever you were thinking of sending my book, forget it. I don't want to do this."

"But I already submitted it!"

"Well, tell them you want it back."

"I can't do that!" (you can) "It'd be embarrassing!" (it isn't)

That put me in the boy-you-really-screwed-yourself-on-this position of hoping my manuscript would be rejected so I wouldn't have to explain this all to Ruthie. Thankfully (I guess), the house passed.

After that, I was wondering if Homer would still have a use for me considering the way I'd flipped on him. But Homer never had the moral qualms I did, and it wasn't long before we heard from him again. This time he was offering us something sounding like the Real Deal, the kind of thing that had all three of us a little drooly.

Homer had a partner in Los Angeles, another lawyer (whom we shall dub Leo), and in 1982, together they'd optioned a 1980 novel called *Free Flight*. The novel had been written by Douglas Terman, a retired Air Force officer who, as I understand it, had done time in the service as a missileer—one of the guys who did their duty in ICBM missile silos. Terman was into a couple of things: he'd started some kind of resort down in the Grenadines (he seemed to spend a nice hunk of the year sailing down to and hanging around in the Caribbean), he ran some kind of phone service in Vermont where he lived, and he wrote. Between his other businesses and his Air Force pension, he was in the enviable position of not having to live off his writing.

Before *Free Flight*, he'd written a novel and a children's game book, then had a breakout hit with *First Strike*. *Free Flight* had been another winner, making it onto some of the country's bestseller lists.

All of his novels to that point took advantage of his intimate acquaintance with nuclear weapons, and *Free Flight* was no exception. This was still the time of the Cold War when the fear of a nuclear exchange was very much in the zeitgeist. Think of movies like *Fail-Safe, Planet of the Apes, A Boy and His Dog* (1975), *Damnation Alley* (1977) etc., and you get the feeling a nuclear holocaust was viewed as an inevitability at the time. *Free Flight* played off that same sense.

Set in a U.S. devastated in a nuclear exchange with the Soviet Union, Russians and their East Bloc allies now occupy what's left of the U.S. Greg Mallen, an ex–Air Force pilot, makes an escape attempt from the new regime to Canada in a powered glider in the company of Wyatt, a black guy who'd once worked for the new authorities in a misguided attempt to make things better. They're pursued by McKennon, an American working with the Soviet occupiers. There's a chase by helicopter, the glider is forced down during a storm near a frozen lake, Mallen and Wyatt find an isolated farm where they think they can scavenge repair parts. On the farm lives Jean, her son Paul, and her great-grandfather. Mallen and Jean fall in love, Paul—who's a member of the local youth group—feels betrayed and rats Mallen out to the local authorities. A patrol comes by the farm, there's a shoot-out, Wyatt is killed, the great-grandfather tells Mallen to get Jean out. Mallen and Jean get to the glider, he's just finished making repairs when a chopper carrying McKennon shows up. There's a fight on the ice between Mallen on the ground and the chopper, Mallen manages to bring the chopper down which crashes into the ice on the lake before sinking. Mallen gets Jean into the glider and off they fly to an unoccupied part of Canada while a penitent Paul watches them soar off.

Homer and his partner had taken a one-year option on the novel, and now they needed someone to do a screenplay adaptation. To them, I was a gift. I was a pro (hell, I'd done a screenplay for Brian De Palma!), and I was also cheap (for which I'd gotten no credit). I was experienced enough to pull it off, had just enough credibility to give it cachet, and hungry enough to do it for nothing with the promise of a pay-out down the road.

Ruthie and I thought it was worth the shot since the contracted-for fee—if the project made it to production—was over three times what a first-time author was typically paid.

Problem was I knew diddley about how to turn a 346 page novel into a two-hour movie (120 script pages give or take).

What I'd remembered from Bill Fox's class and from some interviews with screenwriters and articles in film magazines was the idea of stripping out the narrative spine of the novel; pare the book down to its essential plot.

I read through *Free Flight* making a list of every scene in the book. There was a fair amount of material which was easy to cut: passages which were just Mallen musing on his situation or on the past, a 30-page prologue that was an account of the war and its aftermath by a Soviet historian.

I then did what would become a regular part of my writing process (when given the time for it) and that was to bang out a quick, down-and-dirty pass. All writers are different. Part of the trick to this occupation is learning how your head works, and then working out a game plan playing to your strengths and avoiding your weaknesses. For me, it's easier to rewrite something than writing it from scratch. That first, quickie, outrageously rough pass was for no one's eyes but mine, and was only to give me some idea of what the story would look like on paper so I could figure out how to reshape and refine it.

But even in the rewrite, I stuck fairly close to the novel. I'd complained as much as anyone else about how so many screen adaptations were inferior to their source books. I didn't want to be guilty of the same crime.

Besides stripping out digressions and unnecessary passages (like the prologue), the only major change I made in the novel had to do with those East Bloc occupation forces. In the novel, some are Poles, some are Czechs, and so on, reporting to their Russian chiefs. There was no smooth way to render that on-screen without explanatory exposition, so I junked that element and simply made them all Russian troops.

In accounts by other writers, I had read that one strategy to keep production execs from futzing with material was to deliberately incorporate "fat" into a script for the purpose of trading it off to keep something more valuable. You want to keep the scene where a guy elopes with a goat? Offer to cut the scene where he cheats on the goat with an elephant. The thrust-and-parry is supposed to play something like this:

"Bill, this scene here with the talking walrus and Alice, I mean, c'mon, a talking walrus?"

"It's in the book, Brad, ya gotta keep it. People will be looking for it. Trust me; it'll play."

"Man, I don't know, it's hard for me to see—"

"But as I'm talking to you, you've got me thinking, because I do think you're on to something about being careful about going too far over the top. That scene where the helicopter gunship and the SWAT team come into rescue Alice from the Queen of Hearts? I definitely think you'd be right to call me out on that."

"I would?"

"Yeah, I mean, Brad, you've got a legitimate point, but I think *that's* the scene where it shows up. I'd hate to lose it, but when you're right, you're right, and you're right about that one."

"I am?"

And so Alice doesn't get rescued by the choppered-in SWAT team, but the walrus still gets to talk with her of many things.

As in *Blow Out,* I came up with a visual plan. As in the book, Mallen lives in a mountaintop cabin. I took this Nature Boy image a couple of steps further, opening with him chopping down trees (to clear a takeoff area for his glider), showering in the rain … real at-one-with-Mother-Nature stuff. His cabin is cluttered with artifacts he's scavenged from the ruined towns below: books, works of museum art, etc. (something I stole from the 1959 post-apocalyptic movie, *The World, the Flesh, and the Devil).* And when he makes his break, it's in the quiet, graceful whiteness of his powered glider.

In opposition, the Soviets and their American collaborators work out of ugly, roughly-built cinderblock buildings. They wear odds-and-ends of military uniforms, and drive vehicles (like an old school bus) sloppily painted over with military colors (an approach I borrowed and morphed from *Mad Max 2: The Road Warrior* [1981] with which I'd been greatly impressed). And when Mallen makes his break, they chase him in noisy helicopters.

It's the Road Runner *vs.* Wile E. Coyote: one side representing a sort of naturalistic purity, the other side a harsh, brutal technology.

Mind you, I wasn't trying to make a philosophical statement. I just thought it was an iconography which played nicely on the screen, and gave the proceedings a greater heft than they might otherwise have.

Homer was happy with it (although it's an open question as to whether or not he'd read it), and started shopping the project around.

By this time I was working for Home Box Office. I'd been promoted at Dutton to assistant to a guy who was starting a new Y/A business for the company. The come-on for the position would be that I'd be able to grow with the new division; a chance to finally move up.

HBO, however, was sending me back to the minors: a secretary's job. I didn't particularly want to take it, but...

"Is it money?" my new boss asked.

I nodded.

"I can understand that. I'd hate to lose you. I think I can get you up to $212 a week. Maybe $215. What're they offering?"

"Two hundred and fifty-two."

He leaned across his desk and shook my hand. "You're doing the right thing."

(More right than I knew at the time; the new business never got off the ground.)

I'd become friendly with Bob Conte, and every so often he and I would have lunch and he'd tell me screenwriting horror stories and I'd pretend I was a peer with my one uncredited movie. HBO had just started making original movies, and in those days it was a catch-as-catch can kind of affair. The company was years away from establishing its reputation as a house for quality cable originals. In the mid–1980s, it was more a junkyard where producers who couldn't sell something anywhere else brought properties. I asked Bob if he'd look at *Free Flight,* and he agreed.

After a couple of weeks, he passed, but we took some hope in that it hadn't been an easy call; as he told me, "You'll never know how close that thing came to being made."

Then Homer gave us some exciting news: Elliott Kastner wanted the property.

Even though in those pre-internet days I couldn't Google up Kastner's track record, he'd produced enough movies that even I was familiar with his name; he was an honest-to-God movie guy. If I could've Googled him, I would only have been even more impressed.

A one-time talent agent, Kastner had been producing movies since the 1960s with a particular penchant for smart, often literary-inspired flicks. His filmography included some favorites of mine: the private eye flick *Harper* (1966) which had given William Goldman his first solo screenplay credit; his biggest hit with World War II actioner *Where Eagles Dare* (1968); a culty Robert Altman piece of Raymond Chandler deconstruction in *The Long Goodbye* (1973); the screen adaptation of Peter Shaffer's acclaimed stage play, *Equus* (1977, with Shaffer Oscar-nominated for adapting his work for the screen) (Weber).

Perhaps most impressive about Kastner was that despite a horrific box office record which hardly matched his creative accomplishments, the guy was still in business. *The Godfather* author Mario Puzo once wrote of the producer that "(Kastner) has put together very big films, nearly all of which are flops. And yet he can get the money and stars to produce any movie he decides to. He does it with a phone, irresistible charm, and shameless chutzpah" (Puzo, D1).

Unfortunately, Kastner didn't want me, and Homer wanted the deal too much to debate the point. Kastner was in, and I was out. Kastner took a six-month option (out of Homer's one-year option), and took the project to Warner Bros. But then soon after, Homer surprised me saying he wanted to set up a meeting with me, Kastner, and himself. Oh, not for *Free Flight;* I was out of the running on that. But Homer thought maybe we could get something else going with Kastner.

It would be nice to think this was Homer feeling guilty about me getting the boot on *FF.* Yeah, it *would* be nice to think that. But I think it was just Homer trying to build on his new relationship with a guy of Kastner's industry standing to get as much going as possible.

We met in Homer's office. Homer was wearing a navy blue felt blazer which I suppose was a 1980s brand of flashy. Kastner showed up in a sweatsuit and orange-tinted sunglasses.

Ok, you could take that get-up as a Hollywood kind of cliché, and I guess it was, but I liked Kastner. He was very upfront about looking kind of shabby. He said his wife was gravely ill and he was dealing with that, and had the bleary eyes to prove it.

He may have looked like a Hollywood cliché, but where Homer reeked of hyper, over-eager suck-up, Kastner had a relaxed, veteran's confidence. He knew he was the only guy in the room who'd done anything, and didn't need to showboat it to make the point. And, he had that charm Puzo had written about and for which he was legendary. I was hoping we'd figure out something to do together not just because I wanted the professional break, but he looked like he might be fun to work with.

He had something in mind; a spy thriller. About a spy who, let's see, he has amnesia, maybe he was on a yacht that blew up and he washes ashore and doesn't remember anything. Oh, and no matter what else happens, it has to start in the lobby of the Dorchester Hotel in London.

"Why is that?" I asked.

"Because I *love* that hotel!"

We talked around and around the idea a bit, and finally Kastner came to the bottom line: "The thing is I want to do something like *The Bourne Identity*. But I don't want to have to buy the book."

The old Hollywood prescription: the same ... but different.

(Note: it would be another 20 years—2002—before producer Frank Marshall got the 1980 Robert Ludlum novel up on the big screen.)

After Kastner left, Homer shook his head. "Boy, he's so *crude!* Didn't you think he was crude? And did you see the way he was dressed?"

This from a guy in a felt blazer. I think what bothered Homer most was when Kastner heard what he thought was bullshit, he'd call it bullshit, and that was the word he'd use: bullshit. A bullshit artist like Homer was never going to be comfortable in a room with a guy who called bullshit bullshit.

Over the next couple of days I horsed around with an idea or two but couldn't come up with anything. Didn't matter. Kastner and Warners couldn't agree on a director, they stayed at an impasse until Kastner's option ran out.

And as suddenly as I'd been booted off the project, I was back in.

With Kastner out, Homer needed a writer again, and I was still attractively priced (free). When I got the call, I pretended I hadn't been offended and hurt when I'd been dumped (I had been, not having yet learned the primary loyalty in the movie business isn't to people but to projects and getting them done).

Not long after Kastner's exit, Homer informed me John Kemeny was interested in the project.

Kemeny's name I knew from his recent hit, the prehistoric adventure *Quest for Fire* (1981). What I didn't know at the time was he was one of the biggies in the Canadian film industry, having started out in documentaries in the 1960s, then turning out *The Apprenticeship of Duddy Kravitz* (1974), a landmark of Canadian cinema. His subsequent features included the Oscar-nominated drama *Atlantic City* (1980) (Knelman). Like Kastner, not a bad guy to work for in terms of trying to get my footing in the business.

Homer gave me Kemeny's contact information so I could write him a letter introducing myself. In my letter I also made some suggestions about who he might want to consider as a director for the project. When word about my directorial recommendations got back to Homer, he had a fit.

"You can't do that!" (You can.) "That's an insult!" (It's not; in Hollywood, it's idle conversation.) "You have to apologize!"

Not wanting to blow either the gig for myself or the project, I said fine. Homer gave me a phone number and one evening I wound up on the phone with Kemeny.

Over the phone he sounded a lot like Henry Kissinger; same low, gravelly voice and an accent (Kemeny had been born in Hungary). If he was pissed at me, as Homer had said, he gave no indication of it. In fact, he was quite cordial, never mentioned my supposed presumptuousness in suggesting directors. He was, as one might expect from his movies, articulate, intelligent, and, as we discussed *FF* in unspecific terms, I was getting more and more excited over the idea of working with him. In his hands, the movie would undoubtedly be a class project.

A week later Homer told me he was selling the project to RKO.

I never found out what happened with the Kemeny deal (ironically, Kemeny went on to produce several well-received films for HBO while I was working there), although knowing Homer, I have no doubt somebody waved a bigger check under his nose.

Although RKO was no longer the major Hollywood player it had been in its heyday, the legendary weight of the name still resonated with me. Back during the great days of Old Hollywood, this had, after all, been the studio which had given us all those great Fred Astaire/Ginger Rogers musicals, *King Kong*, and *Citizen Kane*, as well as all those wonderfully shadowy Robert Mitchum *film noirs* of the late 1940s and 1950s. But RKO had never had the financial muscle to match the major majors like MGM and Paramount, and when Howard Hughes bought the studio in 1948, the erratic billionaire's management drove the studio's managers crazy and the studio ever deeper into the red. The company would go through several ownership changes in the late 1950s, and by 1957 RKO was out of the movie business (Finler, *Hollywood...*, 168–170).

In the late 1970s, the company had decided to try to revive its motion picture production arm, and they had turned out some pretty visible flicks like the film adaptation of the stage musical *The Best Little Whorehouse in Texas* (1982), and *Cat People* (1982), but hadn't produced any hits. When Homer was dealing with them, Mark Seiler was the president of RKO Pictures.

Homer told me we needed a rewrite on *FF* to clinch the RKO deal and he wanted me to get on the phone with Doug Terman for counsel. It was the kind of frantic, half-assed advice you'd expect from Homer: "Oh, you want me to ask the author of the novel for better ways to chop up his book for a movie? Great idea! I'm sure he'll be enthusiastic as hell!"

Homer wanted me to call from his office so this could be a three-way discussion, but knowing what an I'm-a-writer-too pain in the ass he could be, I said this had to be a me-to-him thing and closed myself in his secretary's office to make the call. When I got Terman on the phone, I was up front with him:

"If I were you, I don't know how willing I'd be to help somebody butcher my book."

He laughed. "You seem like a nice guy," he said. "Do yourself a favor and do what I did; take the money and run." He told me to do whatever I felt I needed to do and not worry about him. "I got *my* money," he said.

So I did another pass, tightening the script up a bit although it was still fat, running between 130–140 pages as I remember. Still, it was good enough for RKO. They bought *Free Flight* outright from Homer and contracted me for a rewrite.

When I say "bought outright," what I mean is RKO didn't buy an option. They now *owned* the property, and that being the case, I no longer had to deal with Homer.

*   *   *

I did two rewrites working with RKO's development person, a terrific lady named Leslie Werner. Leslie was a movie person; she knew the classics, she knew the new stuff. We had generally similar sensibilities so we always knew what the other one was talking about, we got each other's references. You could argue with Leslie and she wouldn't take it personally, and it was always (well, usually—I'll get to that) about making the material better. She wasn't one of those people who felt she always had to win, although the time-honored rule of Hollywood was still in effect: he/she who signs the checks gets the last word.

She was fun and easy to work with and I learned a tremendous amount from her. Bill Fox had taught us to remember that screenplays have to be read so make them readable. He showed us some pages from his own adaptation of one of his novels (which was never produced) and it was quite prosey. I don't know if things had changed since Fox had been in Hollywood, or maybe this was why Fox hadn't gotten more things done, but Leslie had me strip a lot of that descriptive prose out.

"The first thing people out here look at is the number on the last page," she said. That gives them a ballpark idea of how long the finished movie will run and an even looser idea of how much it'll cost, but as loose as those numbers are, if they're too high, even before they start reading you're screwed.

The other thing, Leslie pointed out, was that most movie people simply don't like to read ... *anything.* That's why they're in the movies and not publishing. They like to see a lot of white space on the page.

(Note: In the early 2000s, I began to hear about a screenplay format called a "ladder." The idea was to keep text to an absolute minimum, to have no paragraph longer than a few lines, preferably even less, to break down action sequences into a series of single sentences. Text on the page was so sparse it resembled a—you guessed it—ladder. This supposedly made reading a screenplay an easier scan, but also boosted the amount of white space on a page considerably, and, as I said, screenplay readers love white space.)

We cleaned out a lot of the prose, Leslie's rule being to write no more than was necessary to get an idea across. We also took out a lot of stage directions particularly for dialogue line readings. "That's the actor's job," Leslie told me. "They'll ignore it anyway." Only if a move or a certain color to a line was absolutely, critically imperative should I put it on the page (say to indicate that a remark was meant sarcastically rather than literally). Don't direct from the page; the director and the actors don't like it. Their feeling is, if you want to direct, become a director.

Some changes were purely practical. RKO had some kind of production arrangement with an outfit in New Zealand and that's where *FF* would be shot. The novel and my screenplay had been set in Vermont in late fall: frost on the ground, snow, climax on a frozen lake. New Zealand does get snow up in its mountains, but we weren't going to be shooting in the mountains. That meant no snow, no frozen lake.

"What happens to the helicopter crash through the ice?" I asked Leslie.

"You're going to have to figure something else out. Doesn't matter; on our budget, we can't do it anyway."

The budget was $3 million, which due to currency exchange rates and that a lot of stuff was cheaper in New Zealand, was going to be the equivalent of $6 million worth of production value. In today's dollars, that would mean an effective budget of $13–14 million; still pretty tight for an action flick with a lot of flying sequences. That's *Spotlight* and *The Big Short* (2015) kind of budget money. *Blue Thunder* (1983), which had come out not long before RKO had picked up *Free Flight,* had featured a lot of roughly comparable aerial work. *Blue Thunder* has cost $22 million.

To try to get costs down, Leslie had me minimize the number of night scenes since it was more expensive to shoot at night during the day. We also had to look at seeing if we could cut down the number of principal actors.

We obviously couldn't cut Mallen, and Wyatt gave us a buddy-buddy dynamic we felt carried the movie through its first act and well into its second. Obviously, we couldn't lose Jean or her son; they were prime movers in the plot. And McKennon was the foil. That left the great-grandfather.

"Well, he's got some nice dialogue," I said, "but yeah, we could live without him."

"That's what I was thinking, too," Leslie said. "But they want to keep his dialogue."

"*They.*" There is always a "they"—people in a production or a studio whom you never meet but have the authority to have their words heeded as if delivered by burning bush.

"I like the dialogue, too, Les, but how do we keep it?"

"They wondered if maybe you couldn't give it to Jean."

"The guy is talking about World War I! Why in hell would this young woman be talking about World War I?"

"They like it, you have to find a way to keep some of it."

I was able to strip out enough lines (which sounded kind of groundless without the weight behind them of being spoken by someone who'd actually survived the carnage of World War I's western front) to make them happy, but I kept bumping into a completely unexpected problem, and the situation with the great-grandfather's lines illustrated it. I'd built fat into the script to trade for stuff I wanted to keep; throwaway stuff like a scene between a pair of plane spotters, for instance. But "they" often wanted to keep the fat and cut the meat!

Then Leslie told me I needed to tamp down the violence in the script.

There was only one scene I thought was a tad excessive: Mallen sneaks up behind an enemy trooper, stabs him with a pitchfork and the tines pierce out through the trooper's chest. No biggie to lose that, but the note about violence was more comprehensive.

"Look, Les, this is a PG-13 movie. There's nothing in there kids aren't seeing on TV during the day."

"I agree with you, but So-and-So says it's too violent."

"Who the hell is he?"

"He represents the bank putting up the money."

So I tamped down the violence.

The story was plagued with the notorious Second Act Sag. First acts usually have the dynamism that goes with setting up a situation, and third acts, well, if you know what you're doing, they have the dynamism of bringing things to a head. Second acts are always the toughest slog and this was no exception. Once Mallen crash-landed, the forward momentum of the story began to slow. McKennon sat around getting grief from his superiors while he waited word from search parties looking for the downed glider. Meanwhile, there was background exposition between Mallen and Wyatt, then Mallen and Jean, and Mallen and the great-grandpa, and Mallen and Paul... But the real time-eater and momentum-slower was the amount of time we had to give Mallen and Jean to go from mutually suspicious strangers to lovers. Even in the movies you can only compress that kind of arc so far before the audience is going, "Oh, pul-*eeeze!*"

Besides trimming down the expository scenes, Leslie also suggested we put some of them on the move; a construct Aaron Sorkin would make famous years later with what would come to be called his walk-and-talks. It doesn't sound like much, but putting Mallen and Wyatt on their feet for some of this exposition gave a subconscious feeling of the plot moving forward (at least that's the thinking). If they had to talk, at least they could talk while they were going somewhere.

We made one significant change from the book and that was to get rid of the Soviet occupiers. A year or so earlier, in 1983, ABC had aired *The Day After,* a graphic, disturbing portrayal of the results of a U.S./U.S.S.R. nuclear exchange which still remains one of the most watched television events of all time (over 100 million viewers during its single network airing). We weren't exactly doing a docudrama with *FF,* but I thought considering how widely *The Day After*'s picture of how little would be left of *anything* in the event of a nuclear war had saturated into the American collective consciousness, the idea that there was enough of a Soviet Union left intact to sends thousands of troops overseas to occupy the U.S. wasn't going to fly. Besides, by the time we were working on the script, relations between the U.S. and the Soviet Union were beginning to thaw a bit. There was a reasonable chance that by the time the movie came out, a U.S./Russia nuclear war would look ridiculously out of date.

Besides, Leslie and I agreed, the story didn't need the Russians. They were a largely off-screen presence anyway, and even in the novel Mallen is mostly pursued by American collaborators. We turned the new oppressive regime trying to exert control over the survivors into a wholly American, quasi-fascist organization, and made McKennon an ex-cop who liked the new authority's idea of law and order.

After I turned in my first rewrite, a few weeks later I got an excited call from Little Ruthie: "I got you another rewrite!"

"Oh, great."

"They asked me if you could do it in two weeks and I told them yes."

I almost dropped my phone. I'd had four weeks to do the first rewrite. "Jesus, Ruthie, couldn't you have talked it over with me first?"

"I wanted to get you the job!"

"Two weeks! It'll take me two weeks just to retype it!"

Before I started to work, Mark Seiler wanted to have a three-way conversation with Leslie and me. Most of the changes weren't major, mostly tightening, but he wanted the Russians back in.

Leslie and I explained to him why I'd first taken out the East Bloc troops and then the Soviets. We explained about *The Day After* influence, and about how U.S./Soviet Union relations seemed to be changing—

"I think the Russians are playing us for suckers!" Seiler declared. "This is our chance to take a shot at them."

I kept trying to make an argument against putting the Russian back in not only on the credibility issue, but taking them out had streamlined the screenplay considerably.

When a screenwriter disagrees with the people who are paying him/her, and cannot change their minds, the subsequent discussion usually goes something like this:

"I respect what you're saying, Bill, and you obviously feel very strongly about this."

"Thank you."

"And we wouldn't want you to make any changes you don't believe in."

"I appreciate that."

"Maybe we need some fresh eyes on this."

"Excuse me?"

"I think you've taken the material about as far as you can go, and maybe what we need at this point is some new thinking."

Translation: do it or you're fired. Either you do it, or someone else will do it, the only difference being in whose going to get paid to do it.

So, the Russians went back in.

We took another look at that nagging second act sag. Leslie came up with a wonderfully simple and elegant idea to move us through the second act more quickly:

"What if Mallen and Jean *already* knew each other?"

Mallen puts his damaged plane down near Jean's farm on purpose, and since he already has a history with both her and her son, a lot of the scenes we had constructed which only served to build their relationships could be junked.

I did the rewrite, managing somehow to get it done in two weeks. After that, Leslie left RKO and I was sorry to see her go. If there was any more work to be done, I was going to miss working with her.

Weeks went by with no word from RKO, then I received a call from Seiler saying he was going to be in New York and he wanted to meet with me to discuss *Free Flight.*

I went up to meet him one evening after work. He was staying at one of the grand old uptown hotels (I think it was the Waldorf). I'd never had a real, honest-to-God movie meeting with an honest-to-God movie exec and had been nervous as hell all day about it. I had pumped friends of mine at work about protocol, making a good impression, all kinds of needlessly paranoid crap.

"He's going to ask if you want something to drink."

"Do I say yes?"

"You say yes. All those guys drink. He's gonna think you're a wuss if you don't have something to drink. What do you drink?"

"I like a nice white Russian."

"You order that and he'll *still* think you're a wuss."

Seiler let me into his suite, offered me the sofa in the sitting room. He was a trim, pre-maturely gray mid–30s, and although this was close of the day and he was in his room, he was still in business attire.

"Can I call room service and get you a drink?" he offered.

"Yeah, sure, thank you. I'll have a seven and seven." My HBO colleagues agreed this was a manly enough drink without too overbearing a sense of machismo.

Seiler picked up the phone. He ordered the makings for a seven and seven, "And I'll have a Diet Coke."

So much for worrying about looking like a wuss.

"The screenplay's still not right," Seiler said, "but we don't think it's you. You've done everything we've asked you to do. So if it's not working, we think the problem is *us.*"

I thought that was an incredibly forthright thing for him to say, so much so that I couldn't think of anything to say in response.

"So we want you to do another rewrite. But this time, we want you to do it *your* way."

Jeez, when in this business does *that* ever happen.

"How long will you need?"

I wanted the breathing room to get it right this time. "Six weeks?"

"Six weeks is fine."

Wow. This was a lottery win.

"There's just one thing—"

And there it is.

"Don't change the first act and give it a big finish."

So, in other words, not *my* way, at least not completely. Still, I was being given a lot of running room.

And I took it.

The Russians were out.

When Leslie and I had been working together, we had often discussed how to get some energy going in McKennon's narrative, and now I thought I'd come up with something. After Mallen escapes, I had McKennon poke around Mallen's cabin and find a photograph of Mallen and Jean. He runs down the photo to a camera shop in a near–ghost town overrun with cannibals and is able to get a bead on Jean's place. In other words, McKennon isn't just sitting around on his ass anymore, and as he closes in on Mallen who doesn't know McKennon is now on his trail, that gives the story a "ticking clock": Mallen doesn't know his time is running out.

And as for the big finish, instead of McKennon's helicopter chasing Mallen on the ground around a big grassy field (the replacement for the frozen lake), he's now in a gunship chasing Mallen's glider around the Vermont hills.

I was pretty happy with the results, felt we had a nice "popcorner" as I like to call them; a fun, entertaining, exciting action flick. I sent the screenplay in, got my check, and then…

Nothing. Weeks of nothing. I was still in touch with Leslie Werner and I asked her if she had any idea what was going on over at RKO. According to her, everything about *Free Flight* should have been ready to go; it only needed Seiler to give it the green light. She wondered if he'd gotten cold feet on the project.

Which didn't make any sense to me. The studio had made larger pictures than this, they'd spent the money to buy the property outright and had kept investing in the screenplay. It just didn't feel like the company would get weak-kneed.

And then another call from Seiler that he was, again, going to be in New York and this time he wanted to talk to me and Little Ruthie.

This time it was a morning meeting at the hotel's breakfast buffet. I had to slip out of work, and Seiler and Ruthie were already waiting for me (later, Ruthie would tell me she was pissed Seiler hadn't offered her anything when they'd sat down together, but that the minute I, the talent, got there, it was, "Hey, Bill, help yourself to some breakfast!" but that's the crap agent's get paid to put up with).

Seiler didn't talk about *Free Flight.* He was trying to set something up where I'd be a kind of "house writer" for him, and he talked about me working on something called "Battle Bus II" (although I'd never heard of "Battle Bus I"). Whatever happened with *Free Flight,* this was a wannabe screenwriter's dream; to be attached as the go-to guy for a production outfit meaning a steady stream of work.

It wasn't long before we found out what he'd been talking about. Seiler and several other executives had been trying to put together a takeover of RKO. That explained the freeze on *Free Flight;* Seiler wasn't going to put a picture in the production pipeline while he was trying to engineer a multi-million dollar acquisition of the company.

And then it was over. No *Free Flight,* no being a house writer, no takeover. In June of 1987, the news broke that Seiler and his group couldn't put together the financing for the $48 million takeover, and what usually happens after a failed coup happened: Seiler got the boot.

And everything at RKO he'd had his hands on died with his exit.

*   *   *

When the RKO arrangement collapsed, I got a call from Homer's partner, Leo, about the possibility of doing something else.

"Before we talk about doing more work together, how about my $1500?"

When Homer had first been negotiating with RKO, for business reasons way beyond me, Homer had had to show them he'd paid me something to work on the script for him. We'd struck a contract in November of 1983 which had stated that I'd been first asked to work on the project in 1982 and that I'd been paid $1500 for that service.

Except I'd never been paid that $1500.

Despite the big house on Long Island and the big Manhattan office, Homer had boo-hooed he didn't have that kind of cash, but for the RKO thing to happen, he had to tell them I'd been paid, I had to sign a contract confirming I'd been paid, and he'd promised me he'd make it up later.

Well, this was later and I wanted my $1500.

"He never paid you?" Leo sounded pretty unhappy. I don't know that this was the case, but the way Leo sounded I got the impression he'd put up some of that $1500 I didn't get.

Then Homer called. "Don't you remember, Bill? I paid you."

"Uh, no, Homer, you never paid me. I'd remember getting $1500 from you. If you paid me, show me the cancelled check."

I told Little Ruthie what was going on and nothing got her ire up like being stiffed on a payout. After she went around with Homer, she called me.

"That sonofabitch says he paid you."

"I know. I asked him to show me the cancelled check."

"You know what that pond scum told me? He says there's no cancelled check because he paid you in cash, and he's got no receipt for it. He's a lawyer and I'm supposed to believe him that he doesn't have a receipt for a $1500 payment? I'm supposed to believe he gave you $1500 *in cash*?"

Little Ruthie agreed with me that Homer had probably screwed Leo along with us. I don't know how it worked out between Homer and Leo, but that was the last we heard from either of them.

But it was not the last I heard *of* Homer.

*   *   *

Homer finally did get to produce something: after years of shopping that tweener mystery series around, he finally got himself a production deal for a television series for cable.

It ran eight episodes.

As far as I know, he never did anything else.

*   *   *

Because RKO owned *Free Flight* outright, the project stayed on the company's shelves. Since they had invested a fair amount of money in the project, I thought if I could get someone else interested in it, they might be willing to give it up for a price, or work out some kind of co-production deal.

Dave Pritchard had been my boss at HBO. Despite the fact I had absolutely no background in corporate PR, Dave had given me a shot at being a PR writer, and, thanks to him, I'd gone from listening to subscribers bitch about how often we ran lousy movies to being HBO's designated corporate writer. Dave and another HBO exec, Tim Braine, had left HBO to start their own production company. By the early 1990s, they'd done a not-bad movie for HBO, and had had a cult hit with the animated television series *Dr. Katz, Professional Therapist,* then Dave had landed at the animation company Film Roman and was credited as executive producer on a number of animated series including *The Simpsons* and *King of the Hill.*

I reached out to Dave, showed him *Free Flight,* and he thought he could do something with it. What about RKO?

"Don't worry about them. If I can find someone who wants to do this, they'll say yes." Dave had an in with director Peter Markle who'd done the Vietnam War flick *Bat*21* (1988) for TriStar. According to Dave, Markle had a "put" with TriStar; he could bring a project in to the studio. I'd seen *Bat*21* and even though it hadn't exactly rocked the box office, I'd liked the movie, and, with its aerial action sequences, I thought Markle would be a good fit.

Markle passed.

I've contacted RKO a couple of times since then about the possibility of reviving *Free Flight.* One time I was surprised to find out they already had, and had a director and a different screenwriter attached. Then both left for better work and *FF* went back on the shelf. Another time, they'd moved offices and nobody could even find the paperwork on the property to ascertain what rights, if any, they still had.

Through all of this, I stayed in contact with Doug Terman. He and I became phone buddies and pen pals, and I kept him apprised of my efforts to land *FF* somewhere while he provided me with sales info on the novel as ammunition. We would trade writer's stories, he even showed me a treatment for a book he was working on to get some feedback. When the RKO gig had finally collapsed, he'd invited me up to his place in Vermont so I could vent about it, but the date fell through when my car wound up in the shop the day before I was supposed to drive up.

And then I stopped hearing from him. It wasn't like him; he'd always been a gracious guy, warm in his responses, supportive about my other writing projects. Then sometime in 2000 or 2001 I received a letter from his wife. Doug had passed away in December of 1999. She hadn't realized I didn't know until one of my letters showed up in the Terman mailbox. Even though we'd never met face to face, I felt a loss. More than that, I'd always wanted to have been able to pick up the phone and say, "Hey, Doug! Guess what? *Free Flight* is happening!"

It still bothers me I never got to make that call.

The Academic:
Dr. Benjamin Dunlap

(A Rhodes scholar at Oxford, a Ph.D. from Harvard, Bernie Dunlap's subsequent awards-studded five decades as an educator include stints at Harvard, the University of South Carolina, and Wofford College where he also served as president for 13 years. Overlapping were also almost 20 years as an award-winning writer-producer for public television, books, essays, and a heap of accolades. Among his television efforts was the acclaimed 1979 series Cinematic Eye *in which he looked at foreign film classics. Point being Bernie is a very smart guy.)*

I know less and less—which, according to Socrates, is the beginning of wisdom ... or, according to my wife, the advent of senility.

More and more, to me the privileged moments on screen are shrewdly contrived accidents (paradox intended) to which writers, directors, actors, and cinematographers contribute, sometimes equally, sometimes not. That moment in *La Règle du jeu* (*The Rules of the Game,* 1939) when, amid the tragicomic nonsense, Robert de la Chesnaye displays his glittering symbolic toy with such proprietary anxiety, pride, and precarious pleasure summarizes for me all the complex nuances of Jean Renoir's uncanny ability to stumble over miracles. That's not a fair assessment of what Renoir does, of course, because he knew the risks he was taking and understood full well how style, script, direction, casting, lighting, luck all played a part. Especially luck, and the big question for me is why some people are more consistently lucky than others.

That's where the question about scripting comes in, in helping create the likeliest circumstances for miracles to occur while never supposing what's on the page is like a chemist's formula. As you can tell, I've moved a long way from a writer's emphasis on plot to a viewer's love of those revelatory epiphanies, sometimes apparently offhand, for which the elements of a good script can at best be a necessary ingredient. In other words, I cling ever more tightly to brilliant "accidents" in films like *L'Avventura* (1960), *Earth* (1930), and Humphrey Jennings' *Listen to Britain* (1942).

Toss in Marcel Ophuls' *Le Chagrin et la pitié* (*The Sorrow and the Pity,* 1969) and I show myself to be the sort of pretentious movie-goer Woody Allen was skewering in *Annie Hall*—except, like Marcel Dalio, I'm revealing what I have truly and persistently loved the most about our intricate toy.

Myth #3: Every Scene Should Move the Plot Forward

As it happens, as I was noodling around with this piece, I happened to catch three great flicks by the Coen Brothers: *The Big Lebowski* (1998), *Fargo* (1996), and *No Country for Old Men* (2007). Joel and Ethan Coen are among the most elegant violators of many of the concepts addressed in this book, and the idea that every scene needs to drive the plot forward is no exception.

Before we go further, we need to get some terms straight. Many if not most people (including myself) use the words "plot" and "story" interchangeably, but they're actually two different things.

"Plot" is what we see on the screen; the sequence of events that carry a movie from its beginning to its end. "Story" is what all those happenings are *about*.

Ok, that's a bit confusing. Let's try this:

When H.G. Wells wrote *The War of the Worlds* in 1898 (yes, youngsters, there was a book, and yes, it's really that old), it was an anti-imperialist reaction to the way Britain and other European powers thought they had some kind of divine right to occupy the lands of what they considered to be "inferior" peoples. Wells' story was him saying, "How'd you like to be on the *other* end of this empire-building business?" So, the *plot* of *TWOTW* is Martians come to Earth, kick hell out of the mightiest powers on the planet and almost conquer the world, but humankind gets bailed out by the aliens' vulnerability to Earth microbes. The *story* of the novel, on the other hand, is that humanity—nearly brought down by a power greater than itself, then saved by something smaller than itself—is taught the humbling lesson that it is not the center of the universe ("Wells").

This is that wild, submerged, invisible, sometimes subversive world of *subtext*.

"Plot" moves; "story" doesn't. Story, for lack of a better way to put it, is a movie's state of mind. It's invisible on the screen, it's a sensibility seeping through, the cumulative, sometimes subconscious effect of what happens in the plot. As much as action, it can manifest through mood, texture, resonance. And, in my opinion, the more plot-driven a movie is, the less likely there's much going on in that subterranean story level.

Plot-driven movies tend to move quickly. Think most big-budget summer blockbusters. They're about what they're about. Not a lot of subtext to the fight between the Avengers and Ultron (*Avengers: Age of Ultron,* 2015). It is what it is.

But some moves are about more than what happens on the screen, and, generally speaking, those movies will tend to have a slower momentum and "waste" time (at least those every-scene-etc., adherents would consider it a waste) watering and fertilizing their subtexts.

Ok, that's a bit vague, so let's look at some examples.

Francis Ford Coppola's Vietnam War epic, *Apocalypse Now,* offers a pretty clear illustration of the point about the separation of plot and story, and that the more weight given the story, it's more likely that not only will every scene *not* drive the plot, but the nature—and aesthetic success—of such a film demands they don't.

Apocalypse is framed by a classic plot form: a journey, that of the assassin Willard (Martin Sheen) upriver to "terminate the command" of renegade American colonel Kurtz (Marlon Brando) "with extreme prejudice." But the journey itself is episodic, and those episodes have little to do with furthering Willard's trek: a USO show gone anarchic, a tragic encounter with a Vietnamese family on their sampan, the Boschian nightmare of the leaderless, never-ending fight around Do Long Bridge, and, perhaps most memorably, Willard's meeting up with the cowboyish, surfing-obsessed Colonel Kilgore (Robert Duvall with his war-lover's treatise on napalm: "I love the smell of napalm in the morning").

That these episodes have nothing to do with getting Willard to his destination is even more manifest in *Apocalypse Now Redux* (2001), Coppola's re-editing of the film to restore footage not in the original 1979 release. Whether one prefers the original or *Redux,* what's clear is that the cut footage changes the central plot of the movie not a hair. Like all of the episodes, they are there not to move Willard up the river, but to cultivate a sensibility extending beyond the plot to nurture the soul of the movie; a thematic core taken from the film's uncredited source, Joseph Conrad's 1899 novella, *Heart of Darkness.*

Apocalypse is only tangentially about the war in Vietnam just as *Darkness* is only tangentially about ivory hunting in the Congo. Conrad's thesis is that what keeps us sane and civilized is living in civilization among sane people. Remove that framework, and something brutally primal emerges: Conrad's off-the-rails ivory hunter, Coppola's off-the-rails soldier (Stafford).

Coppola's Mob epic, *The Godfather,* may have a more emphatic, driving plot, but, again, the subtextual yang to the plot's yin manifests itself in several unforgettable yet irrelevant (plot wise) scenes. Were the movie more conventionally built along the every-scene-etc., model, it would open with the segment where Robert Duvall, adopted son and *consigliere* of Mob chief Don Corleone (Brando again), tells the don of the need to meet with an ambitious drug dealer which, in turn, leads to an unfruitful meeting which, in turn, kicks off the gang war which, in turn, brings Corleone's youngest son Michael (Al Pacino)—whom the don has tried to keep isolated from the family's criminal enterprises—into the family business which, in turn, leads to his becoming the Mob family's soulless chief. That's a nice, clean, by-the-book, runs-like-a-Porsche plot arc.

But that's not how the movie plays. Instead, we have the iconic opening of the undertaker Bonasera pleading with Don Corleone for revenge against two punks who raped his daughter. We have Corleone's actor/singer godson whining about his fading career; a scene which will lead to the infamous—and equally irrelevant—horse's head scene.

These scenes have nothing to do with the plot driving the movie forward, but they do steep the audience deep in the day-to-day immorality which makes up Corleone's universe, and Coppola's take on the immigrant American dream gone twisted and perverse (Muller, 11). Without this kind of "fat" in the script, *The Godfather* would be a more conventional, more familiar gangster flick. It wouldn't be *The Godfather*.

One of the few mainstream filmmakers able to give story primacy over plot was Stanley Kubrick, particularly in two movies we looked at earlier: *2001: A Space Odyssey* and *Full Metal Jacket*. The film *2001* has the barest wisp of a plot; Kubrick's priority was to create an immersive, futuristic experience. The actual storytelling in *2001* is minimal at best. The plotline of *2001* may be barely visible to the naked eye, but *Full Metal Jacket* doesn't even have that much forward narrative drive. Instead, there's a series of episodes and mini-arcs, none with much connection to each other, but all contributing to a frame of mind, a sense, a *feeling*. The words "mosaic" and "collage" come to mind, neither of which makes for a happy marriage walking down the aisle hand-in-hand with plot. Feeling—not the plot dynamics of suspense and anticipation or even character involvement—is what Kubrick's after.

Bringing this back to the Coens as exemplars *par excellence* of filmmakers with a demonstrated ability to weld story to plot (to incorporate "fat" into a driving narrative), it's worth noting these are storytellers not trapped by a specific style. They can write lean and mean (*Blood Simple*, 1984), and also go comedic in a movie so packed with speed freak-paced craziness it threatens to blow apart (*Raising Arizona*, 1987). And, they also have their contemplative, near–Kubrickian tone poems where narrative (plot) plays second fiddle to mood (*Barton Fink,* 1991; *The Man Who Wasn't There,* 2001). But they also have those films where they've managed to seamlessly blend a reflective resonance with an imperative and impressively dense narrative.

Fargo juggles multiple plotlines: its dumbass kidnappers, the hapless businessman trying to engineer a ransom scheme to bail himself out of a financial bind, and the waaay pregnant cop poking into the whole mess. But what gives *Fargo* its distinctive, Coenesque flavor which brought the film a Best Picture Oscar nom and a win for its screenplay is the fat; the throwaway scenes. Think of Steve Buscemi's not-the-hotshot-he-thinks-he-is kidnapper out on the town with a bimbo hooker trying to impress her with his (not really) discerning taste in schlock music; or the digression of preggers cop Marge Gunderson (Frances McDormand) meeting up with an old high school pal, touched by his tale of woe about marrying another fellow high schooler who recently died, then finding out it's all b.s. and that he, in fact, had been stalking the woman. Think of those scenes that are nothing more than Marge having a bite to eat: no dialogue, not even another character present, just Marge at a hotel buffet, Marge in her car eating drive-thru burgers. And then there's the scene with one of Marge's deputies talking to one of the locals about a conversation he had with, possibly, one of the kidnappers. The scene runs over a minute and a half, revolves around a character making his only appearance in the film, and, for the most part, is an unbroken meandering monologue which, in the end, conveys only a single, simple point of information.

So what does all this "wasted," unnecessary, doesn't-drive-the-plot stuff do? Like the fat in a good Italian sausage, it's what gives *Fargo* its flavor, it's what breaks it out of a crowd of thousands of twisty-turny crime thrillers, it's what makes it its own thing and not a clone or variant on a jillion other caper-goes-bad flicks.

The Big Lebowski goes even further. It's Raymond Chandler-on-weed plot is almost an excuse to drop in on the messy, completely unproductive life of an almost permanently stoned, 1960s burn-out case with a thing for bowling, along with his two equally empty-headed (but each in his own odd way) bowler friends. You could strip out the plot from *Lebowski* and without much tweaking, set it in the 1940s with Dick Powell in a snap-brim fedora as Philip Marlowe and carry it off just fine, but then it wouldn't be *Lebowski.* Even more so than *Fargo, Lebowski* is more about the flavorful fat than the familiar meat.

With its brooding, laconic storytelling, *No Country for Old Men* seems a different animal from *Fargo* and *Lebowski,* but the Coens—sticking pretty close to the Cormac McCarthy source novel—come up with a similar paradigm; a lot of plot spiked with irrelevant scenes giving the telling a greater gravity than the plot alone can provide. On the surface, *No Country* is about Josh Brolin stumbling across money from a drug deal gone bad, then going on the run from both obsessive hitman Javier Bardem and local cop Tommy Lee Jones. That's a solid, propulsive arc.

But the movie regularly wanders off onto sidelines: Bardem's long conversation with a gas station attendant who never knows how close he came to being part of the film's body count; Jones chasing after the dumbass who almost loses the bodies he's carting in from the desert drug rendezvous; and several long, talky scenes Jones has—with a fellow lawman, with his crippled ex-lawman uncle, with his wife—about a world descending into drug-fueled, chaotic violence.

And it is this last bit—this sense of an entropic devolution from a world of decent people and understandable motives into unnecessary, even absurd brutality—which gives the movie its poetry, which makes it *No Country for Old Men* instead of a more formulaic, nondescript guy-on-the-run flick.

Not on the same level as these three movies is another Coen Brothers effort, *Burn After Reading* (2008), but it's still worth looking at for how it doesn't play by the rules. An ensemble piece in which every character has his/her own ridiculous arc, all of which do more or less have a three-act architecture, and all of which, one way or another, carom off the other arcs, *Burn...* has plenty of well-sculpted plot which doesn't help it make any more sense. But it's not supposed to. It's a fun tangle of nonsense—kind of like watching someone juggle an egg, an apple, and a bowling ball; pointless but fascinating—that doesn't seem to be going anywhere until it ends in an explanatory conversation in the office of the director of the CIA. Ridiculous and craftily messy, *Burn...* did $60.3 million; almost as much as the Coens' more disciplined, Oscar-winning (for Best Picture and Best Adapted Screenplay) *No Country* ($74.2 million), and a bucketload more than their acclaimed *Fargo* ($24.6 million).

* * *

Screenwriting architecture dogmas—like three-act structure and every-scene-should-etc.—are sturdy conventions which work best for sturdy, conventional stories, but they deny an entire category of filmmaking; a category for which a firm plot is secondary, or maybe even completely irrelevant.

Consider some of the movies we looked at in the chapter on Three-Act Structure. Move the plot forward? *M*A*S*H* doesn't have a plot to move. Neither does *The Bellboy*. Or *Full Metal Jacket*. And there's those superfluous prologues in *The Wild Bunch* and *Saving Private Ryan*.

Look at the Oscar-winning screenplay for *The Big Short* (2015), an adaptation of Michael Lewis' non-fiction bestseller by Charles Randolph and Adam McKay. Move the plot forward? At regular intervals, Randolph/McKay's script actually calls a time-out, stopping the forward movement dead while cameos by the likes of Anthony Bourdain, Selena Gomez, Margot Robbie (among others) are used to explain the esoteric economic concepts at the heart of the movie, using yet another rule-breaking advice: breaking the "fourth wall" to directly lecture the audience.

Or consider works from writer/director Richard Linklater like *Boyhood* (2014), shot over a period of 12 years. How do you structure a screenplay along conventional concepts when you don't even know what your cast is going to look like from one episode (and *Boyhood* is nothing if not episodic) to the next because you're shooting them years apart? Linklater went into the project with only a skeleton of a script, the project would shoot for just three or four days maybe once or twice a year, with Linklater looking at the previous shoot's edited footage before outlining the next sequence, sometimes not even having finished material to shoot until just a few days before filming (Stern). *Boyhood* would go on to become one of the most acclaimed movies of 2014.

And there's the funny, fuzzy storytelling of Linklater's *Everybody Wants Some!* (2016), the "spiritual sequel" (Linklater's words) to his delightfully dizzy *Dazed and Confused* (1993). "Like its predecessor," *Entertainment Weekly*'s Kevin P. Sullivan wrote on the eve of the movie's release, "*Everybody* is light on story, but the onscreen friendships are real..." (90). Linklater's process, as with *Boyhood*, was not about sculpting a well-defined narrative form. Linklater shipped the cast to his Texas ranch:

> ... where they could rehearse and reshape the characters to each actor's strengths. "That workshop process is essential to dialing in the humor," (Linklater) says. "The writer in me gets fired by the director in me: 'That doesn't work. That's not funny. I'm giving these lines to this other person'" [91].

The conventions of three-act structure and a constantly progressing narrative are the equivalent of writing solid, effective, mainstream commercial prose. And these kinds of films are not prose.

I've been lucky enough to make the acquaintance of the award-winning American poet Renee Ashley. She is the only person who ever got me to understand how poetry works (more or less). Prose, she said, comes in the front door and sits down. Poetry, conversely, doesn't come in the front door. It comes in through the windows, through the attic vents, it comes in everywhere *but* the front door (Mesce, "Writers...," 145).

The concept of every-scene-etc., works for some films, can even work brilliantly. One of my favorite thrillers is the 1974 original *The Taking of Pelham One Two Three*, with Peter Stone's express train of a script as flawless an execution of the every-scene concept as you'll ever see. Another favorite of mine is the 2015 winner of the Best Original Screenplay (for Josh Singer and Tom McCarthy) and Best Picture Oscars, *Spotlight*; an information-packed piece, every scene providing another piece in a complicated puzzle about a massive, true-life child molestation scandal involving the Catholic church.

But every-scene is *a* way to go; not *the* way. It brings the viewer in through the front door, sits him/her down and tells them a story straight through to the end. For some stories that's fine. But it rarely allows an opportunity for poetry.

For poetry, you have to break a rule.

The Network Executive: Josh Sapan

(Josh Sapan's first media job after graduating from college was driving around the country with two projectors and a pile of film cans rattling around in the back of his little station wagon, traveling from college campus to campus to show the kind of art house movies that weren't making it to downtown cinemas. He's come a long way since. In 1987, Sapan joined Rainbow Media Holdings LLC, becoming its CEO in 1995. Now known as AMC Networks, the company is most closely identified with its cable channels: AMC, Bravo, IFC, Fuse, Sundance Channel, WE: Women's Entertainment. Sapan is credited with turning AMC from a TCM clone into an original programming powerhouse with shows like Mad Men, Breaking Bad, *and* The Walking Dead, *and expanding original offerings across the company's channel spectrum. In 2010, business mag* Fast Company *tagged Sapan as #21 on their list of the "100 Most Creative People in Business.")*

Great movies and television shows share a simple, common thread; their creators have a bond to the material so deep that it comes to life in a way that transcends fad, genre, and time. The results are unique when they premiere, and continue to engage decades later.

Mass media is often justifiably accused of being transient: those involved must often work within the constraints of market influences that can yield work too beholden to passing trends or imitation, yet writers and directors often have passion projects that—for the lucky ones—get produced after years of effort. The best results are movies and shows that can take on the status of great books: they are unique, fully realized, and deeply individual.

The notion of a singular, driving creative vision being at the center of the best work has long been accepted in art films. Few question that *The Bicycle Thief* (1949) directed by Vittorio de Sica, Orson Welles' *Citizen Kane*, or *On the Waterfront* (1954) directed by Elia Kazan, are everything that the word "classic" implies. And movies critically recognized in recent years, such as *Spotlight* (2015), *Birdman* (2014), and *Boyhood* (2014) are likely to enjoy similarly long lives because of the deep relationships their respective directors—Tom McCarthy, Alejandro Inarritu, and Richard Linklater—have to their work. *Boyhood*'s decade-long vision set a different standard of commitment against significant odds; *Spotlight* languished on the "blacklist" of unproduced screenplays before it marched to Oscar recognition.

Sometimes surprising is the depth of creative synergy between maker and material in a film that, at first glance, looks like it was created for the market but moves well beyond the derivative to a new, personalized incarnation of a familiar story. *The Dark Knight* (2008), directed by Chris Nolan, took a pop franchise and elevated it to memorable, setting a standard for a genre known primarily for its cartoon qualities.

The critical variable of a creator's depth of connection is also at play in television. Early television shows like *Playhouse 90* and *The Twilight Zone*, and, more recently, *The Sopranos, The Wire, Breaking Bad,* and *Mad Men* are commonly referred to as icons of (the first and second) Golden Age of television. *Mad Men* famously was rejected by most networks and kept alive by the tenacity and singular vision of Matt Weiner—a vision he shepherded throughout the entire run of the series.

All in the Family, Maude, and *The Jeffersons* are testaments to Norman Lear's personal authorship. *Seinfeld, Friends,* and *Modern Family* may look and feel like standard sitcoms, but their unusual endurance is derived from the determined, specific vision, and less widely acknowledged depth of connection of their creators, and their dogged commitment to keep that vision sharp and disciplined in a commercial medium over the long run.

It is comforting that entertainment—commercial or art house, wide screen or streamed—can celebrate the vision of the artist, elevating both the product and the medium to a more meaningful, lasting power.

Orphans: *Big Phil's Kid* and *Surrender*

Unless you're one of those A-list, always-in-demand Hollywood scribes for whom producers and directors line up at your door, a screenwriter's professional life is more typically one of short, furious bursts of activity scattered among long periods of waiting around and/or hustling for work. From the time I was first brought on *Free Flight* until Mark Seiler idled the project while he set about trying to buy RKO was a period of about four years. If I add up the actual writing time I'd spent on drafts for Homer and then RKO, I don't think it totaled six months sprinkled across that span.

My biggest concern once *FF* went on the shelf—and it amplified considerably with Seiler's exit from RKO—was this was Little Ruthie's and my only Hollywood connection. If *Free Flight* didn't fly, we had no follow-up moves. But just as I began brooding about my bleak-looking future prospects with *FF* tabled, another gig fell into our laps.

Little Ruthie was still managing Dutton's backlist when she was contacted by Bill Persky, then the executive producer, director, and sometimes writer for *Kate & Allie*, an Emmy-winning, Top 10 sitcom on CBS. Persky was after the film rights for a 1969 Y/A novel, *Big Phil's Kid*, by M.M. Parker.

The kid of the title is Larry Carrett, a 16-year-old New York high schooler who learns, upon the death of one of his uncles, that his father is Big Phil Carrettelli, one of the biggest Mob kingpins in the country.

Neither Ruthie nor I was familiar with Persky's name, and after I got to know him better and learn just how impressive a track record he had, I still wasn't surprised I didn't know him better because Billy, as I would also come to find out, is not a name-dropper, nor a self-promoter, and is probably one of the most self-effacing yet accomplished people I've ever met. Many of his friends, I would find, became his friends initially knowing him only as—for one example—just some friendly guy on the next treadmill at the gym. Like me, it was only after becoming a closer acquaintance that any of them discovered there was a bit more to him.

Not that he didn't have reason to brag if he'd chosen to.

Persky had a writing career extending back to the 1950s when, with his then writing partner Sam Denoff, he had written comedy material for New York D.J.s, then graduated to penning jokes for stand-up comics working the sadly-now-extinct circuit of night clubs in the city (Persky, 21). The pair moved up to television when they were hired to write for *The Steve Allen Show,* a variety series airing on NBC, but after relocating to Los Angeles and working for Allen for just five weeks, NBC cancelled the show (28–30). What happened after that, well, as Billy has often said to me, "Carl Reiner saved my life."

This from Billy's memoir, *My Life Is a Situation Comedy:*

> In 1963, *The Dick Van Dyke Show* was starting its third season and was already considered the high point in the development of situation comedy. Every writer in Hollywood was writing a sample script trying to get Carl's attention [Reiner was producer for the series].... Though our script was flawed, Carl liked the writing so much that he gave us an assignment to do a show, and everything really good in my career started at that moment [42].

Billy would win his first of five Emmys the following season, and an Emmy nomination the season after that.

In 1965, not long after *Van Dyke* went off the air, he and Denoff would move up to producing, creating the ABC series, *That Girl.* A breakthrough in the portrayal of women on TV, *That Girl* was one of the first television shows to feature a single, independent, profession-directed woman, plugging into the decade's burgeoning Women's Lib movement (King).

Billy and Denoff would amicably split afterward, and Billy would score another major hit with *Kate & Allie* which debuted in 1984. Scattered throughout, as a writer, director, and producer, he worked with some of the biggest names in film and television: Julie Andrews, Sid Caesar, Bill Cosby, even Orson Welles (on a television adaptation of the Moss Hart/George S. Kaufman play *The Man Who Came to Dinner*).

Against this I could match my uncredited few minutes of *Blow Out,* and *Free Flight* which had never gotten off the launching pad. So, naturally, Little Ruthie pitched me as just the guy to help Billy turn *Big Phil's Kid* into a movie. Despite my paltry c.v., Persky agreed to a meeting over lunch.

The sit-down was at a small midtown restaurant, nice but not plush, off on one of the quiet cross streets. Little Ruthie and I got there first. I was dressed like I was on a job interview: jacket and tie (which I had long since stopped wearing to HBO). From where I sat I could see out through the glass of the front door. I saw a middle-aged guy pull up on a bicycle, wondering as I watched him lock it up, Is *this* our guy?

Dressed in corduroy slacks and a pullover sweater—a nice middle ground between Eliot Kastner's I-don't give-a-damn sweat suit and Homer's velvet sports jacket—Billy had the relaxed, relaxing, instantly friendly feel of everybody's favorite professor at a small college.

He talked about how long he'd been a fan of the book, and then, inevitably, the conversation got around to me.

"Ruthie showed me your last script," Billy said. "It's obvious you can write. My concern is, can you write comedy?"

Having already oversold me by telling him *Blow Out* was practically all mine, Little Ruthie then went on another hype streak saying, "There's a lot of humor in *Free Flight*," like slipping a few good one-liners into a post-nuclear holocaust actioner indicates you know how to get yuks.

Billy mercifully let Ruthie's comment fly by, and asked me directly: "*Can* you write comedy?"

Let me digress for a moment here. There's a difference between being witty and humorous, and being comedic. You know to give James Bond or Iron Man a couple of zingers during all the explosions, but that's not comedy. Comedy operates in another universe, requires a different sensibility; one that not only sees the laugh in any situation, but knows how to extract it and keep a consistent tone throughout a piece. *Dr. Strangelove* has one kind of comedic voice; *The Hangover* another. Kubrick cut a pie fight from *Dr. Strangelove* because as comic as the movie is, it's never silly-funny (there being a significant difference between absurdity and silliness); the pie fight would've broken the mood. But it would've been fine in the anything-goes world of *The Hangover.*

Billy asked me a straight question, I gave him a straight answer: "I don't know. I've never tried it before."

"See, because I'd hate to hire you and then find out you can't do it."

"Well, I'd hate for you to hire me and then *I* find out I can't do it."

"So what do we do about this?"

There were a few seconds of quiet around the table, then I had a thought. It was a mechanism that had gotten me the gig for *Blow Out:* "Why don't I take a scene from the book and adapt it," I offered. "It'll be kind of like an audition piece."

Billy seemed happy with that idea, so that was the plan.

I had made the offer knowing I had an ace to play. Early in the book, there's a scene at an Italian wake for the main character's Uncle Angie "No Nose" Carrettelli. Coming from an Italian family, I'd been to more family funerals than I could count. For those of you who've never been to one, they're a cross between grand opera, soap opera, *The McLaughlin Group*, and a raucous family reunion. Like the old movie posters used to say: "Thrills! Chills! You'll laugh! You'll cry!" My family's funerals were so ripe with material that, for years, I'd been jotting down bits of dialogue and business I'd witnessed at them, storing them away, just waiting for the right opportunity to use this stuff; the kind of material usually followed by the addendum, "You can't make this stuff up!"

In the book, the wake runs about six pages. I wrote the hell out of it, incorporating damn near everything in my Family Funeral file into the scene which consequently ran somewhere around 10 script pages. I knew that was a ridiculous scene length for a finished screenplay, but I felt this was the time for showboating.

Apparently that was enough; that and the "button" for my submission. I ran the scene a page into the next scene when Larry's family arrives at a house they keep in Palm Beach while things cool off back in New York in the wake of Uncle Angie's assassination. Big Phil's limo pulls up in front of their opulent vacation house along with a car full of bodyguards. As Big Phil steps out of his car, he notices a dead goldfish in the pond in front of the house. He turns to one of his goons. "Fix the fish," he commands.

"I love that line!" Billy said to me, and from someone with his comedy pedigree, I consider that one of the highest compliments I've ever gotten.

*   *   *

There was a hitch to signing with Billy, and that was to work for him required my joining the Writer's Guild. Little Ruthie, having researched the pay scale for Guild writers, was ecstatic. Me, not so much.

Look, nothing against the WGA at all. Besides providing practical assets like guaranteeing certain pay minimums and screen credit protections and offering health insurance, they're often the only friend a screenwriter has in the world. But at that time, entry into the Guild required me to pay a $1,000 join-up fee, 1½ percent of all earnings, plus $50 each year whether I worked or not. If I had been working regularly (or thought I might be), that wouldn't have been such a big deal. But what it meant was that on my first big-time contract, between the WGA, Little Ruthie's cut, and taxes, I was going to clear a little less than fifty cents on the dollar.

My bigger worry was about what would happen *afterward.*

The way you're *supposed* to exploit these situations is that while you're on your current gig, your agent is out there bragging about the job you're on at the moment trying to make you look attractive enough for someone to offer you your next gig (or for a couple of someones to offer you your next several gigs). You do it this way because it can take a couple of years for a movie to wind its way through development, production, post-production and release ... providing it ever gets made. Obviously, you want to minimize what could, considering those circumstances, be substantial downtime.

Little Ruthie didn't have the movie and television connections to do that. Her strategy was that I would write this movie, the movie would get made, be a big, big hit, and people would chase me down to get me to write for them, and all those WGA-sized paychecks would start rolling in. I tried—gently—explaining to her that the movie world didn't work like that; not only did most movies flop, but most screenplays don't become movies. I don't know what the numbers were back when I was working on *BPK*, but today about 50,000 screenplays are registered with the WGA each year. Any one of those screenplays has only a .3 percent chance of eventually becoming a studio release (Meslow). Little Ruthie didn't have a strategy; she had an opium smoker's fantasy.

If you belong to the WGA, you can't take non–WGA work. Up until Billy hired me, non–WGA work was the only screenwriting work I'd been able to get. Little Ruthie looked at WGA membership as a road to riches. If her fantasy didn't come true, it was more likely membership would make me unemployable to the only people who would probably want to hire me.

* * *

The writing had to take place around Billy's work on *Kate & Allie.* There were times when we would have a run of meetings once or twice a week, and other times we wouldn't meet for weeks at a stretch. He had a townhouse on the Upper East Side; nothing gaudy, but comfortable, low-key classy. We worked in his office/den which was a lovely, book-lined room looking out on the street. I'd be sunk in a sofa, Billy'd be slouched in his desk chair. Sometimes he might be strumming his guitar (he was always into something; classical guitar lessons, calligraphy, gourmet cooking). In those sessions, for the most part we would talk and spitball ideas, me taking plenty of notes, then I'd go off and write pages, drop them off, and the next time we got together we'd go over them and spitball some more.

Billy's writing process was 180 degrees away from mine. When I sit at the keyboard, I tend to have a pretty good idea of the story I'm going to tell. Not that things won't change over the course of writing the piece, and especially over the course of rewriting, but rarely do the fundamentals change. My first novel went through at least 10 full rewrites over more than 20 years. Style changed, voice changed, secondary characters were cut and/or added and likewise some subplots, but the story—what the piece was about, what it was I wanted the reader to come away with—didn't change, nor did the basic elements of the plot and main characters. In other words, I know the story I want to tell going in; it may just take me a number of tries to figure out the best way to tell it.

Billy's process would drive any how-to guru or writing teacher insane. In my experience with him, I felt he tended to go into a piece with only a vague idea of the story. He discovers a piece in the writing (I think of it as the literary version of panning for gold). We worked together over a period of about six months, and much of that time involved getting part-way through a pass at the script only for Billy to feel it wasn't working right, and we'd go back to square one and try again. Billy was the writer's equivalent of those stories you hear about Stanley Kubrick calling for take after take from his actors, dozens of them.

"Just tell me what you want, Stanley!"

But Stanley didn't know. He only knew what he had wasn't working … until it worked.

If my co-writer had been anyone else, I would've clubbed him to death with the tons of notes I made during those sessions. But Billy was one of the most pleasant and fun people I've ever worked with, and over the course of our work together, we went from co-workers to friends.

He only ever treated me as an equal. I never felt I rated that, but he did. Our sessions in his den were completely give-and-take; anything I had to offer was considered just as good as any suggestion he made. He would always introduce me as "this terrific writer I'm working with."

One time he invited me to watch a taping of *Kate & Allie* which was taped at the Ed Sullivan Theater. I walked over to the theater from work and got in line with the tourists and day-trippers from Jersey. After a bit, I saw Billy's assistant, Clare, walking along the line looking for—I assumed— me. I waved and called out.

"What're you doing here?" she asked.

"Billy asked me to come watch the taping."

She smiled in a way that was the equivalent of patting me on the head and saying, "You poor, poor idiot child." "Bill," she said, "*you* don't wait on line," and she took me by the arm, escorted me past the queue, into the theater to the VIP section where there was a reserved seat marked with my name.

As we made pass after pass at the story, I may have sometimes felt like we'd be working on that goddamned screenplay forever, but working with a guy like that, I didn't really mind it so much.

Little Ruthie, on the other hand, did mind. A lot. She assumed every pass we took constituted a draft (a "draft" is what you have when you think you have a finished script ... until you realize it sucks, or someone willing to produce it tells you it sucks, and you have to write another draft). She never understood what Billy and I were doing was less writing a draft than experimenting with how to tell our story.

We had a lot of experimenting to do.

*　*　*

When Little Ruthie had first gotten it into her head to pitch me to Bill Persky to work on adapting *Big Phil's Kid* for the big screen, I had somewhat arrogantly thought that since I'd done a decent job adapting *Free Flight,* I had this adaptation process knocked.

But *FF* had been easy because Doug Terman had made it easy. *Free Flight* had a rather tight, almost completely linear, forward-driving narrative arc. It was more or less an every-scene-moves-the-plot kind of novel which was easy to transform into an every-scene-moves-the-plot screenplay.

The problem with *Big Phil's Kid* was it didn't have a narrative arc. At all. It was the very definition of episodic. The opening chapter sets up the situation: Larry learns his dad's a mobster; he meets Courtney, a high school girl from a well-to-do family that becomes his romantic interest. At the other end, there's an affecting if somewhat inconclusive closing chapter where Courtney dumps Larry because he doesn't seem to know his ass from his elbow about what to do with himself. In between...

Well, there's a lot of fun stuff in between, and it ranges from charmingly funny to laugh-out-loud slapstick. It's inarguably a fun read (there's a reason it had stayed in print for almost 20 years; hell, *I* laughed reading it!), but there's no real direction to it; no build. The construction of the novel is less like a, well, like a novel, and closer to that of a television series. A debut episode sets up the situation and introduces the running characters, but thereafter the episodes are mostly stand-alones, and there's no evolution in the characters. You can almost picture the *Entertainment Weekly*'s "What to Watch" write-up for each chapter: "In this week's episode, Larry plays off his father's Mob reputation to impress a stripper. Hilarity ensues."

The book's adaptive problems were not all structural. The novel had been published in 1969. Seventeen years later, we might not yet have had the internet, but the cable television spectrum was exploding, and that included the (then) all-news channels CNN and CNN Headline. The 24-hour news cycle had been born, and Billy and I didn't think it was possible that a kid growing up in the most media-saturated media market (New York City) in a media-saturated country could reach the age of 16 without ever hearing a word that his father's business activities weren't the kind you see listed on the NYSE.

We briefly considered setting the book at the time it was published, but that replaced one problem with others. Parker, writing in his time, had been able to get by by placing his story in a bit of a bubble untouched by the cultural currents of the era. But in the nearly two decades since the book's first publication, the 1960s had become too freighted with the iconography of the time: Vietnam, urban riots, Nixon, campus demonstrations, hippies... In our time, we didn't feel we could credibly insulate the story in its time the way Parker had done in his.

A story with no structure that was no longer credible, even in comedic terms. Sometimes I wondered what the hell Bill Persky had been thinking when he had bought the rights on the book.

During one of our sessions, Billy, who'd recently gotten interested in working with glass beads, puttered with a tray of colored beads making bracelets and necklaces for his friends while we tossed plot ideas back and forth. At one point, he held up the string of beads he was working on and announced, "This is what we have to do with our script. We've got to find the right pattern. A red bead, then a white bead, then a blue, a green... We have to build this screenplay the same way."

* * *

Billy was old enough to remember that in 1950, Tennessee Senator Estes Kefauver headed up televised committee hearings which introduced the American public to the idea of a nationally organized crime syndicate. People had always known there were big mobsters like Al Capone and "Lucky" Luciano, but the FBI had consistently denied that all these regional crime world headliners were in league with each other. The Kefauver Committee changed that ("Estes..."). As soon as Billy suggested setting the story against the background of the hearings with Big Phil slated to testify, it immediately sounded like the perfect time setting. Larry would be learning about the Mob—and his father's place in it—at the same time the rest of the country would.

That setting also helped us with our narrative arc issue.

Having a problem with the episodic nature of the novel might seem hypocritical coming after my chapter on three-act structure in which I went to great pains to show that episodic pieces can work. And so they can. But neither Billy nor I wanted a broad *The Hangover* kind of comedy in which a tight structure didn't matter much as long as the big yuks kept coming. Art house fare like *Smoke* (1995) or almost any film by writer/director Jim Jarmusch also carries off episodic storytelling with aplomb, but we weren't looking for an art house audience. We both knew that a mainstream, life-sized comedy would need a more perceptible narrative arc than the novel had in order to engage a mainstream audience in any serious way.

After the set-up of the opening chapter, Parker's book is a generally a series of episodes where Larry sometimes rebels against the perception that, as Big Phil's kid, he's a mobster in the making, and other times where he tries to play off of it. But there's no evolution in his thinking, there's little connecting thread from one episode to the next, no cumulative effect. Then, in the final chapter, the book takes on an unexpected gravitas when Courtney drops Larry not only for being aimless, but for blaming his father for his own shortcomings. Larry grimly heads back to college.

It's not only quite a downbeat ending for a story that's been light and fun up to that point, but also emotionally ambivalent. As a movie ending, it would be the kind of close that would have an audience going, "That's it?" All of these weaknesses became apparent when I did my ritual quickie-down-and-dirty first pass just to see how the book would play on the script page.

Fortuitously for our story, the summer of the same year Kefauver began his hearings also happened to mark the outbreak of the Korean War. Billy got the idea Larry should join the Army as the emotional climax of the piece as both a declaration of independence from his father (who has arranged for the draft to skip his son), but also as a sign that he's decided to grow up. It was an arc—from Larry overwhelmed by the revelation about his father, through Larry trying to figure out what this means for his own identity, to Larry declaring himself to be his own person by defying his father and joining the Army—that made an obvious emotional sense.

(Here I feel I need to pay tribute to Billy's assistant, Clare. Pre-internet, research could be a quite a pain. On *Big Phil's Kid,* it fell to Clare to find out when events happened and where, what the New York City geography of 1950 was—particularly where the Army induction center was located—and what the process of induction was. Clare even managed to find a manual detailing the physical exam for military service. Clare, if you ever see this, you were amazing!)

We decided the climax would have more dramatic gravity if we condensed the timeline of the novel. The book begins with Larry in high school and ends while he's into his first year of college. With its inconclusive ending, that gave the book a sense of drifting along until it ended. We put the story wholly within Larry's senior year in high school (another obvious, well-defined arc), him joining the Army after graduation; a clear affirmation on Larry's part that, with his schoolboy days behind him—to borrow a bar mitzvah cliché—"Today I am a man!"

We toyed with the idea—for no good reason I can recall—of telling this story with a fractured timeline, flashing back and forth between Larry's processing at the Army induction center and the narrative leading up to that point, but we couldn't find enough smooth points of transition throughout the piece, and the device came to seem gimmicky. Worse, there was a point too early in the plot where this device telegraphed to the audience where things were going to end up, undercutting any suspense the latter part of the story might have. We pared the back-and-forthing down to bookends: starting at the induction center, then flashing back to tell the story, then ending where we started. But then the bookends seemed so scant they had a what's-the-point feel, so we wound up telling the story in a straightforward A-B-C manner.

As happens with so many screenplays, the hardest part to tackle was the second act, which wasn't really an act at all. Through all our experimenting, it was becoming evident we were going to wind up with a hybrid structure; yeah, it would have forward movement, but it would be episodic in construction, with some episodes pushing the plot forward, while others functioned to give us a sense of the morally/emotionally/psychologically confused world Larry was living in. And some episodes we included just because they were fun.

But finding the right arrangement of those episodes—Billy's string of colored beads—was a chore and a half. At one point, since we couldn't seem to find an effective combo on our own, Billy hired a script analyst to get an outside opinion. I was very struck that this guy with three decades in the entertainment business and five Emmys on his mantle was so lacking in ego that he didn't have a problem going to someone and asking, "What do *you* think?"

The analyst put on a good show. The report came back with color-coded graphs showing characters' and the plot's emotional hot and cold spots along with a pretty detailed analysis of where the piece lagged and where it worked. But it didn't tell us anything we didn't already know (we had second act problems), and offered only broad-stroke suggestions on how to fix it.

Let me digress again. Here's the thing about script analysts. To repeat my point in the chapter on screenwriting gurus: this is not a science. There's no objective measurement device you can put on a screenplay to tell you if it's good or bad, or if it's weak and where and why. Show the same screenplay to three script analysts and there's a good probability you'll get three different analyses because this kind of thing is purely subjective. *Purely.* No matter what all those damned writing books say. In the end, it's somebody's opinion and nothing more.

Whether you buy into that somebody's opinion or not, in the end you have to make a gut call, and the only thing that's going to fix what you think might be your script's problems are your imagination, creativity, judgment, and skill.

I'm not saying analysts aren't worth the money. Sometimes having to justify why you should turn right when an analyst is telling you to turn left forces you to examine your thinking, challenge it, demand that it validate itself. If it can't, the analyst is right. Maybe.

The troubling part is you'll never know which of you is right until (and if) the movie ever gets made, made the way it should be, and you get to see how your calls play in front of a paying audience. Until then, you, the analyst, studio development people, the director, the cast, and everybody else whose creative decisions affect the finished product are guessing.

Off and on, we banged away at *Big Phil's Kid* for maybe six months. At the end of that time, we still didn't have a screenplay we were happy with, but according to Billy, "You've done a lot more work than you should've." He paid me ten percent more than we'd contracted for. "You earned it."

* * *

Billy continued to work on the screenplay on his own, and I began to see that my function had been to be something like a booster rocket, getting the screenplay to a certain point where Billy's thinking on what it should be could crystallize, and then he could take it the rest of the way into orbit.

He kept me apprised every step of the way, showing me his new pages, asking for feedback and suggestions. I think he worked on that thing for maybe another year. In the end, the finished version was mostly Bill Persky (there was little left of my funeral and even "Fix the fish" was gone; sigh), even though, as far as he was concerned, it was still a collaboration and he kept my name right next to his on the title page. And, while most of the material was his, the screenplay did nicely mix our sensibilities.

Early in our sessions, I had confessed to Billy that, "I don't know how to write funny stuff."

"You just do what you do," he said comfortingly. "I'll take care of the funny."

So I didn't try to be funny, and when I felt the plot needed to turn seriously dramatic, I let it. In his rewriting, Billy sometimes found the smile and even laugh in those scenes, and other times he left them alone. What we wound up with was a comedy grounded in a family drama.

A year and a half all told went into that piece. But that wasn't the hard part. Trust me on this: no matter how much sweat and blood you put into a piece of material, no matter how long it takes for it to take on a form that satisfies you, that's the easy part.

Finding it a home is the hard part.

*   *   *

When we had first started working together, Billy had been pretty confident he could get *Big Phil's Kid* made. "At the very least, I could get it done as a TV movie," he said.

That wasn't ego or arrogance or hubris. Billy knew the business, and he knew his stature in the business. He was arguably in the best position of his career as the executive producer and director of a highly-praised, award-winning hit. He hadn't been bragging; he'd been making a simple statement of fact.

The problem for *BPK* was that the entertainment business Billy knew was suffering tectonic changes in the late 1980s, and what had been true in the early part of the decade was no longer true by its end. At the time, neither of us understood that.

As a prospective feature film, Billy and I had had our eyes on Garry Marshall's 1984 flick, *The Flamingo Kid* (written by Marshall, Neal Marshall, and Bo Goldman) as a model. It was a small, charming movie set in the early 1960s about a kid (Matt Dillon) having generally similar crises of conscience and identity as Larry Carrett. *TFK* had been a comfy mid-range hit: $24 million domestic making it #43 for the year.

Like *Flamingo*, *Big Phil* was going to be a life-sized comedy; life exaggerated to the point of being funny while still resembling life, an approach allowing both stories, although generally comedic, to touch points of drama. In this way, we thought *Big Phil* could fit in the same niche *Flamingo* had mined so well.

But by the time Billy had a screenplay he was satisfied with, it was 1988/89 and it was getting harder to find those kinds of small, sweet movies out in the mainstream. And as for a television movie, the presence of the form on the broadcast networks was evaporating.

The 1970s and early 1980s had been a golden age for network made-fors with television movies like *That Certain Summer* (1972), *The Day After,* and *Duel* (1971, the television movie which would bring its director—a 25-year-old Steven Spielberg—his first big screen feature). But toward the end of the decade, the three major broadcast networks had lost approximately one-half of their audience to cable. As their audience drifted off to HBO and TBS and ESPN and a growing spectrum of cable channels, the networks made fewer made-fors, and even fewer good ones (Mesce, *Inside...,* 149). In one of its early original programming successes, HBO—after floundering for a few years—had finally found its voice in original movies, and it became a regular network complaint at the Emmys that the pay–TV channel was monopolizing the Outstanding Drama Special (TV movies) category with classy efforts like *Mandela* (1987), *The Josephine Baker Story* (1991), and *Murderers Among Us: The Simon Wiesenthal Story* (1989) (147).

Meaning: Nobody needed *Big Phil's Kid.* Not the networks desperate to lure back their ebbing audience, not an overly serious HBO.

Big Phil's author, M.M. Parker, had let Billy extend his option once, but when it didn't look like we could make anything happen with the project, Parker refused to extend the option a second time.

And that was that.

I still think of that project as a win. I have a lot of actor friends, and a common experience among them is that in the intensity of working on a play, people draw close, there's a feeling you're making friendships (or having romantic liaisons) which will last forever. Then the play is over, the intensity dissipates, everybody goes their own way and you may never hear from any of these forever-friends/loves again.

Screenwriting can be like that: the same, compressed, intense bit of work which breeds a sense of connection. And then it's over.

That didn't happen with *Big Phil's Kid.* I came out of the experience with one of my best friends. How could that not be a win?

*   *   *

Billy might've had more leverage getting *Big Phil's Kid* mounted as a television movie—at least on CBS—if he'd still been with *Kate & Allie,* but he'd left the show after its fourth season, feeling that after having directed 100 episodes he'd pretty much done everything he wanted to do with the series. (Note: the series ran one more season, but the show had lost its spark when Billy left; the ratings nose-dived, and it was cancelled after season 5.)

After Parker refused a second option on the property, Billy went back to network television with *Working It Out* which aired on Saturday nights on NBC during the fall of 1990 facing off with ABC's *The Young Riders,* a kind of Y/A fictionalization of the Pony Express. He had said that there was a possibility, once *Working* had established itself, he might be able to bring me on the show in some capacity. Instead, Billy's show became another illustration of how the network television currents were shifting.

Saturday night had once been the crown jewel of the network programming week with hits like *The Mary Tyler Moore Show, The Bob Newhart Show, Mission: Impossible, All in the Family, M*A*S*H, The Carol Burnett Show,* but by the late 1980s, it was becoming a programming graveyard. A new generation of viewers was just as often watching cable, or a movie rented from the video store, or had decided Saturday nights were for going out, not for watching TV. Consequently, although *Working* and *Riders* alternated winning the time slot, the numbers even for the weekly winner were feeble.

Billy's best work has often been comedy grounded in a recognizable reality. Dick Van Dyke may have played a television writer on *The Dick Van Dyke Show,* but much if not most of the show plugged into his character's white collar suburban commuter lifestyle, a social development which had exploded in the 1950s. It's almost a comedic version of *Mad Men.* *That Girl* rode the wave of Women's Lib, and *Kate & Allie* took its cue from the fallout of the rising divorce rate. *Working It Out* followed in the same vein, being the story of two mature, divorced people who meet in a cooking class while they're trying to re-start their lives.

As the networks' audience numbers ebbed, to compensate for the loss of bulk viewers, network programmers became more concerned with appealing to specific target demographics; the audience slices that most appealed to advertisers, the most appealing slice being young viewers. *The Young Riders* skewed young; ABC moved the series to another night where it managed to run for several seasons. *Working It Out* skewed older; NBC cancelled the show at the end of the fall season.

Billy and I continued to talk, to get together, sometimes he would have an idea and we would horse around with it a little bit. He would look for writing opportunities for me, recommending me to anybody whose ear he could catch. Year by year, we became closer, and he would become not just a mentor, but one of my dearest friends which was why it pained me so much when he stopped pitching projects to the networks. But that, too, was the result of another evolutionary change in the television business.

The Big Three—ABC, CBS, NBC—once mighty, independent corporate entities, had all been absorbed by larger media empires (ABC is currently owned by Disney; the current CBS is the result of several changes of ownership and reconfigurations; NBC is owned by NBCUniversal, itself a subsidiary of cable giant Comcast). Once, I asked Billy why he'd stopped pitching.

"Everybody I know in this business is either retired or dead."

When Billy and I had first begun working together, he had invited me to an informal get-together honoring Sheldon Leonard. More people outside the television business are probably familiar with Leonard as an actor; anybody who's seen *It's a Wonderful Life* would immediately recognize him as the sideways talking, tough-guy bartender who throws George Bailey and his guardian angel out in the snow. His arguably greater impact, however, was as a producer. From the 1950s into the 1960s, Leonard had been associated, as a producer, with a string of classic television shows including *Make Room for Daddy, The Andy Griffith Show, I Spy,* and *The Dick Van Dyke Show* ("Leonard..."). But by the 1980s, Leonard hadn't had anything on the air in over a decade, and hadn't had a hit since the *Andy Griffith* spin-off, *Gomer Pyle, U.S.M.C.* in the late 1960s. Billy felt Leonard's contributions to the medium—particularly in the many talents, like Billy, whom he'd mentored and who had gone on to create their own memorable work—had become unjustly forgotten. Billy put together an evening to show Mr. Leonard that he was still remembered.

I would remember that event often when I saw Billy's frustration with a younger generation of programming executives who'd replaced his network of long-standing connections. They didn't know his work or his name. Hollywood doesn't respect a body of work, but measures you by the last thing you did.

Billy had stopped pitching, he told me, "Because I'm tired of trying to explain myself to children."

*   *   *

It must've been somewhere around 2003–2004 when Billy called me with an idea for another feature screenplay, and he wanted to work with me on it. He'd heard former New York City mayor Rudy Giuliani on some talk radio station talking about a program during World War II managed out of a command center on Long Island in which Italian prisoners of war worked as laborers for the U.S.

Just a few years before, I'd written a trilogy of World War II novels for Bantam. It had taken me twenty-odd years of writing and rewriting to get the first book published, and then Bantam had arm-twisted me into two sequels. I was so burned out by the time I'd delivered the third book that I'd asked to be released from my contract. Billy's request rekindled a paranoia I'd had when I was doing the books; that I'd be labeled, "The World War II guy," and not be thought of as anything else (an embarrassingly grandiose paranoia since even though the books had been critically well-received, they hadn't sold in the kind of numbers that were going to get me branded as anything but a respected flop).

As much as I liked the idea of working closely with Billy again, I confessed to him that having gotten World War II behind me, I didn't relish going back to it.

"But you're perfect for this! You love doing all that research shit!"

"I *hate* doing all that research! I only did it because I *had* to!"

"But you're so good at it!"

Well, like I said; it was going to be working with Billy again, and that would've been hard to say no to in any case. And even though it was a World War II story, it was a story that had never been told; the proverbial footnote in history. And, it was the first time since I'd begun writing professionally that I would be dealing with a subject touching on my ancestral roots. This one, I thought, could be for the family.

Billy envisioned a kind of left-handed *The Great Escape.* Like that 1960s classic, Billy saw our project as an ensemble piece, a mix of humor and drama (tipping more toward humor than its predecessor). The twist was that instead of the prisoners trying to escape to get home, they would be trying to escape to *stay* in the United States.

Even though we now had the internet at our disposal, at the time there wasn't much to find on the topic: one online article, and one academic book: Louis E. Keefer's *Italian Prisoners of War In America 1942–1946.* From this scant pool of information, this is what we learned:

The Allies had taken an enormous number of Italian POWs during the fight for North Africa and then again during the taking of Sicily. The Americans were holding so many prisoners at detention camps in North Africa—around 130,000—that they became a serious drain on the Army's resources (Keefer, 28), so the Army decided get some of them off their hands by shipping 50,000 of them to the U.S. where they were held in camps mostly situated in the western and southwestern states (1). At some point in 1943, an offer was made to the prisoners that they could work as paid laborers to make up for the manpower shortage on the American home front (approximately one in every nine Americans—nearly all males— served in the military during the war). Thirty-five-thousand of the Italians volunteered for the program (59).

When Italy surrendered in the fall of 1943, there was some dispute between the new Italian government and the U.S. about returning the POWs to Italy since, technically, the two countries were no longer at war. But the U.S. couldn't afford to give up tens of thousands of laborers, and reorganized the work program into Italian Service Units with its own command structure (the place in Long Island Giuliani mentioned), and in which the Italians were no longer considered prisoners but helpers in the Allied war effort. While the U.S. didn't make any overt promises, the idea was in the air that ISU volunteers would be given special consideration for remaining in the States after the war. But, when the war ended, the U.S. repatriated them all to Italy, taking its time doing so with the last ISU volunteers not being sent home until 1946 (Calamandrei).

Billy no longer had the townhouse, so we would meet to work at a suite of offices he had taken uptown with three of his close friends; kind of a base of operations for them to do business professional and personal, and just hang out together.

Wrangling with what Billy dubbed *The Italians Are Coming* and what I called *Surrender* was a hell of a lot harder than the process had been for *Big Phil's Kid.* As I said earlier, when I sit at the keyboard, I know the story I want to tell. It'll percolate mentally for months, in some cases even years, until I get a more or less complete picture of it, and that's when I sit down to write it. I had never been through the experience of creating a screenplay from nothing before. For all the narrative weaknesses of Parker's novel, the book had still given us a firm concept and raw material to work with. This time, we were working from scratch. Billy's panning for gold process was going to require a lot more panning this time around.

The first idea we tossed around was that among our ensemble of Italian POWs, one was a kind of Vittorio De Sica, a cutting edge filmmaker back in his native land. He would help an American film crew making a propaganda piece about their camp, introducing them to Italian neorealism in the process, and the film shoot would act as a cover for the prisoners' escape plan. We horsed around with the idea for a bit but it never jelled.

Since we had set our POW camp in Arizona, we then got the idea of the prisoners participating in a rodeo, and that, too, would act as a cover for the escape plan. Again, it didn't spark and we tossed it.

As we tried out first one approach then another, the initial concept of who would comprise the ensemble also began to shift.

Ok, I don't want to get artsy-fartsy here, and I don't pretend to understand the psychology of how this works, but sometimes a story tells you where it wants to go, and there are characters who tell you, "I'm real," and others that never crystallize.

I once overheard a college psychology class lecture in which the professor said the human mind was incapable of creating a face; that all those people you see in your dreams that you don't know are faces tucked in your memory. They may have been people you only glanced at on the street and of whom you have no conscious memory, but they're real people.

Writing characters can be like that. I'm not saying you can't construct a wholly unreal character and make him/her work on the screen. Quentin Tarantino is great at writing fun characters who couldn't possibly exist off the movie screen. But what I am saying is that unless you're Tarantino, what generally happens when you slap together a bunch of tics and traits you think are cool, that's what you end up with; a construct, not a character. When you tap into something real and human, even in the most fantastic circumstances (think of Han Solo in the first *Star Wars* and how every time something goes bad around him, the first words out of his mouth are, "It's not my fault!"—who doesn't identify with that?), it resonates with an audience in a way the cool but unreal stuff doesn't.

Initially, Billy and I had spitballed some characters who were more functions than characters, and as we started trying to find their story, most of them evaporated. Who we were left with, however, became more full-bodied; they came alive.

Again, not to get too arty, but you know a character has truly come to life when you know what he/she will say or do—or not say and not do—in any given circumstance. You are now no longer writing a character, but describing the actions of a person who—at least in your head—is, for all intents and purposes, real.

Our "anchor" characters, around who orbited a number of supporting players, were:

Colonel Barth, camp commandant whose humanitarian impulses are regularly in conflict with his military responsibilities. Barth has to wage a war on two fronts: with the prejudiced townspeople, particularly their mayor Raymond Florette; and Don Aldo, the imperious senior Italian officer who was an aristocrat back in Italy and continues to conduct himself as such.

Helping Barth is Miss Irvine, a spinster obsessed with all things Italian and who has never gotten over a one-nighter with Caruso decades earlier.

Of our ensemble of Italian POWs, besides Don Aldo, the only ones who jelled were:

Carlo, a one-time Catholic priest defrocked because his artist's admiration for beauty including that of the female form particularly in its unclad glory. Carlo winds up working for Miss Irvine and manages to get her to stop burying herself in the past and live in the present.

And Fredo, a not particularly committed communist who sees in the labor offer an opportunity to prove his abilities as an engineer in a way not possible back home. His construction of an aqueduct for Florette's ranch brings him in contact with Florette's fiercely independent daughter Eileen with romantic results.

What made these characters jell in a way others we discarded or relegated to supporting functions was that their actions and interactions became immediately apparent. Barth, for example, the humanitarian soldier, immediately sprang to life with his diplomatic efforts with Florette, his frustrations with Don Aldo, and fending off interference from the Army high command in Washington.

The true history of the Italian POWs provided us with our arc. Our story began in an empty patch of Arizona desert in May of 1943, and ended just after New Year's 1944 when the POWs would be transferred to ISU units around the country. Covering that stretch of time and following several character arcs meant the story would be episodic in nature (not unlike Billy's original model, *The Great Escape*). In terms of tone, however, my model was the 1963 movie, *Captain Newman, M.D.* (adaptation of Leo Rosten's novel by Richard L. Breen, Phoebe Ephron, Henry Ephron).

Newman and *Surrender* came to have a lot in common. *Newman* concerned the head of a psychiatric hospital on an Air Corps base in the southwest dealing with what today we'd call PTSD cases during World War II; it dealt with several character arcs over a substantial period of time resulting in an episodic structure (not unlike the Rosten source novel); and it deftly balanced between the comedic and drama (some of it quite dark). It was sort of a military *One Flew Over the Cuckoo's Nest;* often funny, but not really a comedy. That's the same posture we tried to give *Surrender.*

But getting to that point where we had a reasonably clear idea of what the main characters and plot should be involved a lot of let's-try-this-nope-it-doesn't-work. We believed in the concept, but couldn't find the story. Billy's solution to that frustration was to give me a taste of writer's heaven.

"What we need is a couple of days with no distractions," Billy declared. "No job, no nothing, just focusing on the script."

The place for that, Billy said, was his house on Shelter Island.

Accessible only by ferry, Shelter Island sits of the eastern end of Long Island, and a lot of very comfortably well-off people keep getaway houses there. When I say comfortably well-off, I mean like the guy whose playhouse for his daughters, designed like a Dutch windmill, was bigger than the house where I lived with my family. "Do you think I could get him to adopt me?" I asked Billy.

Billy's house sat close to the water and was curtained off from his neighbors by woods. It wasn't a huge place, but a sleek piece of modern design so visually striking it had been featured in *Architectural Digest*. The house had a little sister; a small but no less a beauty of a guest house. Billy's plan was we spend three days at his Shelter Island house in a kind of writer's camp.

Those three days spoiled me. To this day I still look back on those days thinking, "*That's* how writers should live!"

We'd wake up between eight and nine, maybe do a lap or two in his pool, then sit for a bit in the corner of the pool walled off as a hot tub. Completely relaxed, we'd rinse off in an outdoor shower (I didn't think I'd be self-conscious being ogled by a deer but I was), then Billy would fix us a light breakfast, and afterward out would come the laptop and we'd work in his eat-in, family-style kitchen for a couple of hours. Then we'd break for lunch and a little R & R. One day he took me for a drive around the island, showing me the sights. Another day he took me out in his little motor boat, put-putting around the harbor which turned unexpectedly suspenseful as gas ran low and we found the fueling dock closed. Then we'd work a couple of more hours, and go out for dinner at one of the many fine eateries on the island.

Both the focus and relaxed atmosphere worked. By the end of those three days, we had a pretty good idea of the story we were going to tell which only vaguely resembled the story we had started out with. Even the escape attempt was gone, with the plot evolving into a more relatable tale of strangers overcoming their suspicions and prejudices as their interactions worked them through a begrudging mutual respect, then friendship, and, in a few cases, romance. The length of the finished draft came in somewhere in the mid-130s; a hair long, but not too bad (later, for the purpose of submitting the screenplay to a contest, it was trimmed down to a tighter 128 pages).

But now, again, the hard part: finding it a home.

If Billy had been complaining how few people in the business he had a connection with in the 1990s, they were positively scarce by the time we had a screenplay to show around (I believe this was around 2005–6 or so).

One guy we both agreed was a natural fit was producer Sonny Grosso.

A garrulous bear of a guy given to hugs, Sonny's story is worth a movie. Actually, part of his life was one.

Before he'd gotten into the movie and television business, Sonny had been a decorated cop with the N.Y.P.D. for twenty years, and whose police career included, along with his partner Eddie Egan, being part of one of the all-time biggest drug busts in the history of American law enforcement: the so-called "French Connection." In 1969, eight years after the Connection case, author Robin Moore turned his account of the bust into a bestselling book, and three years later, the book had been turned into an acclaimed hit movie, winning five Academy Awards including those for Best Picture, Best Director, and screenplay adaptation by Ernest Tidyman (Mesce, "A Conversation…," 44).

Sonny and Egan were both hired as consultants for the movie, and this led to more gigs for Sonny advising on cop movies. By the time he retired from the police force, it was almost a natural transition for Sonny to movie into the movie and television business, partnering with producer Larry Jacobson to form Grosso/Jacobson Communications. Over the next thirty or so years, they would turn out over 750 hours of television programming ranging from hard-nosed made-for-TV cop dramas like *A Question of Honor* (1982, based on Sonny's book *Point Blank*), to the inspired silliness of *Pee-wee's Playhouse* (Mesce, "A Conversation…," 47–48).

Billy and I both thought *Surrender* would hit Sonny square in his passionate connection with his Italian heritage and so it did. As it happened, Sonny was working with another retired cop (a former FBI agent, I think), who had connections with people in the Italian government working with a government fund providing financing for film production. The Italians had gotten on the wrong side in World War II, and their poor performance on the battlefield had often been treated by the movies as unimpressive at best, at worst a joke (Everson, 128). Sonny was sure the Italians would see *Surrender* as a strong step in the opposite direction, and, for a while, they did.

What happened next, I was never quite clear about. From the little bits and pieces filtering back to Billy and I, evidently another film financing arrangement involving some of the same players we were dealing with went bad. The fallout from that collapse somehow spiked *Surrender*.

Not long after, Sonny called Billy and I in for a meeting; he had another possibility. Sonny wanted to pitch the piece to Hallmark for their cable channel.

Billy and I looked at each other with the same uneasiness. While television movies typically occupy a two-hour time slot, they're not two-hour movies. Deduct the time set aside for commercials and it's closer to 90 minutes, meaning we would have to cut our screenplay by something like 25–30 percent. Hallmark's made-fors had a reputation for sentimental romance which told us what would probably get cut. We had intended *Surrender* to be a layered look at how supposed enemies could get past their wartime-bred prejudices to see each other as people and find common connections. Those connections ranged from professional respect, to brothers-in-arms camaraderie, and, in a few cases, romance. We were sure a Hallmark version would probably shave off all but the romance, and probably sugar it up as well. Maybe we were a bit snooty about this, but Billy and I both thought *Surrender* deserved better and passed.

Considering how sporadic my screenwriting "career" (and it's been *so* sporadic, it's hard not to say "career" without putting it in quotes) has been since then, it's been hard for me not to go back to that decision and wonder if that was the right choice. What would have been better? A bad movie which was made and which had a paycheck attached to it? Or a good screenplay that never saw the light of day?

Hmmmm... You tell me.

* * *

That was the last time *Surrender* seemed to have any real chance of making it to the screen, but I thought then—and still do—it's one of the best things I've been attached to. I couldn't give up on it.

Billy and I showed it to the few people we knew in the business, but there were no takers. It was a period piece which made it pricey, people wondered if anybody still gave a damn about World War II, it was a war story with no combat, and we know they were thinking of the 2001 box office dud *Captain Corelli's Mandolin* (domestic gross of $25.5 million against a budget of $57 million) which had dealt with generally similar themes.

With no other cards left to play, I began submitting the piece to screenplay competitions. *Surrender* would make it to the quarter- and semi-finals, but never finish in the money.

In 2015, I submitted the piece to the Capital Fund Screenplay Competition which not only promised a nice paycheck for the Grand Prize winner, but circulating winning material to film production entities and investors. Actually, I sent in *Surrender* along with another piece: *Carjack*, a cops-and-bad-guys action thriller that was the kind of mercenary piece whose entertainment value was directly tied into its body count.

Neither piece won the big prize, but *Carjack* won in the suspense/ thriller category. *Surrender* won nothing.

The prize for a category winner was a phone conversation with a production exec, so I had a nice chat with a guy involved with some sort of production investment outfit. Over the course of our conversation it naturally came up that I was hardly a screenwriting virgin.

"I could tell," he said. "There's nothing I can tell you. You know how to write, and it's just a matter of luck as far as you getting anything made."

"Frankly, I'm surprised *Carjack* won," I said. "It's a fun script, but it's not a smart picture. It's a shoot-'em-up. I thought if one of them was going to win, it would've been *Surrender*. It's the smarter piece, it's the classier piece."

He chuckled. "That should tell you something about where the movie business is at."

The Screenwriter: Robert Conte

(I interviewed Bob Conte of HBO about the same time I interviewed Dave Baldwin. I felt Conte's piece, like Baldwin's, is still relevant to what we're looking at here, particularly considering the difference in Conte's perspective. Conte not only helped HBO pick projects for its various programming divisions; he also wrote—and still writes— movies.)

Bob Conte is one entertainment industry veteran not inclined to join in the hand-wringing over the present state of American movies. "I don't think of movies as being worse than they used to be. That seems like cheap cynicism to me. Movie nostalgia works like this: you remember the 20 great movies from the last 70 years and forget the 2000 bad ones. If you've been to twenty movies *this* year, you forget the one or two good ones, and focus on all the bad ones—at least when you're characterizing the state of the industry."

Conte's take on the business comes with more than a little informing experience behind it. Looking around his office at HBO where he's been employed for over 30 years, the shelves bow with the weight of scripts. As Senior Vice President of Creative Affairs, it's Conte's job to read scripts, hear pitches, review DVDs of film projects—in stages from first draft scripts to completed movies—to look for material which might be suitable for the company's HBO and Cinemax services, its DVD arm, or possibly even as an original HBO film.

But Conte's also served on the other side of the desk. He and his writing partner, Peter Wortmann, have worked steadily as a screenwriting team for over two decades. Working on originals and as re-write men, they have lent their talents to projects at companies like Columbia, Universal, Disney, and Warner Bros.

His situation as both acquirer and talent, and his years served on both counts, seem to have left him with a sanguine imperturbability. He gives the sense of understanding the freakish combination of insanity and sagacity which are often simultaneously involved in the Hollywood decision-making process.

Conte dismisses the complaint that the tide of big-budget blockbusters is a sign the movie business has become inordinately obsessed with making money. "It's *always* been about making money." What is different these days are the market dynamics. "I think in mainstream movies there is that desire for characters and events to be larger than life." He feels that may be a necessity when one considers the environment in which a movie must survive. "With a TV show—as quick as the networks are to pull the plug on under-performing but promising shows—you have time; time to let the characters develop, time to set up your story, time for the audience to get hooked and tell their friends. With a movie, you have a few months, or as little as a few weeks to create awareness (before the picture is released), and then a week in theaters—maybe two—to sink or swim."

Conte himself, however, has managed to avoid any pressure to overinflate his works.

I haven't often had the experience of being told to pump up the action. It's more often the opposite: I've written stories with expansive set pieces, and then been asked to scale them down for budgetary purposes. You write "big" because it makes for an entertaining read, and it doesn't cost a dime until someone tries to put it on-screen. If you're writing an action script on spec, and you hope to sell it to the studios for one of their summer tent poles, you don't worry so much about the script being too big. You just want to hook the reader.

Another thing he feels hasn't changed as much as the doomsayers claim is good material: it's *always* been hard to come by.

> On a production level, you can do more things these days. You can hire a top stunt coordinator, an A-list special effects house, and chances are—if you give them enough money—they are going to deliver.
>
> Great scripts are more elusive. Not many people can write them; not many producers and executives can even consistently recognize them. It's not just a matter of spending the time and money. A terrific writer—or twenty talented writers lined up in a row—won't always deliver that great script.

And even then, he points out, those movies that do have a distinctive, quality flavor may also have their box office limits built in. "It's very difficult to sell the idiosyncratic charms of pictures like *Wonder Boys* (2000) and *L.A. Confidential.* What are you going to see in the trailer? With something like *The Fast and the Furious* (2001), you see the 'pop' in the trailer. Studios are always looking for what they can sell, and the shiny bauble is easy to sell."

Myth #4:
The First Ten Pages

In Hollywood terms, it would be tantamount to criminal negligence on my part to counsel you to ignore the First Ten Pages rule: that you only have those few pages to convince the reader your screenplay is worth reading to the end (let alone acquiring).

The First Ten Pages rule *is* a true, real fact, as much as death and taxes. And about as pleasant. Here's how real I believe that rule is: I'll put money down on the table right now that says a lot of script readers won't even give you *that* much breathing space; you're lucky if they give you the ten (remember Gerry Abrams saying how you can tell within the first *five* pages if a screenwriter is any good?).

So, Bill, you might ask, if this is a real thing, why is it on the list of

Six Screenwriting Myths? You've spent all these pages telling us one supposed rule after another is a lot of crap, and now you start off this chapter telling us this myth isn't a myth? Bill, ol' boy, we are confused.

As well you might be, but as a work-up to an answer for you, let's poke around into what this First Ten Page thing is all about.

*   *   *

I first heard about it back in the 1980s when it was posited as a brutally practical tactic for dealing with The Pile.

And what, may you ask, is The Pile? It's that mountain of scripts that has to get plowed through by the poor low level Morlocks who do the reading for studios and producers and agencies and stars and etc.; it's their share of the 20–30,000 screenplays registered with the Writer's Guild every year (Bloom). According to screenwriter William Goldman, "a major star may read two hundred scripts a year, an executive twice that many" (*Adventures...*, 106). Pity, then, the luckless executive's assistant valiantly trying to winnow down The Pile and only pass on those scripts he/she thinks are worth the boss's time. If the boss is reading 200–400, and those are only the ones the reader passes through, how many were read that *didn't* get passed through? The numbers stagger.

No matter how fast you read, no matter how much you cheat by skimming, The Pile never goes down. You're reading into the night, you're reading on the weekends, on the ride to work, you're reading on the toilet, but as fast and as much as you read, there's more stuff coming in the door, in the mail, over the transom, getting foot-nudged to you from the bathroom stall next door. The First Ten Page thing came about as a way to keep that poor reader from being found in his/her cubicle one day, crushed to death when The Pile toppled over (or from suiciding, or going berserk and setting the office on fire, or running screaming naked into the streets completely out of what was left of his/her mind).

Why ten pages? Totally arbitrary number. Sounds better than nine or eleven. Has a nice, round, heft to it. And it's not carved in stone, either; according to Goldman, during the time of *Adventures in the Screen Trade*—1983—screenwriters were aiming to score within a script's first 15 pages (106).

Ok, so a two-time Oscar winner says this kind of thing was a fact over 30 years ago, and, if anything, it's five pages harsher now (or maybe ten if you go by Abrams). Let me ask the question again: Mr. Bill, why is it on your hit list?

Because, my friends, somewhere between then and now, some people in the movie business have gotten it into their heads that this constitutes good writing. Horrifyingly real and pragmatic as the rule is, it has *nothing* to do with good writing, and I'd put more money down on the table that says, in fact, it's probably responsible for a lot of truly crappy storytelling.

*   *   *

Like all the other myths we've addressed, First Ten Pages isn't in and of itself a bad thing. Look at *Jaws* (with a screenplay by Peter Benchley, author of the source novel, and Carl Gottlieb as well as several uncredited script doctors). That picture's opening—its first ten pages—are about as perfect an illustration of the concept as an effective tactic as you're going to find: young lady goes for some moonlit skinny-dipping while her would-be partner passes out on the beach in a drunken stupor. Said young lady then gets whipped around in frothing water like a puppy's chew toy as some unseen denizen of the deep takes hold of her. She screams, the passed-out dude back on the beach barely stirs, and under she goes, a midnight snack for the monster shark which has now staked out this stretch of ocean as his personal buffet.

Even on the page, this hooks you from the beginning. Even in Benchley's not particularly well-written book, he's reeling you in from the outset.

Or consider the Coen Brothers' *Raising Arizona*. The brothers pack more story into the opening minutes of *Arizona* than is contained in some entire movies, as the flick whizzes through H.I.'s (Nicolas Cage) criminal career, his meeting up with police officer Ed (Holly Hunter), their romance, marriage, discovery that Ed can't have children, failed attempt to adopt, and their plan to kidnap one of the quintuplets born to a furniture magnate and his wife ... and that's all before the credits run.

These are the kind of openings First Ten Page proselytizers proselytize about.

But one of the bad side-effects of the concept is a nasty tendency for some writers, desperate to grab a reader's eyeballs and not let go, to front-load their scripts with a lot of over-the-top action and broad-stroked characters, essentially bludgeoning the reader into submission rather than craftily hooking him/her.

Let's look at the opening for *Lethal Weapon* (1987, screenplay by Shane Black). Young girl stoned out of her mind walks off a high-rise balcony to smash into a car floors below. Cut to undercover cop Riggs (Mel Gibson), making a bogus drug buy. Riggs crazily flashes his badge, guns come out, Riggs drops two of the four dope dealers, and when another takes him hostage, he calls for his fellow cops to not worry about him and to go ahead and shoot the bad guy. When the bad guy remarks how nuts Riggs is, Riggs head-butts him and that's that.

There's no denying these opening minutes set the stage. This ain't exactly *The French Connection* we're watching: over-the-top characters, more bad guys dropped than most cops shoot in a career, a self-destructive sharpshooting detective... Well, we could go on and on. It's an opening where it's impossible *not* to get an idea of how the rest of this flick is going to play.

Is this effective screenwriting? After a box office success and three money-minting sequels, you can't argue with it.

But is it *good?*

As The Bard said, aye, there's the rub.

If you like what Stephen King refers to as "moron movies"—movies you can kick back and enjoy while disengaging the thinking parts of your brain (as I have the many times I've watched *LW*)—I'd say, yeah, ok, *Lethal Weapon* is good. If, on the other hand, you're more of a *French Connection* or *Ronin* (1998) guy (movies I've also sat through many times) ... well then, no, not so good. In fact, by comparison, it's absurd, it's comic book story-telling.

But it's symptomatic of a kind of screenwriting that's come to dom-inate the commercial mainstream over the last 20–30 years: movies that pretty much play all their high cards up front. The characters and the plot are set up quickly (and to do it quickly usually demands simplicity and going over scale) and we spend the next 110 minutes watching a plot unspool pretty much the way those first 10 minutes told us it would unspool.

You see it in thrillers, romcoms (Nora Ephron's 1993 *Sleepless in Seat-tle* is an easy example; let me guess, these two cutsie-sweetie adorables—Tom Hanks and Meg Ryan—end up together? No kidding!), broad comedies (*The Hangover;* gee, what're the chances these arrested development types will get into trouble? No kidding!) ... actually, it's hard to find a mainstream flick these days that *doesn't* do this.

Look at the movies that led the 2015 box office: *Jurassic World, Avengers: Age of Ultron, Furious 7, Mission: Impossible—Rogue Nation, Ant-Man, San Andreas.* C'mon, seriously, you didn't know where these movies were going even before the first 10 minutes were up? Did the characters intro-duced up front evolve in some sort of surprising, unpredictable way?

If you said you didn't know, and yes, that the characters and the movie still surprised you... Well, my friend, I'd say you don't go to many movies.

The thing is, for big budget whammo-blammo flicks like these, that's fine. Nobody's coming to see great revelations of the human paragon when they plunk down their money at the ticket counter for one of these action-and-FX behemoths. But that First Ten Page thing has killed (at the major studio level) what used to be a Hollywood storytelling standard: the slow build.

Let's start with one of the all-time greats and look at an aspect which makes it one of the all-time greats: *Citizen Kane.* Movie opens with the camera crawling around bazillionaire Charles Foster Kane's lavish estate gone to seed, winds up in his bedroom just in time to see him—his face obscured—whisper, "Rosebud" and die. Cut to a *faux* newsreel account of this big shot's life and death, then there's a lot of exposition among the journalists who've watched this film-within-a-film (and whose faces we never see) about trying to find out the *real* story behind this guy, the clue maybe being his last word: "Rosebud."

By contemporary standards, it's not much of an open: slow-paced, heavily expository, and offers only the most arm's-length introductions to the two characters who'll carry us through the movie: Kane (Orson Welles), whom we'll only ever see as others see him with all the contradictions that entails; and the reporter tasked with digging into Kane's bio (William Alland), whose face we will never see, and who is less a character than a device, a microphone for those who knew Kane to talk at.

Let's get a bit more modern-day and look at a movie we've already cited several times: *The Godfather* (with Francis Ford Coppola and Mario Puzo adapting Puzo's novel). The movie opens on a character we will only ever see once more in the movie, and then only briefly—Bonasera the undertaker (Salvatore Corsitto)—who has come to the Godfather looking for revenge against the young men who assaulted his daughter; a throw-away as this story element will never be revisited. Bonasera is followed by a parade of other visitors to the don, looking for either favors or to pay tribute on this, the day of the don's daughter's wedding. We are introduced to an ensemble, not really knowing at this point who the pivotal players are (and with no indication the movie's focus will change, as Marlon Brando's don is sidelined for part of the movie by an assassination attempt, replaced by his oldest son [James Caan] who will be murdered, placing leadership of the family with youngest son Michael [Al Pacino]); or what the major plot driver will be (there's just a few tossed off lines during this opening sequence about setting up a meeting with drug dealer Solozzo, and it is not until that meeting—which occurs well into the movie—that *The God-father* finally gains its forward momentum).

The slow build may not have been the only opening stratagem, but it was certainly a mainstay for decades in movies of all sorts. In the 1962 World War II epic *The Longest Day*, the first hour of this nearly three-hour extravaganza consists of nothing but the movie's all-star cast (there is no central character; the movie, like its source book, is a mosaic portrait of the Normandy invasion) fretting about whether or not the D-Day landings are going to go off or not. That's it; no action, no main character, just a lot of jabber from dozens of characters about will-we-or-won't-we.

Despite being considered a classic actioner, another World War II thriller—*The Dirty Dozen* (1967, Nunnally Johnson and Lukas Heller adapting E.M. Nathanson's novel) also takes, by contemporary standards, a hell of a long time getting going. Granted, the movie starts with a shock as Major Reisman (Lee Marvin) stands witness to a hanging, but he then proceeds to an extended yak-fest of a briefing about his assignment leading a behind-the-lines mission of a dozen convicted criminals. Reisman then meets the prospective Dozen for the first time at a military prison, then there's another long stretch of jawing as Reisman interviews the principals among them. We're a good 20 minutes or so into the movie's 2 hr. 30 min. running time before we've got a handle on the basic plot and major players, with all of that info delivered through nothing more dazzling than expository dialogue.

Consider that just about every private eye movie ever made—from 1941's *The Maltese Falcon* (John Huston adapting Dashiell Hammett's novel) to 1966's *Harper* (William Goldman adapting Ross Macdonald's novel, *The Moving Target*) to 1974's *Chinatown* (screenplay by Robert Towne) starts with similar gab parties: enter the client, there's a ton of exposition to set up the case (most of which, we usually find out at the end of Act One, to be b.s.), and then there's still more exposition as our gumshoe begins his initial poking around into the case.

Even in movies from that more patient era which did opt for a punchy opening, it was hardly the shoot-the-works kind of opener that seems *de rigueur* now.

I mentioned *The French Connection* earlier (Ernest Tidyman adapting Robin Moore's book). The movie opens in Marseilles, we follow a man never identified who seems to be tailing a certain car, the man is abruptly assassinated by hitman Marcel Bozzuffi, there's some cryptic conversation between Bozzuffi and his boss (Fernando Rey), then the movie cuts to Brooklyn where two NYPD detectives (Gene Hackman and Roy Scheider) bust a street-level dope dealer; an action with no connection to the main plot. It's a beginning with a lot of First Ten Page pop: the killing in Marseilles, Hackman and Scheider on a frantic foot chase through a stretch of New York which looks like war-ravaged Beirut, but, unlike *Lethal Weapon*, it's all life-sized, taking place in the same world where the rest of us live ... and has kept us interested by *not* telling us where this ride is taking us. We're about 12 minutes into the 104-minute movie before Hackman tips to the low-level hood he suspects might be involved in something worth his interest. It'll be another 12 minutes before Hackman and Scheider connect the hood with a major narcotics figure and now—24 minutes into the movie—the main plot finally kicks in: Hackman/Scheider's investigation and their cracking of the—ta da!—French Connection.

So, what's the point of the slow build? What advantage does it have over today's standard, over-energized, breathless First Ten Pages?

The idea is to give the audience a baseline; a sense of what "normal" is before taking us to more highly dramatized levels, in giving us the chance to get to know the "before" of a story's characters before a plot's action begins to energize, twist, and possibly even pervert them. What would the nightmarish last half of *Deliverance* (James Dickey adapting his novel) be without its four-suburbanites-on-a-lulling-backwoods-idyll first half? Or would the introduction of the titular big ape in the original *King Kong* (screenplay by James Ashmore Creelman, Ruth Rose, and an uncredited Merian C. Cooper, Edgar Wallace, and Leon Gordon) be as impressive early in the movie instead of coming about one-third of the way into the film? Or how disturbing would Jack Nicholson's descent into homicidal, delusional madness have been in Stanley Kubrick's *The Shining* (Kubrick and Diane Johnson adapting Stephen King's novel) if it had been tipped early? Would Pixar's lovely tale of love between robots, *WALL-E* (2008, writing chores handled by Andrew Stanton, Pete Doctor, Jim Reardon) have the same heart-aching sweetness if we hadn't first spent almost 20 minutes alone with WALL-E, getting acquainted with his loneliness, his childlike wonder and respect for vestiges of a past he never knew, and his longing for connection?

From classic thrillers like Alfred Hitchcock's *The Birds* (1963) to rat-a-tat comedies like *The Out of Towners* (1970), arty tours of the demimonde like *Midnight Cowboy*, high cinematic art like *2001: A Space Odyssey*, vintage sci fiers like the original *The Thing from Another World* (1951), goofs like *The Big Lebowski*, stately docudramas like *The King's Speech* (2010), John Wayne punch-punch bang-bang Westerns like *El Dorado* (1966), and art house faves like *The Artist* (2011), the slow build demonstrates both its pliability and its strength in drawing an audience into the texture and flow of cinematic storytelling whether it was Saturday matinee schlock (any John Wayne flick) or convention-defying high art (any Stanley Kubrick flick).

To Robert Towne, Oscar-winner for his brilliant neo-*noir Chinatown,* this business about front-loading scripts to provide a hook defies common sense. Interviewed for the 1981 book (see? This was an issue even *then!*), *The Craft of the Screenwriter,* Towne pointed out the routinely overlooked yet obvious fact that even if the beginning of a movie sucks, movie-goers have "paid three-fifty or five dollars.... They're there. They're not going to go anywhere" (Brady, 424).

William Goldman quotes his *Butch Cassidy and the Sundance Kid* star Paul Newman as saying, for storytelling's sake, it's not the first ten pages that are important, but "the final fifteen minutes are the most important of any movie." Newman had enough hits and misses over his 57-year career to learn people who've plunked down money for a flick care more about how satisfyingly it ends than how it begins (106).

So, with such a tonnage of examples to the contrary, how did the First Ten Pages doctrine evolve from a tactical option to a time management tactic to a dominating aesthetic?

Like Queen Eleanor said, one step at a time.

* * *

Once upon a time, people used to read books. For fun. And now they don't.

Ok, that's an unfair, monumentally broad generalization, and an overly simplistic explanation of how First Ten Pages got where it is today.

But I think you'll find, as you look back over cinema history, that what was, once upon a time, a new medium trying to find its voice often aped the architecture of the novel (which some cinema aestheticians have argued is—or was—the movies' closest structural relative). The slow build—the patient, careful laying down of a foundation of circumstances and character—was a regular part of literary storytelling (Svetkey, 39). One could even argue that at least some clearly artistically ambitious films—say Kubrick movies, David Lean epics, Francis Coppola's best work, just to name a few—aspired toward the same dramatic gravitas of a fine novel, and often did so by mirroring the same stately elegance of one.

But in terms of both content and sensibility, the Hollywood mainstream has moved away from that stance. On the issue of content, "The problem with screenwriters today," entertainment lawyer David Colden told *Entertainment Weekly,* "is they don't write from experience. They write from having watched 25 years of television." (Svetkey, 39)

Five-time Emmy-winning producer/writer/director Bill Persky, on a 2005 NYU panel honoring Sid Caesar, was asked about the difference between Persky's early days of writing for television sitcoms in the 1960s and the present, and said pretty much the same thing:

> Most of the scripts for (*The Dick Van Dyke Show*) started with one of (the writers) coming into the writers' room on Monday saying, "Let me tell you about what happened to me over the weekend." Today, it's TV shows inspired by other TV shows.

(Warning: shameless self-promotion approaching!)

In my 2007 book, *Overkill: The Rise and Fall of Thriller Cinema* (still available on Amazon, kids!), I spent three rather dense pages explaining how the literary aesthetic which was a part of cinema storytelling for decades, and particularly prominent in the 1960s/1970s, was steamrolled by a more rushed, action-driven dynamic beginning in the late 1970s and which now dominates the commercial mainstream. Let me boil it down for you:

The MTV generation of the 1970s/1980s—the first generation growing up with cable and who spent their youth flipping through the cable spectrum—begat an even more ADD-sensibility as their kids grew up enveloped by videogames, the internet, and smart phones (I recently read an article showing how kids as young as four are comfortable and adept with portable tech like tablets). And now those kids have grown up to become the first rank of script readers sincerely believing faster is better (199–202).

Entered into evidence, Exhibit A:

Interviewing writer/director John Dahl in 2010, (probably best known for his neo-*noirs Red Rock West* [1992] and *The Last Seduction* [1994]), he recalled speaking at a west coast film school and being approached by an aspiring young filmmaker who told him "the audience only had a long enough attention span to see an image for four seconds, then it had to change." The proof, the young man said, could be founding watching "a classic movie like (Michael Bay's) *The Rock* (1996)" (Mesce, "Neo...," 188).

Exhibit B:

In a 2003 article, "Plotting 101," for *Hollywoodlitsales News,* the case is put forth that plots of certain genre movies had "improved" because they had "taken to cramming 20–30 percent more plot beats into two hours ... than your average action movie or thriller made before 1990" (Peel). So, by those lights, Francis Coppola's paranoia classic *The Conversation* (1974) isn't as good as Tony Scott's vaguely similar (plot-wise) bang-chase-boom thriller, *Enemy of the State* (1998); and the slick but improbable, they-lived-happily-ever-after 1999 remake of *The Thomas Crown Affair* is better than the moody, almost melancholic 1968 original. That's like saying a six-pack of Budweiser is better than a bottle of Moet & Chandon champagne because it has more fizz.

The First Ten Pages concept isn't something these perusers and evaluators use as a method of chipping away at The Pile; it's the way they think.

*   *   *

Screenwriting, as a profession, isn't about personal expression, about telling a story one feels compelled to tell, about exploring the possibilities and limitations of the form. To be blunt: it ain't art. Never was. It's about survival.

You don't get to do diddly unless you write stuff readers think (and I emphasize this point: "think," not "know") people will pay to see. If the readers are afflicted with Hollywood's particular brand of attention-deficit mindset, and they're serving an audience with a similar affliction, well, as I said at the top of this section, you'd be making a serious career error ignoring the idea of kicking off what you'd hoped would be a meditative piece on the human condition with some huge explosions and a cigar-chomping protagonist declaring, "Long, dark nights of the soul are for wusses."

You want to work? You want to get paid to work? You want to work again? Then you do what you have to do.

I wouldn't be the first person to compare the screenwriting profession with prostitution. The purpose of this particular entry is to remind you that, yeah, you do what you have to do to eat ... just don't confuse screwing with making love.

The Triple Threat:
Adriana Trigiani

(With a 35-year career which includes producing and writing for network television [credits include The Cosby Show*], turning out a string of bestselling novels [latest being* All the Stars in the Heavens*], writing, producing, and directing her first big screen feature [Big Stone Gap, 2016], Trigiani has seen the writing profession from a dizzying variety of angles.)*

There are enormous differences between writing for film and television. When I write for television, I am part of a team, stories are broken in a room, script assignments are handed out by the show runner, we write the scripts, writers come together to re-write, and during production, we serve several roles on the stage for re-writing, often in casting, and while production is in force, we work on future scripts. It's a lot of work on several levels, which is why you find a lot of television writers married to the craft, putting in a chunk of years and then snapping their laptops shut and getting out. It is grueling and can wear you down. Most television writers will tell you that the work load, hours, and stress take a terrible toll on their families and personal lives. It's the very reason you find 20-somethings (and that included me) writing television. It's not just a craft, it's a lifestyle.

Writing for film, if you're a screenwriter for hire, ebbs and flows with the marketplace. There are times when the studios buy up spec scripts and take pitches, then they go into lockdown and develop from within, or re-fashion projects they already own, or work on their franchise projects. The bottom line is profit. Follow what a movie makes, and you will find the director and writer re-hired, flush with success, and when a movie flops, a fallow period. Perception is part of a screenwriter's career, but what drives the screenwriter's career is the success of their last movie. Many writers make a living re-writing movies that never get made, or ones in trouble in mid-production, so you have to decide what kind of artist you want to be, and if writing fills you up regardless of the outcome, you'll be very happy re-writing movies, and probably, in terms of material success, very rich. If you want to write original screenplays, it will be your responsibility, with your agent's help, of course, to put the team together to get the movie made—you'll have to find the director, the producers, the financing, and often the casting is key. Sometimes, the casting is everything. Making a movie is like building a house, and if you want to make a great one, you need the best elements in every department. Phillip Dunne (and I'm paraphrasing here) said you need three things to make a great movie:

a great script;

a great cast;

and a great production.

That is true, and I know it for sure, because I lived it when I made *Big Stone Gap.*

As a writer and director, I relished both roles because the storytelling was clear. There was no question of the romantic nature of the storytelling, there was a clear communication between the great Reynaldo Villalobos, our cinematographer, and me, so there was no way, with a brilliant cast, we could fail. We would make the movie I had written—or set out to make—that is, until all manner of things happen that are out of your control. It is then that the writer has to save the day, pivot quickly and re-write, keeping the entirety of the story in her head and knowing where the scene will go and how it will fit.

You write the movie three times they say: on the page, on the stage, and in the editing room. And I say you write it four times: on the page; on the stage; anew on the stage because the script you wrote was missing elements, or the actors show you such colors and emotions and skill that you, as writer, have them there and must write to their brilliant strengths, or you, the writer, are an idiot, and you, the director, have not taken advantage of the magic of your performers, which, on a movie set, is a crime; and finally and of course, in editing.

Editing is a challenge because you see all you couldn't get if you were on a budget, and frankly, in my mind, every big budget movie should be grand, because they have all the tools they need to make a great picture. I understand here and there why a movie might be a turkey, but as someone who watches these blockbusters, and I know my CGI tricks, I want to say, Come on! Can we write a story that moves the audience, not a thin premise speckled with visual hyperbole? A lot of great minds work on these movies, and that may be the problem.

A singular vision in storytelling on the page is essential in my opinion. Then, when the script is magnificent, the world is clear and original, the characters new and surprising, the dialogue fresh, crackling, and yet familiar in some sense, do you get a movie that you, as an audience member, will remember and treasure. The director can make that world come to life in her imagination and with her skills of leadership and vision and artful scope, but only when she has it on the page.

A screenplay, to me, is a work of art akin to an epic poem—it has a journey built into it, with vivid characters traveling through a world where they will be forever changed by the end of their sojourn. Or at least, that's how I look at it!

*   *   *

When it comes to the discussion of film and television, or film versus television, here are a few courant thoughts:

A dramatist in this day and age has to be adaptable, facile, and open to changes in the world of how we deliver storytelling to audiences. Fundamentals still apply, but the writer has to adapt to fit the distribution element—no longer is the theater the primary source of income for studios, or the television set the primary source of profit for television producers and studios.

This has huge ramifications for the writer, who must adapt her story-telling to the expectations of the audience and devices upon which her stories will be dramatized and transmitted. Now, what does this mean to the writer who sits down to create a show? The writer now has to pay attention to rapid changes in the marketplace and figure out how to flow with the tide. No longer does a writer visit four networks to pitch a show; you have 60-plus places to choose from, and while this may seem like a boom for the writer, it has also created a work load—figuring out where a project fits and who to bring it to—whereas it was simpler in the past. Change is the order of the day, and that might not mean you change the way you write, but it will mean you will change the way you sell what you write, and surely the way you market it once you have made the show.

*   *   *

I have always, and I mean from childhood, savored the process of creating a work of art on the page. By that, I mean the part that doesn't take place with a pencil and paper, but out in the world where I'm just liv-ing in it, walking around, making notes and breathing in the moment. I have so many notebooks, you might be able to stack them to the moon and back. Whenever I'm without paper and pen, I'm a wreck. I hear things and see things and then have to memorize the moment, or I turn to my daughter or my husband, and in the old days, my friends, and would say, "Will you remind me?" I'm famous for bugging people to remember things for me because I couldn't find a pen.

That said, the process begins in my sleep, in my dreams. And I have now seen a real ribbon in the novels and the television writing and the movie, and the development of movies that is strong and clear, and if I chose a color for this ribbon it would be bright red: I write to remember people. People I love, people I miss, people I wish I knew, people.

I am fascinated by decisions made, failures, mistakes, illusions, allu-sions, people's relationships with one another, with the past, with sex, with money, with their sense of self-worth, and their sense of what their pur-pose is and why they were put on earth. The themes of love and work are strong and unknowable ultimately, but I crave deeper and deeper knowl-edge on those fronts.

If you talk to people who are married a long time, many years, they know something about commitment, and the same goes with art. I don't flail and I don't panic at the whims of anyone or anything in the marketplace.

I never have because I know the audience, the people are interested in exactly the same things I am interested in. They want to go home to someone they love after a day of doing something they like. And they want to feel safe when they walk in the door. That's it. That's all. And that's what I write about, it's what I'm obsessed with, you might say, because in my estimation, all unhappiness comes from lack of connection to one person to love, and a flailing about purpose—anybody can figure out how to make money, but how do you make a living, meaning how do you want to live and survive by the labor of your own hands?

Teachers know the secret, and cops and nurses, and, back in the day, farmers, you can even say inventors, scientists, people who yearn to find answers—these are people who survive by their wits, by the labor of their own hands, and, most importantly, are in service to the world.

That's my job. I'm in service to you. I'm here to uplift, entertain and enchant you, because my role as a dramatist is to have you rest and relax, to laugh and to remind you how important we are to each other. Now, that's my mission. And low and behold, some pretty smart people have been very generous and hired me, and been very generous and sustained that vision; they see it as I do. Those are the folks I have worked with, and will work with again.

*   *   *

I never change how I write when I'm directing my own material, but I change and challenge and re-frame, always, what I have written as I'm writing. And, once on the set of *Big Stone Gap*, I was very clear, if I saw two actors spark, I wrote more material for them. If I saw a particular skill in an actor, I wrote a speech to highlight their skill as it served the story. If, in the middle of a scene, it wasn't working, I shot it, then pulled elements out that didn't work, refashioned it for the actor, and shot it again, this time better and more to the point, and perhaps with what I already had, and with what I had re-written, I could do something wonderful with it all later. Later because ... the clock is on and it's not your friend.

You have to move quickly and stay calm and centered and focused. You have to be warm and loving and kind and a leader, and also deep as a river. You have to know everything you've shot and everything that you need to get, and, as a writer, you have to be there for the director (in this case it was one person!) and give her what she needs to make the story better or make the story work or fix what isn't working. If you cast well, and I hit it over the fence with my cast in *Big Stone Gap*, and you love actors, which I do, and you write for actors, which I do and always have, and if you understand their process, which I savor, you will write for them, and they will love the work, and when they love the work, it sings.

So often actors are saving movies, television shows, and plays with their skill and ability to make clunky dialogue and moth eaten arcs work when we haven't given them what they need to do their jobs. Actors are the great fixers of show business and dramatizing. But it should not be so. They are gold and should be given rubies, emeralds, diamonds in the dialogue and action, because they are your orchestra, your instruments, your conduits to the audience. They are the storytellers, and, frankly, they deserve the best scripts and direction we can give them. They are worth all the years of being alone in a room because they dramatize what you have been feeling as a writer, what you know and have seen, and that right there is what it is all about.

Bottom Crawling: Take 2 and Pan Am Pictures

It was during my first lunch with Bob Conte—sometime in the 1980s—when I asked him what now seems to me a painfully naïve question about his screenwriting career: "When do you think you'll feel you've 'made it'?"

"What do you mean, 'made it'?"

"You know; where you won't have to hustle so hard to get work."

"Bill, you're *always* hustling for work."

"You know what I mean; where you feel like you've turned a corner, and you don't have to worry about getting your next job."

He smiled in that that same, tolerant way Bill Persky's assistant had smiled at me when she found me waiting on line to see a taping of his show. "It's like going around an octagon," Conte said. "There's always *another* corner."

You know that old Hollywood axiom that you're only as good as your last picture? I don't think the business is that inflexible; you may get a little more slack than that. William Goldman says, "Producers do not forget your name if a movie loses lots of money. Because *most* studio movies lose lots of money..." (*What Lie...*, 5). Still, careers—even blazing careers—can turn on a dime.

Take Shane Black, for example, who, at one time, was one of the highest-paid screenwriters in Hollywood. Black had hit big as a 26-year-old hot-shot with *Lethal Weapon*, then turned out a series of high profile shoot-'em-ups: *Lethal Weapon 2* (1989, story credit only), *The Last Boy Scout* (1991), *Last Action Hero* (1993), and then his biggest pic, *The Long Kiss Goodnight* (1996). Black was paid $4 million for *Long Kiss...*, making him one of the highest-paid screenwriters in the business. The movie cost $65 million to make, earned just $33.3 million, and Black didn't get another screen credit for nine years (Collis, 44).

But Black was lucky. Working with Robert Downey, Jr., on *Kiss Kiss Bang Bang* (2005), a nifty but little-seen neo-*noir*, eventually led to him co-writing and directing *Iron Man 3* (2013), and, for the moment, his career is alive again. But it was close. On the eve of his 2016 release, *The Nice Guys*, he told *Entertainment Weekly*, of those bad days, "I was drifting off the map at a very alarming rate" (Collis, 44).

Black's may have been one of the more meteoric rise and falls (and apparent resurrection) in the business, but it's an old paradigm. In his follow up to *Adventures in the Screen Trade—Which Lie Did I Tell? More Adventures in the Screen Trade*—William Goldman tells of being a "leper in Hollywood" over the stretch 1980–1985 (*Which Lie...*, 3). Keep in mind that, at the time, this was a guy who had not only written (among other films) two critically acclaimed Oscar-winning classics—*Butch Cassidy and the Sundance Kid* and *All the President's Men*—but had won himself a statuette for each. Not to mention that each of those two flicks was one of the top-earning releases of its *decade: Butch Cassidy* being the eighth-biggest moneymaker of the 1960s (above flicks like *Patton*, *Goldfinger* [1964], *Bonnie and Clyde*, even *Lawrence of Arabia*); and *President's Men* coming in #54 for the 1970s (ahead of *The French Connection*, *The Spy Who Loved Me* [1977]), and *Deliverance*). But then he wrote four movies in a row which died in development, and, for a while, it looked like even an ace like Goldman might be shown the industry's door (5). Goldman did find his way back to write some terrific flicks like *The Princess Bride* (1987, based on his novel), and hits like *Misery* (1990) and *Maverick* (1994), but you have to admit, the idea of a guy with his track record finding himself in a hole has to be, at the very least and especially to those struggling for even a toehold in the business, unnerving.

As I said earlier in the book, this business gives you no credit for your body of work. It's like that line from *The Hustler* (1961, screenplay by Sidney

Carroll and Robert Rossen): "This isn't football. You don't get paid for yardage. At the end of the night you count up your money and the one with the most wins."

That's Hollywood: "Yeah, you wrote some hits in your day, but what've you done lately?"

In Tom Batiuk's comic strip *Funky Winkerbean*, one of his characters becomes involved in the movie business. In a line I've considered having engraved on a plaque to hang over my desk, a veteran actor says that in Hollywood, "You're only a flop away from being discarded" (J5).

By the early 1990s, I had worked with Brian De Palma and five-time Emmy-winner Bill Persky; I had had conversations with Eliot Kastner and John Kemeny; I had adapted a bestselling novel for RKO, and a cult favorite in *Big Phil's Kid;* Mark Seiler had wanted to make me a house scribe for a resurgent RKO. I had had a lot of at-bats, but they'd all been strike-outs. By that time, I'd been at this business long enough to know I'd had more shots at the brass ring than anybody taking a run at a screenwriting career has a right to expect. Hell, most people who try this don't even get *one!*

I have a very old and dear friend who had, at one time, been a struggling young stage actor, and then, when he wasn't young anymore, had switched over to the business side of theater. I once asked him why he'd made the switch. "Because," he said, "you reach a point where you realize it's just not gonna happen for you."

As the 1990s began, for me, that realization was sinking in.

* * *

The only move I had open to me at the time was the screenwriter's equivalent of being sent down to the minors: checking out want ads.

Pre-internet, the two main sources of hard news about the entertainment industry were *Variety* (both the daily and weekly editions), and the weekly *The Hollywood Reporter.* Both publications had a classified section, and occasionally among want ads for accountants and tech people would be "Screenplays Wanted" ads. Who runs a "Screenplays Wanted" ad? It ain't outfits like Paramount and Universal. Typically, they were tiny start-up companies that were often one- or two-head operations, those heads rarely having ever produced anything. One I remember, for example, was a woman who had done some local television production and wanted to get into features as a producer. Another was a pharmaceutical magnate's son who had quit film school after his first year because "I didn't think they had anything to teach me," and was being bankrolled by his daddy. There were minor actors and wannabe actors and recent film school grad wannabe directors and wannabe producers looking for a vehicle to showcase their talents in the hopes said vehicle would carry them up the first rung or two of the Hollywood career ladder.

None of them were WGA signatories, nor were they interested in becoming WGA signatories. Hell, they usually couldn't afford to pay themselves let alone WGA minimums. The very thing I'd been afraid of when Little Ruthie had been doing her victory dance over my joining the Guild had come to pass; the only people I could pitch myself to couldn't afford to hire me.

I remembered an old interview with director Robert Aldrich. With a career in Hollywood running from the 1940s almost up until his death in 1983, Aldrich had been through enough career ups and downs, hits (*The Dirty Dozen,* 1967) and misses (*The Choirboys,* 1977) to know something about survivability in the movie business. He talked about the necessity of "staying at the table": you did anything to stay in the business in a position where you could dig yourself out of a hole, including cutting your price (Silke, 145). If the WGA wouldn't let me cut my price to be affordable to the few it seemed would hire me (and they wouldn't), then I had to leave the Guild.

I wrote to the WGA about resigning from the Guild only to learn that, not unlike the Mob and the CIA, you can never leave the Guild. Unless they throw you out, once a Guild member, always a Guild member. However, they would allow me to go on "inactive" status, where I'd no longer have to pay dues or be bound by WGA strictures.

That was the perfect word for my circumstances just then: "inactive."

＊   ＊   ＊

At about the same time, I had gone through a creative spurt banging out five spec scripts in short order covering a spread of genres: sci fi, horror, mystery, action thriller, drama. But they all had one thing in common. They were designed to be cheap.

A few years before, I had sat in on a living room reading of the screenplay for a small-scale, intimate drama set up by the writer and his director partner. Their intention was to scrounge up enough money to independently produce the flick, their first. Someone asked the director if this was some sort of personal passion project.

No, he said. The choice had been purely pragmatic. It was a small enough piece he and the writer were sure they could get it produced and score their first feature credit. "You don't make the movie you *want* to make," I remember him saying, "You make the movie you *can* make."

All five of my pieces were designed to be makeable: limited and isolated settings (no traffic issues, easy permits), limited casts, minimal effects for the sci fi and horror pieces, etc. I don't know how many pitches or submissions I made before I finally connected with a Florida-based outfit called Take 2 Productions.

Take 2 was George Barnes. George clicked with my sci fi piece *Lab 7*, about a remote government lab futzing with genetic mutations. On our first phone call, he and I connected immediately. We were both Jersey boys, spoke the same effing-this/effing-that language, had all the same reference points (best American hot dogs? The "rippers" at Rutt's Hutt on the Passaic River; best Italian hot dogs? Dickie Dee's in Newark), liked the same things in movies.

George was a non-stop, Eveready bunny of a guy already on his third career. He'd grown up in Jersey helping his dad build houses, and then, one day, while lugging buckets of concrete in freezing rain, decided, "This ain't for me." He relocated to Florida to build houses where there was no freezing rain. He drifted into acting for a while, then found himself more interested in what was going on behind the camera than what was going on in front of it, landed a few gigs as a production assistant, then made his producing bones on a low-budget schlock fest called *South Beach* (1992), and from there decided to launch Take 2 Productions. He wasn't quite 25 yet (Mesce, "Guerilla...," 175–177).

Superficially, *Lab 7* looked like an *Aliens* (1986) clone, but actually it was a riff on the 1950s B sci fiers which were (I felt) the inspiration for James Cameron's flick; movies like *Invaders from Mars* (1953), *The Thing from Another World* (1951), *Them!* (1954). I had also taken a cue from the monster movies of Jack Arnold who'd pumped out a string of solid creature features for Universal in the 1950s, most of them set in stranded little towns in the deserts of the southwest. While the location had been practical (isolated, easily controlled), Arnold had gotten a tremendous amount of mileage atmosphere- and tone-wise out of all that sunbaked desolation (Baxter, 118). So, *Lab 7* was set out in Jack Arnold's southwest.

"We have a problem," George said. "This is Florida. We don't have deserts in Florida."

"What do you have?"

"I have access to a small island, it's not far off the coast, nobody lives there. We can have the run of the place."

So a quick rewrite of *Lab 7* exchanged sand for sea.

A few months into the option, the financing George had been trying to put together fell apart. I offered to give him back some of the option money he'd put down on *Lab 7,* but he wouldn't hear of it. "You earned it for the aggravation," he said.

Before long, Eveready George was back in touch with a more ambitious plan. He'd gotten a job managing Greenwich Studios, a production facility, and was trying to navigate them toward making their own movies along with providing shooting facilities for other production companies. Greenwich had gotten their hands on a script called *In the Mikx,* which was a messy blending of blaxploitation and martial arts flicks with a film school dropout attached as director along with his buddy as the writer.

Every other word in the dialogue was some variant of "fuck" which I think they thought gave the piece a sense of gritty urban authenticity. It didn't. It was a by-the-numbers revenge tale; the cousin of a black Bruce Lee knock-off gets involved with a drug ring, winds up dead, and the martial artist goes on a revenge spree. After the set-up, it was little more than a parade of scenes of guys getting their ass kicked by the hero. Forget about the storytelling; these guys couldn't even spell. George wanted to hire me for a rewrite, but as I looked over the script, I felt a bit overwhelmed.

"Jesus, George, I wouldn't even know where to start!"

"Bill, the thing is in such bad shape, even if you just retype it, that'd be a 100 percent improvement."

Back in my college days, I had put my head together with those of two friends of mine to concoct a redneck revenge story. There was a guy named Earl Owensby in South Carolina who had his own small production company, and who was pumping out low-budget exploitation movies for the regional so-called "bubba" market—shotguns-and-pick-up-trucks stuff—to capitalize on the then popularity of flicks like *Walking Tall* (1973) and *Billy Jack* (1971) (Mesce, "Bubbas...," 129). We were never able to place our piece, but now I lifted the general outline of the plot which involved the escalating war between an Army veteran and the corrupt sheriff who murdered the vet's father.

Having thus taken care of the plot, more or less, I was still stumped as how to write the martial arts combat scenes.

"You do it like they do in porn scripts," George explained. "When you get to the fight, you just write, 'They fight,' and the director'll work it out on the set."

But *In the Mikx* didn't happen. Greenwich wanted to lock George up in an office and that wasn't him, so he walked (Mesce, "Guerilla...," 177).

He went back to trying to make Take 2 fly and called me with another possible rewrite gig on something called *Catch the Wind.* It was a vanity project, some physician wanting to bankroll a small family movie about a high school track star who gets in touch with her mystical side when she meets a Native American living in the woods. The movie would star—surprise!—her high school track star daughter.

Having no touch for kids' films, I passed on a rewrite but offered to do some script analysis, my biggest suggestion having to do with doing something about the Native American mystic. The script had him talking like Indians in old Westerns; you know, no prepositions, very solemn. I made the point that Native Americans talked like the rest of us, wore sneakers like the rest of us, watched baseball like the rest of us. The producer/physician liked my comments, enough that she kept trying to talk me into taking on a rewrite, but then her track star daughter got mono, and by the time she'd have recovered, she'd be off to college. *Catch the Wind* was scrapped.

The next time I heard from George, he'd gotten *really* ambitious.

He'd partnered up with a guy who was supposed to be some kind of financial wiz. The idea was to put together a package of properties and pitch the package to investors. They had already landed one project, now George wanted to use all five of my spec pieces to fill out the proposal. "You don't have to stick with us," he told me, "there's no obligation. Right now, we just need something for the presentation. But I would like to make these flicks."

With visions of being some sort of B-movie ace, I told him I was in.

Actually, they had landed two projects, both from a special effects maven named Brett Piper they'd discovered living in his grandmother's house in Maine.

Piper was expert in old-school FX techniques: forced perspectives, modeling, glass mattes, stop-action, etc. He'd made an absolutely charming thirty-odd-minute stop-action-animated piece called, "The Return of Captain Sinbad" (1995), shooting it all on a table top in his grandmother's basement, and had somehow gotten Roddy McDowall to supply the bedtime-reading narration.

With "Captain Sinbad" an impressive showcase of his abilities, Piper was pitching The Boys—George and his partner—on a feature called *Dinosaur Babes* (1996). It was a loopy, off-the-wall concoction of cave men, Amazons, and a crashed UFO (Mesce, "Guerilla...," 177–178). The Boys wanted my opinion on "Captain Sinbad," to vet Piper's screenplay for *Babes,* and help them out with contracts for both since I was the only one of us who'd ever signed an honest-to-God feature film contract.

"Captain Sinbad," I told them, was lovely, and I even offered to show it to the Family Programming staff at HBO. As for *Babes*, I thought it had the potential to be goofy, campy fun if it was handled with a light touch. I thought some "bookends" might help set the piece better, and quickly wrote an intro piece where archeologists discover some puzzling prehistoric cave paintings, and that would lead into the story proper, and then I had a tag where we see that what's left the cave explorers scratching their heads is wondering what the hell the picture of a flying saucer is doing among the drawings of dinosaurs and early humans. As for the contracts, I lifted language from my screenplay agreements. As thanks, The Boys gave me billing on both projects as "co-executive producer." Those were my first screen credits which was kind of a buzz ... until I saw the finished *Dinosaur Babes*.

The Boy's had scraped up $300,000, brought Piper down to Florida and told him to go to it. One of the things which had puzzled them from the outset was why someone with Piper's obvious talents was still living at home with grandma. They soon found out. Evidently, Piper was much better at dealing with his tabletop dinosaurs than with full-sized human beings. At one point, he threw a snit and wouldn't come out of his motel room. On such a small budget, the production couldn't eat an idle day, so George had to play director.

The finished product was, to put it diplomatically, a disappointment. The movie looked like it had been cast off of Florida's beaches, with everybody—especially the female cast members—looking great in their loin cloths and animal hide bikinis. If only they hadn't had to act, everything would've been fine. It didn't help that, according to George, Piper was no actor's director.

Nor did he have much of a sense of humor about his story. When I'd read it, I'd told them I thought it could be a great laugher, but apparently Piper—who discarded my bookend pieces—took it seriously. Cave men and a crashed flying saucer, and you're taking it seriously? Seriously?

But the bigger problem was they'd all made the movie they *wanted* instead of the movie they *could*. Piper had told them he could make the movie for $35,000, but even $300,000 wasn't enough (Mesce, "Guerilla...," 178). To stretch their budget, they'd shot without synchronized sound, looping in dialogue and effects later, which gave the movie a tinny, 1970s-porno-flick sound quality. Worse, some of the not-so-great actors had ad-libbed some of their lines, and it was impossible to accurately loop in that off-the-cuff dialogue, giving those scenes something of a Japanese monster movie look. But the FX work was impressive; in fact, it was so well done it made the rest of the movie look even shoddier.

George eventually was able to sell *Dinosaur Babes* to a regional video chain and make his money back, but nobody felt like this was a win.

Even "Captain Sinbad" had been a disappointment. The problem was its odd length; something between 30 and 40 minutes. It was too long to circulate in short film competitions; they typically wanted works 30 minutes and shorter. That was also the problem with trying to sell it to TV; it was too short for an hour special, even with commercials, but too long for a half-hour spot. "Sinbad" went on the shelf.

As frustrating as the experience had been, what happened next was a soul-crusher. I received a call from an uncharacteristically dreary George (George is never down; enthused, puzzled, curious, frustrated, downright pissed, but never down) telling me, "It's all over." Evidently, his partner, the supposed financial wiz, hadn't come through with the financing for Take 2's package of films, and had quit. George was calling me from the beach where he sat moping, appropriately enough because he was feeling stranded. He was considering returning to Jersey to build houses again.

"Take some time," I told him, warning against making any hasty decisions. "Right now, you're hurting. Give it a while, go to the movies, take it easy, lie on the beach, don't do *anything* for a bit. Heal up. Then, when your head is clear, sit down and do some figuring on your next move."

He said he thought that was good advice, and we hung up.

By this time, I considered George a friend, and it hurt to hear him so beat up and bruised. I was trying to figure out if I could come up with the money to fly down to Florida so he'd have someone to vent to when I got another call from him that afternoon. The old George. Eveready George ready to give moviemaking another whack.

"What happened?" I said. "I told you to take some time off!"

"I did. I sat on the beach for an hour."

"An *hour!* I was thinking maybe a couple of *days!*"

"Nope. An hour. That's a long time for me" (Mesce, *Artists...*, 208).

By the next day, he was back in business.

* * *

He was working with an outfit called Pan Am Pictures run by a guy named Sam Lupowitz.

Lupowitz was a survivor of the collapse of Cannon Films. Cannon had been a tiny film company in Los Angeles which, in 1979, had been taken over by two cousins, Menahem Golan and Yoram Globus. By the mid–1980s, the cousins had turned little Cannon into something of a mini-powerhouse, minting profits by grinding out a steady flow of low-budget schlock like Chuck Norris's *Missing in Action* movies and Charles Bronson shoot-'em-ups for just a couple of million dollars. Key to Cannon's success was their being one of the first movie companies to understand how new platforms—premium and basic cable, home video, and the growing overseas market—were changing the financial architecture of the motion picture business. By aggressively pre-selling their movies to these ancillaries, the typical Cannon movie was in the black before it ever appeared on a movie screen (Fabrikant).

But then the cousins got creatively ambitious. They started making more upscale movies on larger budgets. Maybe Cannon had been making dreck for so long they'd forgotten how to make a good movie ... providing they ever knew. In any case, they went from a company making movies that couldn't lose money to a company making movies that only lost money, and, by the end of the decade, Cannon was on the rocks (Fabrikant).

Lupowitz, a lawyer by trade, had been with Cannon, and had now relocated to Florida to try to recreate Cannon's initial low-cost model on a much smaller scale. Florida, in the early 1990s, was a smart choice for that kind of strategy.

In this day of downloadable movies and Netflix, it might be hard to understand the enormous impact of VHS in the 1980s, but the video rental business had caused nothing less than a seismic shift in how movies were financed ... and watched. For the first time, viewers could watch what they wanted to watch when they wanted to watch it. Enormous video chains, like Blockbuster and Hollywood Video, exploded across the country, mom-and-pop video stores sprang up like mushrooms in every neighborhood, and establishments from local 7-11s to gas stations made shelf room for rental tapes (Mesce, "Appendix C...," 260).

There wasn't enough theatrical product available to fill those hundreds of miles of video shelves, and a few enterprising souls figured out that certain genres—horror, action thrillers, porn (of course)—had a generic appeal. Throw some blood and bouncing boobs on the screen, put a barely recognizable star at the head of the cast, and *somebody* was going to rent it (Mesce, "Appendix C...," 260).

Production of direct-to-video movies found a welcoming home in Florida. The cost of labor and materials were cheaper than in the New York and Los Angeles film centers, and perhaps most strategically, it was a "right to work" state meaning producers were under no obligation to deal with the film industry's unions. George Barnes had hoped to ride that wave, and now so had Sam Lupowitz with what he'd christened Pan Am Pictures (he'd bought the old logo and name of the defunct Pan Am Airlines thinking—for God knows what reason—it had some kind of brand name value).

George and Lupowitz were coming to New York on business, and George wanted to bring Lupowitz by my office at HBO to introduce us in the hopes of getting me some work. Lupowitz was a prematurely gray-topped guy radiating an energetic, let's-go-make-movies charm. It was hard not to like him. We didn't talk very long, then he abruptly stood up, held out his hand, said something about how he could tell if someone was a good bet right off, and he was sure we were going to do a lot of business together. We shook hands and he was off.

By that time, I'd learned not to get too optimistic about such glowy opening moves, but it wasn't long after Lupowitz was back in Florida he was on the phone with me wanting me to work on two projects.

Miami Models was a screenplay for what I think was supposed to be some kind of co-production with a Swedish outfit. The script had been written by a pair of Swedes which probably explained why it was written in a kind of English reading like someone making fun of the way non–English speakers try to speak English: words that didn't quite mean what the writers thought they meant, English words jammed into non–English syntax, no contractions, etc. But the Swedes had more problems than a poor command of the language.

The story concerned an ex-model who splits from her Latin American drug smuggling boyfriend in the middle of the night, taking a computer disk filled with incriminating information with her, and then heads for Florida to meet up with an old girlfriend who is running a floundering modeling agency deep in hock to some local mobsters. Now partnered, and helped by a novice lawyer, the ladies are able to turn the agency into a success and get the local mob off their backs. Then the boyfriend shows up and havoc ensues.

There was the practical issue of just how much glamour a Pan Am production could put into the glamorous world of modeling when their typical budgets were under $500,000 (Mesce, "Guerilla…," 179). One also had to ask how interested the direct-to-video audience was in the modeling world no matter how much glamour was on display.

The screenplay also had a lethal second-act sag. Once the two old girlfriends met up, the second act was parade of scenes of ever-more-glitzy modeling shoots as their agency takes off. There was no real tension until the boyfriend showed up to kick off the third act.

Besides cleaning up the English, my first move was to downsize the agency's success, making them an outfit that wasn't getting glossy national magazine shoots but doing quite well locally with commercials, car shows, and the like; stuff both more credible and, for Pan Am, more affordable.

To get some tension into the second act, I introduced a ticking clock; I put the drug boss boyfriend on his cabin cruiser (since this was Pan Am, it was going to be a particularly small cabin cruiser) and headed him north to Florida. I gave him a couple of scenes we could cut to, including a juicy one where he throws the member of his crew he knows helped his girl-friend escape overboard to the sharks. I liked the idea that while the two ladies were enjoying a bit of local success, they were oblivious to this threat coming closer day by day.

To give the script some pop, when the boyfriend shows up, I had the lawyer, who's a bit enamored of both women, play the local mob off against the drug boss boyfriend, channeling them into a shoot-out with each other. George's Take 2 offices were in an otherwise empty building, so we placed the modeling agency in that building—a setting over which we could have total control—and that's where the shoot-out would be staged.

I didn't think it was a particularly good or commercial piece, but I felt I'd left it in better shape than it had been when Lupowitz had acquired it. The important thing was he was happy with it, and especially happy I'd turned it around in two weeks.

With *Miami Models* I'd had a draft to work with. But as for the second project Lupowitz tossed me...

"It's called, *Carjacked! Welcome to Miami Beach.*"

"What's it about?"

"I don't know. That's all I've got is the title."

This was an old exploitation movie-maker's move; find a sensational topic or some hot-button headline in the news, and pump out a quick flick to capitalize on the topic's momentary notoriety. You know; like your average episode of *Law & Order.* Just then, Miami was making national head-lines with a frightening spike in carjacking, and Lupowitz wanted to catch that wave.

My first reaction was, Oh, shit, I'm blank, I'm screwed, but then I had a couple of quick epiphanies. By luck, just a few weeks before, I'd caught *Winchester '73* for the first time and had been knocked out by the Rich-ards/Chase screenplay which waltzes from one set of characters and plot-line to another as it follows a prized Winchester rifle passing from one set of hands to another. Hell, I thought, I could do that with a stolen car! Compression can often create tension, so my second epiphany was to have all this baton-passing occur over the course of a single night.

The screenplay (whose title I would later consolidate to simply *Car-*

jack) came together with a quickness which surprised me. As Bill Persky said, the trick was to come up with the right string of colored beads; in this case, figuring out whose hands the stolen car could pass through, so the plotline I came up with has the initial carjacker bringing the stolen car to a Midnight Auto–type chop shop whose owner realizes that since the car is an import, he could probably sell it to some Latin American drug smugglers who would prize its lack of American registration. But, before the sale can take place, the car is stolen by some stoner stick-up men, then stolen back from them. Because these kinds of low-budget pics are all about action, each exchange of the car was accompanied by a lot of gunplay.

As the car is wending its way through the Miami netherworld, on its trail on one side are a burned-out cop partnered with a cop nobody will work with because he'd hesitated on a shooting putting his previous partner in the hospital; and an ultra-violent gang of ex–Russian KGB men for whom the imported car, carrying contraband smuggled out of Russia, had been intended.

As both something of an ensemble piece and a project more plot-driven than is usual for me, I held in mind Alfred Hitchcock's old caution that, "Usually, in a suspense story there isn't time to develop character" (Humphries, 76). Characters would have to declare themselves boldly and quickly on introduction, so *Carjack*'s leads tended to be archetypal: the burned-out cop, the hesitant partner, the raging Russian mobster... There wasn't anything particularly subtle about them, but since the focus of the movie kept rotating, I thought I could get by with that kind of overstatement.

Even though this was intended as nothing more than a low-budget action fest, I liked the way the screenplay twisted and turned as the car passed from hand to hand, hopefully keeping the viewer guessing as to how this would ultimately play out. If Lupowitz didn't completely screw it up in production, I thought I could wind up with a "calling card" piece; a movie I could show more upscale companies saying, "Here's something I wrote for people who had no money. Imagine what I could do for you."

Carjack was a clever but dumb flick, and here it's probably worth talking a little bit about believability in a movie.

I have my own, private scale for this:

Credible: Keeping it real, the kinds of things that are likely to happen under a set of believable circumstances; the probable.

Plausible: The kind of things that *could* happen under the right circumstances, but it's hardly a common occurrence, say, like the car chase in *The French Connection*. Not probable but possible.

Playable: The kind of things that are unlikely, but you can probably get an audience to buy into it, like Ulysses shooting an arrow through a dozen axe handles. This tends to play on what audiences don't know; how hard it is to hit a moving target; that when someone cracks you over the head with a frying pan, at the very least you'll be suffering for days from a concussion; that pistols never shoot as far as they do in movies; that it can take weeks to get ballistics and forensics reports; that it only takes two seconds to empty the magazine of most automatic weapons; etc. In movies, people can shoot from the hip and hit a target dead center, quickly recover from getting conked on the head, get forensics reports by the next scene, and never run out of bullets and the audience buys it because these things *look* possible, even though they're not. Most of *Carjack* floated in this category.

Gimme a Break: No way, no how. That ancient GM bus in *Speed* (1994) jumping a 50-foot gap in an overpass.

Again, I'd banged out a screenplay Lupowitz liked in just a few weeks, and, impressed, he quickly paid on the deal. That paycheck would come to cause me an infinite amount of aggravation to the point I'd wish he'd never written the check.

Over the next couple of months, Lupowitz kept throwing headline-based topics at me for screenplays, regardless of Pan Am's ability to carry them off. I don't remember much about them: *Cuba: The Time Is Now* which was about a conspiracy to assassinate Castro; and *Paparazzi: Anything for the Shot,* which was about the victim of a sleazy tabloid photographer turning the tables on the guy with the camera.

I remember just enough about *Cuba* to give it as an example of Pan Am overstepping its budget constraints. Lupowitz had gotten the idea from a news story about a Cuban air force pilot who'd defected to Florida in a stolen MiG fighter. Lupowitz wanted to kick off the movie with a similar event. I tried to get around the money problems by setting the event in a radar room with U.S. Air Force personnel watching the defection play out on a radar screen. It was hardly exciting—like watching people watch TV—and I wasn't even sure Pan Am could produce a decent-looking radar room.

None of these four screenplays went into production, which, with the exception of *Carjack,* was fine with me since I didn't think much of them. I wouldn't've minded pumping out a few more … except I wasn't getting paid (again, with the exception of *Carjack*).

You might reasonably ask, Gee, Bill, how big a sucker are you? When were you gonna wise up?

It had to do with *Carjack.* Lupowitz had paid for *Carjack;* that meant he owned it. It was his. And it was the one thing I'd written for Pan Am I thought could be executed on the usual company budget and still come out well; well enough that it could be a braggable piece in my portfolio. I kept writing for Lupowitz hoping that at some point I could convince him it was worth making.

But he didn't make *Cuba,* and he didn't make *Paparazzi* and he didn't pay me for them, and he didn't make *Carjack.*

I wasn't the only one he wasn't paying, either. George Barnes had separated from Pan Am complaining about money owed as well. *Carjack* or no, maybe it was time for me to walk away.

And then on July 15, 1997, Gianni Versace—the famed clothing designer and founder of the brand—was gunned down in front of his house in Miami by a male prostitute named Andrew Cunanan. Sam Lupowitz saw a gold mine in the tragedy, and despite the "ick" factor of exploitation, I thought maybe I finally had some leverage with him.

* * *

Two days after Versace's murder, Lupowitz was on the phone with me saying, "I want to be the first person to make a movie about the murder of Gianni Versace!"

"Jeez, Sam, the guy's not even cold yet!"

Lupowitz assured me this wouldn't be a sleazy exploitation flick, but he was convinced bigger companies were sure to jump on this. He offered to pay the lion's share of the writing fee up front, with the rest paid on the back end (after the movie's made and is generating revenue).

As it happens, I was planning my wedding at the time, and my wife-to-be and I would be picking up most of the tab. And, I also thought if this played out the way Lupowitz thought it might, I might finally be able to get him so enthused about my work he would move on making *Carjack.*

That didn't mean I didn't feel a bit slimy. This was worse than the Ted Kennedy allusions in *Blow Out.* No allusions here; these were real people, real people with real sensitivities, real people with real lawyers.

What about permission from the involved parties or their estates—

"We don't need that," Lupowitz assured me. "We're going to work straight from public sources, newspapers and that stuff. Just stick to what's in the news accounts and we'll be fine." He said he was going to send a package of newspaper clippings and magazine articles to me as soon as he got off the phone.

I held my nose, said a prayer of penance, and told him I'd do it.

I spent a week poring over the material Sam sent me, and by that time at least the story had an ending; with SWAT teams closing in on where he was holed up on a Miami houseboat, five days after killing Gianni Versace, Andrew Cunanan shot himself. With that closing of the arc, this at least seemed a less pointless project.

I had never written a true story before, and had to wrestle with the same ethical dilemma I imagine anyone dealing with factual material faces; how much do you make up? It is not a simple question, nor is there a single answer.

Real life is messy; it rarely follows neat, narrative arcs, it doesn't concern itself with one plotline at a time, characters drift in and out. For the practical reason of jamming a life into a two-hour running time, and for the commercial obligation of telling a story in a way which incents people to pay money to sit through it, the screenwriter has to omit a *lot* ... and also make stuff up. But as for what you leave out and what you make up ... that's a hell of a decision.

Ron Howard's 2001 multi–Oscar-winning (including a statuette for Akiva Goldsman's screenplay) biopic, *A Beautiful Mind,* about John Nash, the math genius plagued by schizophrenia, took a few solid raps for completely leaving out Nash's history of homosexual relationships (Henry). You ask, does it make a difference to the essential story? And there's the practical question: would the movie have made $171 million if it had included that side of his life? It's a worthwhile if uncomfortable question. The highly praised *Milk,* the 2008 Sean Penn starrer about gay rights activist Harvey Milk, the first openly gay person to hold elected office in California, copped an Oscar for Dustin Lance Black's screenplay, but grossed only $32 million.

Facets and offshoots get eliminated, characters are dropped and/or combined, time periods are compressed... I suppose you make the choices you can live with, and that won't get you sued.

Generally, it was not a hard script to write. The mandate of sticking close to public accounts of the case meant I was essentially writing a moderately beefier version of the crime reenactments on prime time true crime TV shows like *48 Hours* and *America's Most Wanted.* Naturally, the dialogue all had to be created, and interactions guessed at from what had appeared in the news, but there wasn't a lot of dramatic substance to the piece. The only wholly fictional characters I created were two detectives. The real case had no central law enforcement figures, so I devised these two guys to provide some kind of connecting line to provide information on the manhunt for Cunanan.

And then I got the idea of stealing a device from Warren Beatty's *Reds* (1981).

Beatty's period epic is the story of idealistic American journalist and socialist sympathizer John Reed who covered the Russian Revolution in his milestone book, *10 Days That Shook the World*, and then was caught up in the Revolution, and ultimately victimized by it. As interstitial pieces between the 195-minute film's many episodes (despite being—horrors!—episodic, Beatty and co-writer Trevor Griffiths still managed a nomination for the Original Screenplay Oscar), Beatty used face-on interviews with "witnesses" who could provide insight and commentary on Reed, the socialist movement both in the U.S. and in Russia, and The Revolution. Beatty's testimonials came from individuals ranging from one of Reed's college classmates to novelist Henry Miller. These testimonies place the narrative against a larger canvas, giving a sense of how the story was connected to its times, and the times to its story; the modern day, cinematic equivalent of a Greek chorus (Canby). While it's a common device today (you even see it used in mainstream sitcoms like *Modern Family*), it was impressively novel in 1981, and still so when I was working on the Versace project.

In reading the accounts Lupowitz had sent me, it eased my discomfort with the material a tiny bit in seeing that there was a story worth telling here which went beyond just that of a celebrity murder. I knew very little about Versace at the time; he was a guy who designed glitzy clothes for his high-priced label and rubbed elbows with a glitzy international crowd. While that was true, I also learned he was a hard worker in a long-term, stable relationship, that he truly loved what he did, and it seemed like all the trappings of success he enjoyed—sumptuous houses here and there, friends among the glitterati, etc.—were the rewards for a job well done, not an end in itself. There were times, so I read, when he was just as likely to curl up at night with a book from his well-stocked library as hit the town with his star friends. In fact, the night before his death, he was out with his partner and a friend for pizza. He was an artist who cared about his art, who knew how to market it, and, as the cliché goes, reaped the fruits of his labors.

Andrew Cunanan, it seemed to me, was the funhouse mirror of that kind of life; someone who wanted to skip to the rewards, but had no means or talent to achieve them, a circumstance that doesn't usually dissuade these kinds of people from thinking they still deserve them.

Put more broadly, and perhaps oversimplifying and over-interpreting the tragic intersection of Versace and Cunanan, Cunanan killed Versace because Versace lived the life Cunanan wanted but knew he could never have. It's a guess, I admit, since Cunanan left no clues as to the reasons behind his actions, and to this day no one knows why he did what he did.

I thought using Beatty's *Reds* device of interstitial interviews might give the story some context, some heft, providing both connecting exposition as well as insight into America's sometimes disturbing fascination/obsession with fame and being famous. Unlike Beatty's witnesses, mine would all be fictional, but provide the same Greek chorus function and, hopefully, give the movie some reason for being beyond trying to exploit a headline murder.

As I wrote the screenplay, it was clear that while there was a story here worth telling, this was not going to be the project to tell it. It was being slapped together quickly, on the cheap, and despite his proclamations that this was going to be a "classy" project, I didn't think Sam Lupowitz had the skill or the sensibility to deliver on that promise.

I banged out the screenplay in six days. I wasn't particularly proud of it; the best you could say about it was it was serviceable, but Lupowitz was pleased, and since he was the one signing the check, that was all that mattered. Sensing there was no way this project was going to come out well, I called him up.

"Look, Sam, I appreciate the opportunity, but I don't want to do anymore on this. I'll keep the upfront money and we'll call that payment for the draft. You use the backend money to pay whatever writer comes on for rewrites if you need them. And you can give that writer sole screen credit."

"You don't want a credit?"

"I figure between now and the time you shoot this, someone's going to have to do some heavy work on this and they should get the credit."

"Are you sure?"

Bless him, Lupowitz thought I was missing a career-boosting opportunity here. I didn't have the heart at that time to say that what was really going on was the equivalent of a fighter pilot who's lost his engine, seen his control panel aglow with red warning lights, and reaches for the ejection lever.

"If you change your mind," Sam said, "you let me know and you're back on it!"

Lupowitz brought on his old Cannon boss, Menahem Golan, to direct and to do any rewrites. Somehow Lupowitz got it into his head that me and Golan would make a good team. He also got it into his head that the perfect next-project for this cinematic dynamic duo would be the 1996 hostage crisis in Lima, Peru, when members of a radical revolutionary movement broke into the Japanese embassy during a party and held several hundred hostages until Peruvian commandos raided the embassy to free them.

There were a couple of reasons I wasn't interested, one of them being Lupowitz chasing another headline story meant no *Carjack.* He thought he'd found a winning formula with the Versace project, and now he wanted to keep mining that vein.

Then there were more practical reasons which I explained when he and Golan called to pitch me the project, with Golan—a blustery, circus ringmaster-sounding kind of guy—declaring, "You will write it, I will direct it, and it will be great!"

"I don't know anything about Lima, Sam. I don't even know anything about Peru."

Golan had the solution: *"We will send you to Lima!"*

With Lupowitz's dodgy finances, I had this quick, horrible fantasy that even if he managed to come up with the money to send me to Lima, it wouldn't be long before I'd be selling myself on the streets to come up with the money to get home.

Evidently, I wasn't the only one worried about the expense. As soon as Golan had made his announcement, I could hear Lupowitz behind him, "Menahem, Menahem, Menahem, wait a minute, we have to talk...."

I have no doubt that, on that count, Lupowitz was more relieved than disappointed when I passed.

As the Versace movie came close to being completed, I did begin to wonder if Lupowitz had been right and I had made a strategic error in not remaining formally attached to the project. He was managing to generate an impressive amount of buzz: there was a half-page story in the Sunday magazine supplement of *The New York Times,* an article in the *Times'* coverage of the Cannes film festival where Lupowitz had gone to shill his flick, and then the movie was given a segment on an *Access Hollywood–*type show.

Lupowitz had called to alert me about the television piece, and as I sat down to watch it, I did start to wonder if some of my career problems stemmed from my being an idiot and missing these kinds of opportunities.

But then I saw the piece.

Even in the brief film clip featured in the segment, it was clear the movie was a stinker: cheap-looking, badly acted. That feeling was confirmed when Lupowitz sent me a VHS of the movie.

It was bad. Really bad. Really *really* bad. *Mystery Science Theater 3000* bad. Filmmaking 101 bad.

Most online sources cite the budget at $4 million, I remember Lupowitz touting it in the press as $5 million, although George Barnes estimated it was probably closer to $3 million.

Lupowitz and Golan would claim Golan did 10 rewrites on the screenplay, although I'll be damned if I can tell what all that work accomplished. He did away with the witness interstitials, and the dialogue was even flatter and more perfunctory than mine, and he added some badly psychedelic party scenes with Cunanan for, well, I don't know, I guess he thought they looked cool or something. But it wasn't that much different from the draft I'd turned in.

Examples of the production's extreme badness: One of Cunanan's murder victims is supposed to be found deep in the Minnesota woods (the whole movie was shot in Florida), but one shot in the discovery of the body is framed so badly you can see this is taking place near a highway overpass. You can actually see the cars go by; the national manhunt for Cunanan consists of two actors playing detectives chatting on phones at desks in front of a blank wall on which is tacked a small map of the United States, the kind school kids put on their bedroom walls. That's it, that's your task force, and; the actor playing Cunanan runs out of his hotel just ahead of the cops. He runs down the block, away from the camera, and turns a corner. Through the shrubs at the end of the block, you can see the actor thinks he's out of camera range and stops running.

If you think this is just me pissing on the picture to distance myself from it, well, let's look at the scorecard.

The Versace Murder officially came out in 1998. It received no U.S. distribution deals, no sales to premium or basic cable, Lupowitz couldn't even get a home video deal for the flick (it would finally be released on DVD in the U.S. in 2005). It's never been reviewed (thankfully). As far as I know, the only distribution Lupowitz got for the movie were a few overseas video releases.

Sam Lupowitz did achieve his goal of being the first guy to make a movie about Gianni Versace's murder. In fact, for years, he was the *only* guy who'd made a movie about Versace's killing. Among his other missteps, he'd woefully miscalculated interest in the tragedy. Go online and there's a thin smattering of documentaries, a 2014 Italian miniseries about the fashion mogul, and the 2013 Lifetime television movie, *House of Versace,* which isn't about Gianni Versace but his sister Donatella's efforts to pick up the reins of the brand and keep it going after her brother's death.

In short, even as a low-budget, exploitative quickie, *The Versace Murder* was as much of a flop as a flop could be.

* * *

I thought I was done with Sam Lupowitz at that point, but after *Versace* had been completed and sat around with no one wanting it, he called wanting me to work on something called *More Body Heat.* It was a surprisingly low-key piece for him; I guess after *Versace*'s failure, he'd gone sour on the headline-chasing thing. *More Body Heat* was intended as a knock-off of Lawrence Kasdan's classic 1981 neo-*noir, Body Heat.* As I remember it, it was a soapy bit of murder and mayhem surrounding various parties jockeying for control of a car lot. If it doesn't sound like much, it wasn't, but I thought I finally had the lever I needed.

"I'll do it, Sam, but I want the money up front. I'm not even going to sit at the keyboard until the check clears."

"Awww, Bill!" he said, sounding offended. Lupowitz was like those surveillance systems which wipe their memory clear every 24 hours. He really seemed to forget you had reason to be suspicious of him. I reminded him he still owed me for three screenplays, and he seemed equally offended that—shame on me—I would hold that against him.

"Up front, Sam, or no script. You do that and I'll forget about the money you *haven't* paid me, and one more thing: you give me back *Carjack.*"

He was reluctant at first, I suspect not because he was ever going to make it, but that I wanted to negotiate for it showed it was something of value. Make it or not, he didn't want to give up anything that was worth something. Still, he finally agreed.

After I delivered the screenplay, he called me, very angry. "I feel like you took advantage of me."

"How?"

"This isn't very good. I feel like you just banged this out to get your money. In fact, I think the last couple of things you've done for me weren't very good, and you just wanted to pick up some fast money."

Now it was my turn to be angry. "I didn't put any more or any less time into this thing than I did with any other script I wrote for you *including* the stuff you said you liked. Maybe you ought to consider that if some of these things aren't very good, maybe it's the ideas you wanted me to work with weren't very good."

I'll give him this; he paused there for a second and I honestly think he was considering the point.

"I *gave* you a good script, Sam: *Carjack.* I've kept begging you to make it, and you didn't want to make it. So now it goes to me. As far as I'm concerned, we're square."

Sometime after that, Pan Am Pictures folded. According to George Barnes, the company's failure fell on Lupowitz's head. George had put together what he'd thought was a workable, Cannon-like model for Pan Am: make movies cheap, for under a half-million, then aggressively negotiate distribution deals which could bring in from $3–7 million (Mesce, "Guerilla...," 179).

The flaw in the model was Lupowitz. According to George, Lupowitz "was crazy. He'd take the money, go out and buy a Jaguar or something, and wreck it." Lupowitz would piss the money away on everything but recoupment (179).

There was no formal announcement Pan Am had gone under. Lupowitz just disappeared from Florida still owing George Barnes money.

Talking about this years later, George would sigh, since Lupowitz was not the only moviemaking wannabe George would deal with during his Florida days who'd left him hanging. "People *always* owe me money" (179).

*   *   *

You would think that'd be the end of our business together, but several years later, I got a call from Lupowitz. He was now in Los Angeles, trying to put together a package of low-budget, soft-core skin flicks, hoping to sell the package to cable TV. He wanted me to write them.

It was that surveillance erase thing, again. He was cheery and friendly and showed no sign he remembered (or would admit to) the bad way things had ended with us.

He was nice, so I acted nice, and politely declined. With all respect to my colleagues in the skin trade, nothing against them but that was a place I didn't want to go (I'm not being snobby; in college I once tried to write a porn book to pick up a few dollars but gave up on page three; I had neither the imagination nor the experience to go any further). Besides, Lupowitz's track record in mind, there was a good chance I'd do these things and not get paid for them.

Somebody came out of that whole Florida chapter better than they went in. George Barnes kept working with low-level wannabes for a few years, but grew tired of the frustration of dealing with tight money, unfulfilled financial promises, and the outsized expectations of novice moviemakers (Mesce, "Guerilla...," 179). And, Florida was no longer the easy-to-work locale it had been in the early 1990s. The costs of production and locations had gone up, and getting shooting permits had become a ball-busting process (181).

By then, however, he was doing more business in commercials, music videos, industrials, and even some political campaign work. He eventually moved back to Jersey, although he kept an operation going in Florida, and even expanded into Europe. He told me once of shooting an Audi commercial in Manhattan which required closing a section of Park Avenue. The budget for such spots dwarfed anything he'd produced in Florida (180–181).

*   *   *

From 1992, when George Barnes had optioned *Lab 7*, until 1998 when I'd written *More Body Heat* for Sam Lupowitz, as a writer, script doctoring rewrite man, and consultant, I'd been hired on a total of 11 feature projects being handled by both guys. Of the 11, only two were produced, and I don't have a screenwriting credit on either which, considering the end product, is just as well.

On the plus side, it was a learning experience: I learned to write quickly without writing (too) badly, and to write to a budget. I'd also learned to get the money up front.

Dealing with Sam Lupowitz had been extremely frustrating, but I came out of those years with a good friend in George Barnes who continues to do well *not* dealing with the inherent aggravation of making movies.

And I made enough money to pay for most of my wedding to my very best friend who would go on to give me two beautiful, smart daughters. How is that not a win?

As for *Carjack...*

Having put up with Lupowitz for years hoping to either get him to make the movie or give the property back to me, I haven't been able to get anything done with it. I've submitted the piece to a number of screenplay competitions. It would sometimes make it into the final rounds, and was a category winner in the Capital Fund competition.

It was the screenplay that beat out *Surrender.*

The Artistic Director: Mark Hoebee

(In the earliest days of motion pictures, with no precedent to look to, the first moviemakers drew on the aesthetics of what they saw as

movies' closest relative: theater. The camera was set in a fixed position, approximating the view of a theater patron sitting in the front rows, viewing the action through an unmoving frame—a proscenium, in effect—with all the action presented in a single shot (Brownlow, 9–10). Even as early films evolved from short skits to full stories (although rarely longer than a single reel), individual scenes were filmed from the same theatrical point of view, and encompassed by a single shot.

In time, the movies developed their own, distinctive aesthetic; their own visual vocabulary and grammar and syntax. But the dynamics of storytelling still owed something to principles developed millennia before on the ancient stages of Hellenic Greece; principles that, in time, would be refined and expansively applied to media ranging from prose to film to TV to comic books to, well, you get the idea. The essentials of good storytelling have, surprisingly, changed little; only the vehicles and techniques have changed. There is, then, something to be learned about what constitutes good storytelling in that oldest and most traditional of mass media: the theater.

Mark Hoebee is both the producing artistic director of the Paper Mill Playhouse—New Jersey's signature professional theater as well as a regional institution of national renown—and a director in his own right. His directorial credits include the Actors Fund benefit of The Best Little Whorehouse in Texas *on Broadway starring Academy Award–winner Jennifer Hudson, national tours of* Victor/Victoria *and* Dreamgirls, *as well as such Paper Mill offerings as* Miss Saigon, Smokey Joe's Café, The Full Monty, *and many, many more.*

Hoebee has been with the Paper Mill organization since 2000. As the company's producing artistic director, he has been instrumental in not only raising the company's visibility for its reimagining of classic musicals, but developing new works including turning the failed 1992 movie into the 2011 stage hit Newsies; Honeymoon in Vegas *in 2013;* Ever After *in 2015; and* A Bronx Tale *in 2016. For such accomplishments as well as the consistent high quality of its offerings, Paper Mill Playhouse was the recipient of the 2016 Regional Theatre Tony Award.)*

There is definitely a formula to storytelling in traditional musical theatre that seems to work. We are all familiar with the 2½ hour-one-intermission-following-a-cliffhanger model which includes an opening number setting up the context of the piece typically followed by an expository scene where we meet our major players. Early in the show we hear an "I want" number which establishes the goal for our main character, and we also discover the conflict at the start which sets the story in motion. What is it that is preventing our hero from achieving what he or she wants? As the evening progresses, we travel through a series of scenes and numbers which illuminate the emotions and thoughts of our main characters, explore relationships (there's usually a romance that will develop along the way), introduces our antagonist, bemoans the trials and celebrates the successes of the journey we are taking. Eventually, we get some closure at the finale, and even occasionally are treated to an epilogue which may comment on what we have just seen or further explain events that occurred after our "story." But these are just the tools that we have come to know and use in musical theatre; they aren't necessarily, in my opinion, what makes great storytelling.

When I look at a new musical, or revisit a successful older show, there are some common threads about why the show works. Of course, for a show to be a successful musical, the score is key. A pleasing melody does not, in itself, make a good song. Each song must be a kind of mini-musical with a plot, clever and intelligent lyrics, a rhyme scheme, a voyage, and it must be born out of the emotion the character is feeling at that particular moment in the arc of the story. Also, the song must forward the plot. What it is that we learn in that musical moment that couldn't be told in spoken dialogue or simple action? So, the score must tell its own story.

Then, of course, there is the element of dance. Since the days of Agnes De Mille and the ballet in *Oklahoma*, "Laurey Makes Up Her Mind," we are no longer content to simply watch bodies move around the stage in a musical comedy. They must have purpose, intent, character, mission, and they must highlight, explain, or solve a problem. Of course, dance can be celebratory as well, but the point is that the dance must continue, or, better yet, advance the story. Both of these elements—dance and music—which aren't a part of other forms of storytelling, have very important functions in a musical, but they rely on the underlying plot of the piece and how that unfolds for them to do their work. The best torch songs or ballets or opening numbers or big finales fall flat if they are not presented as integral parts of the whole of the musical.

So what we return to is the story. What makes a good story and what makes good storytelling in musical theatre? For me, one of the answers is the element of surprise.

The basic story of many, many musicals is the traditional "Boy meets girl. Boy loses girl. Boy gets girl back." This simple plot has been retold a million different ways, but it is still satisfying if the method of *how* the tale is told seems somehow novel. Even if you hang this tried and true through-line directly on the traditional structure musicals have followed for decades, the audience can be surprised in a variety of ways. The characters that tell the story can be untraditional or somehow more interesting than the average boy and girl. The conflict and complications that are in the way of their relationship can be unique. The more insurmountable the challenge seems at the start, the more satisfying it is when our characters conquer it. Even the style in which the story is told can be novel.

The sound of musical theatre scores has changed with the times. The traditional sound of a golden age musical morphed into the electric instrumentation of the '60s and '70s, and then took on the pop sound of the '80s and '90s, and today we have arrived with shows like *Hamilton* which mesh the disparate styles of the most contemporary rap music and storytelling with the traditional forms of musical theatre to create an entirely new way of looking at historical events.

And speaking of history and good storytelling, I am reminded of the musical *1776* (adapted for the 1972 screen version by its playwright, Peter Stone). I love this show for many reasons. Long before *Hamilton,* this show told the story of our founding fathers using the tools of musical theatre. It took these stuffy, statuesque figures and painted them as passionate, flawed human beings trying to solve the issues affecting their daily lives. But the true success of this piece, for me, is in the storytelling.

Everyone who enters the theatre to view a performance of *1776* knows that, by the end of the show, those men are going to sign the Declaration of Independence. It's a historical fact that we all learned in grade school, so there is no surprise to how the show will finish. Yet, as the story unfolds and as we watch these men struggle with doubt, fear, uncertainty—and as we watch them work through their own personal and political relationships—we struggle and agonize along with them. During the vote on whether the initiative will pass, we worry along with them. "Will they get enough votes to move forward? Will the warring factions of this young country unite?" We all know what happens, and yet we are on pins and needles wondering how it will all come together. The reason for this is how the story is told. Which moments of conflict and resolution did the authors choose to highlight? How and why must our characters sing the emotions they are feeling? Which are the segments of this story that absolutely must be included and how do we showcase them? Those are the questions successful musical theatre story tellers ask themselves constantly.

When all of these elements are right, the audience knows it, and they leave feeling satisfied, excited, and changed. When the audience learns something by the end of the evening, there is great joy in the theatre. It doesn't have to be a fact of history that they have learned. They may have learned something about the potentially fictional characters on stage and their relationship. They may have learned something about the human condition. They may have learned to see life and events from a new perspective. Most importantly, they may have learned something about themselves. This is the moment when musical theatre is operating at its height and only occurs when the story is well told.

There are many times I will sit down to read a new script or go to see a new show, and I've heard a bit about the story, and I think to myself, "Wow, this is a great idea for a musical!" But when it's done, I am not moved, or worse, I've been bored. As I leave, I try to examine where it all went wrong. What is it that didn't come together?

Unfortunately, there are many shows that somehow just miss the mark. The idea is good, some of the music is good, the book is good, but the show doesn't succeed. It is at that point that the great minds always go back to the story and ask themselves, "What is it we are trying to say and how do we best say it?" When you get that right, the rest of the pieces inevitably fall into place.

Myth #5: Show, Don't Tell

Of all the myths we've looked at, none of them drives me up the wall as much as this one. Not coincidentally, I find it the easiest to deconstruct. Maybe because among these arbitrary rules, it's the most arbitrary.

I landed *Blow Out,* my first professional screenplay job, in 1978, and made it through the next dozen years or so without once hearing anything on subsequent jobs even approximating "Show, don't tell." But by the 1990s, I was finding a creeping change in the lexicon of screenplay development. There were a lot more references to "story/character arcs," "beats," "three-act structure," and—you guessed it—"Show me; don't tell me" (sometimes punctuated with a condescending, "There's a reason they call them motion *pictures,* Bill").

Not to keep picking on these two guys, but I peg the change as starting in the 1980s with Robert McKee and Syd Field. Field doesn't even get out of his Introduction before defining a screenplay as "a story told with pictures" (3).

By the time I started getting hit with "Show, don't tell" as a screenwriter, I had already had enough experience under my belt to know that,

as an overriding cinematic aesthetic, and Messers. McKee and Field not-
withstanding, the concept was more or less bullshit. The "Show, don't tell"
people may have the writing gurus on their side. I have Aristotle.

In his book *Aristotle's Poetics for Screenwriters: Storytelling Secrets
from the Greatest Mind in Western Civilization* (2002), one-time Miramax
story analyst Michael Tierno, inspired by Aristotle's *Poetics*, rates "spectacle"—in Aristotelian terms, the physical elements of production i.e., the
visuals—as the *least* important element of drama coming behind, in descending order of importance, plot, character, character thought, dialogue, and
music. The art of visual spectacle belongs to the set designer (or, more
often these days, the CGI FX department); the art of drama to the poet
(Mesce, "The World's First...", 351–352).

I grant you, the justification for "Show, don't tell" as a screenwriting
axiom *seems* obvious; movies are a visual medium. You're forced to work
with only what you can show. What shoots holes in the concept is that in
the decades before people who didn't write movies started writing books
telling people how to write movies, there were any number of films that
did more telling than showing (or showed characters doing more telling
than doing).

Take that classic early *noir, The Maltese Falcon.* John Huston's screenplay is nearly scene-for-scene, line-for-line taken from the 1930 Dashiell
Hammett novel. For the most part, the movie, like the book, is nothing
more than scenes of exposition and explanation. Its characters do little
more than yak and yak and yak, including about a number of key events
that happened off-screen. The aesthetic of *Falcon*, with only a few tiny
exceptions, is that of "Tell, don't show."

In the film's "climax" (I use quotes because, like most of the movie,
Falcon's cathartic moment is still *more* gab), *Falcon* demonstrates the cinema's frequent *need* to go interior—to get at the turmoil going on inside
a character—and does so through that hoariest of dramatic devices: the
revealing monologue. Humphrey Bogart's private eye Sam Spade feels
compelled to explain at length to *femme fatale* Bridget O'Shaughnessy
(Mary Astor) why he's "sending her over" to the cops for killing his partner,
even though he's in love with her and didn't seem to care much for his
colleague. But Bogie's soliloquy is as much there to provide a window for
the audience into his bruised and roiling soul as it is an explanation for
desperate, uncomprehending Bridget:

> Listen. This won't do any good. You'll never understand me but I'll try once and then
> give it up. When a man's partner is killed, you're supposed to do something about it.
> It doesn't matter what you thought of him, he was your partner and you're supposed

to do something about it. And it happens we're in the detective business. Well, when one of your organization gets killed, it's bad business to let the killer get away with it. Bad all around, bad for every detective everywhere.... I've no earthly reason to think I can trust you, and if I do this and get away with it you'll have something on me you can use whenever you want to. Since I've got something on you, I couldn't be sure you wouldn't put a hole in me some day. All those are on one side. Maybe some of them are unimportant; I won't argue about that. But look at the number of them. And what have we got on the other side? All we've got is maybe you love me, and maybe I love you ... maybe I do. I'll have some rotten nights after I've sent you over but that'll pass. If all I've said doesn't mean anything to you, then forget it and we'll make it just this: I won't because all of me wants to regardless of consequences, and because you counted on that with me the same as you counted on it with all the others....

Bogie's full speech runs a little over two minutes of screen time, barely interrupted by Mary Astor. Mind you, this follows another block of jaw-flapping where Bogie—in another supposed contemporary no-no—dishes up another two minutes of pure exposition laying out the facts behind the 95 minutes of lying, duping, and manipulating that have come before.

Film critic Stephen Whitty offers a more recent example of telling playing better than showing:

> In *Jaws* ... (the character of shark hunter) Quint (Robert Shaw) remembers a time in World War II when his ship sank and sharks circled the stranded sailors. As visual a filmmaker as (director Steven) Spielberg is, he resists the urge to give us a flashback and show us the bloody water, the hungry fish, the screaming men. Instead, he just lets Quint tell us—and makes *us* fill in the horrible details. What we imagine is far more horrible than anything he could show [Mesce, *No Rule...*, 18].

Quint's quite lengthy monologue—which doesn't exist in the source novel and runs close to four unbroken minutes—not only explains his Ahab-like obsession with shark-killing, but gives his ball-busting hard-ass character a tragic, even sympathetic underpinning the action of the movie cannot provide.

And thanks to Shaw's underplayed melancholy, and Spielberg's willingness to let the speech roll out in long takes *sans* such contemporary post–MTV gimmicks as moving cameras and quick cuts, there's no visual that can equal the haunting quality of the actor delivering lines like: "Ya know the thing about a shark? He's got lifeless eyes, black eyes, like a doll's eyes. When he comes at ya, he doesn't seem to be livin' ... until he bites you and those black eyes roll over white...."

"If you think of films often cited as 'perfect' movies," says Whitty, "whether it's old Hollywood films like *Casablanca* (1942) or more modern classics like *Chinatown*—it's not just the pictures you remember. It's the characters' voices" (Mesce, *No Rule...*, 18).

There are entire film genres which are dependent on telling: stage adaptations, mysteries with reams of exposition ("The killer is here in this room!"), courtroom dramas ("You can't handle the truth!"). When I hear "Show, don't tell" in connection with screenwriting, one of the first titles my mind goes to is *12 Angry Men* (1957), Reginald Rose's big screen adaptation of his live TV drama. *12 Angry Men* not only depends on telling, it's *about* telling, with the dozen titular jurors grappling with iffy testimony about off-screen, never-seen events as they stumble toward what they think might be the truth of a murder case. The only thing we're shown are people arguing about what they've been told.

Across genres, for one reason or another, various filmmakers—sometimes even those considered the most visual of directors—have drawn on devices dating back 2500 years to the days of Hellenic theater because there are limitations to showing; showing can't always get us inside a character, or inside a character's story.

These "telling" devices include self-revelatory soliloquies (like the *Maltese Falcon* and *Jaws* examples above) and any variety of voiceover approaches often operating as another form of soliloquy and/or cinema's version of a Greek chorus. Says Stephen Whitty, "The device encourages us to see the events through these (characters') eyes, to take their point of view.... Words seduce us in ways images never could" (Mesce, *No Rule...*, 19). Martin Sheen's hushed, first person voiceover in *Apocalypse Now* gives Francis Ford Coppola's Vietnam epic a narrative cohesion and tonal underpinning the story on the screen doesn't always have ("It's a way we had over here for living with ourselves. We cut 'em in half with a machine gun and give 'em a Band-Aid"); in *Raising Arizona*, Nicolas Cage's low-key narration keeps the movie's screwball express train montage sequences from flying apart, and also provides a certain soulfulness to the rapid fire comedy ("Sometimes it's a hard world for little things," juxtaposed with the Biker of the Apocalypse blowing up a desert hare); in *Little Big Man* (1970) and *Barry Lyndon*, voiceover narrations are even more true to the nature of an ancient chorus, offering both editorial commentary and a bit of historical context along with a peek into characters' interior workings (from *Barry Lyndon*'s omniscient narrator: "No lad who has liberty for the first time, and twenty guineas in his pocket is very sad, and Barry rode towards Dublin thinking not so much of the kind mother left alone, and of the home behind him, but of tomorrow, and all the wonders it would bring"). The comic Westerns *Cat Ballou* (1965) and *Waterhole #3* (1967) have a literal chorus; troubadours (an on-screen Stubby Kaye and Nat King Cole in *Ballou;* an off-screen Roger Miller in *Waterhole*) who sing narrative bridges, flashes of character insight, and even a bit of frontier philosophizing (from Miller: "The code of the West is to do unto others ... before they do it unto you").

And then there are those movies where telling isn't about getting us to some interior place that showing can't get us, but where telling is— and yes, I'm going to say this remembering that they are called motion *pictures,* Bill—the best, most effective, most impactful way of telling the story.

One of my favorites is *Fail-Safe* (1964, screenplay by Walter Bernstein adapting the novel by Eugene Burdick and Harvey Wheeler), a nuclear holocaust scenario played out, for the most part, in four interior settings: the Strategic Air Command's Omaha war room, a small war room under the Pentagon, the President's shelter under the White House, and the cockpit of the lead plane in a flight of nuke-armed bombers accidently sent off to obliterate Moscow.

Even in those scenes taking place aboard the bomber, director Sidney Lumet (unsurprisingly coming from the guy who directed *12 Angry Men*) only ever shows some flash cuts of exteriors, mostly keeping his camera on the faces of the men in the shadowy cockpit. Like the men on the ground trying to recall them, most of what they understand of the situation around them is told by their cockpit instruments.

And it works. The suffocating interior-bound nature of the film—the only windows to the outside world being display screens showing animated versions of what's happening in the skies over Russia—echo the characters' helplessness, their utter inability to influence a countdown to destruction. They are literally watching what may be the coming end of the world on television and can do nothing more than narrate it for the uninformed.

To have taken the camera out of those bare, oppressive environments— to show—would've been a relief. And Lumet and Bernstein—just like the authors of the source novel—refuse to offer that relief.

About the time I started seriously studying film, Paddy Chayefsky— arguably one of the all-time best screenwriters—wrote two of his strongest pieces, both Best Screenplay Oscar-winners, *The Hospital* (1971) and the classic *Network.* In his later works, Chayefsky—who began his career as a playwright which may explain his lack of aversion to talky scripts—was famous for his dense, literate dialogue, often volleying between characters not in one-liners, but in cannonades of verbiage. In fact, the highlight of *Network* is a series of on-air screeds by ranting television anchorman Howard Beale (Peter Finch) including the oft-quoted "I'm mad as hell and I'm not going to take it anymore!" speech.

In the same period, William Goldman was in the process of winning his second Academy Award for *All the President's Men*, a movie in which the main characters do nothing more than talk to people in person, talk to people on the phone, and sift through documents and clippings. That's the whole movie. The Big Climax is watching a teletype machine spit out the stories of a series of White House staff resignations culminating in the resignation of President Richard Nixon. *All the President's Men* became one of the top-earning movies of the 1970s.

Now I can hear those same carpers who keep telling me, "They're called moving *pictures*, Bill," saying, "Look, Bill, we get what you're saying, but tastes change, ya know. Maybe this stuff would've played back when you were a kid, but these are different times."

And so they are, and there's truth to that remark. Sensibilities are different, tastes are different. Rhett Butler told Scarlett O'Hara "Frankly, my dear, I don't give a damn," and audiences were scandalized (and delighted). Today, Rhett could probably tell her to kiss his ass as it's going out the door and still get a PG-13. Yeah, tastes change.

But telling can still work and in impressively profitable ways.

Two of 2015's most acclaimed releases—*Spotlight* (Oscars for original screenplay and Best Picture) and *The Big Short* (Oscar for adapted screenplay) are nothing but exposition. They're investigative pieces following an ensemble of question-askers talking to answer-givers.

Spotlight avoids gimmicks like reenactments, flashbacks, and all those other visual tricks which suggest a mistrust of the smarts of the audience. Scenes where adult survivors of childhood molestation painfully recalling those traumas of their youth are infinitely more uncomfortable—as they should be—then some lap dissolve to a recreation. Director and co-writer Tom McCarthy wants us to feel the victims' pain, and that means sitting there watching the shame and rage and anguish on their faces. To "show"—like the example of Quint's recalling his World War II sinking—would, ironically, be a cop-out.

The Big Short is another exercise in exposition, and there's so much of it on so many arcane elements of economics that the Charles Randolph/ Adam McKay script has to freeze the narrative in order for one of its "guest lecturers" to explain to the audience what the hell is going on: exposition on top of exposition.

So, how did these two gab fests do out there in the marketplace? I mean besides all that critical acclaim and the Oscars and such?

Out of the 698 films released in 2015, Best Picture *Spotlight* came in #88 at the domestic box office. By the end of the year, worldwide earnings tallied $88 million against a budget of $20 million.

The Big Short did even better: #44 in the U.S., with a worldwide take of $132.3 million against a budget of $28 million.

I grant that's not *Star Wars* or *Avengers* money, and nobody's going to be buying *The Big Short* piggy banks or *Spotlight* videogames. It's not even *All the President's Men* money. But consider this: *ATPM* was a major studio release (Warner Bros.) with a budget to match, based on a best-selling book about a national trauma still fresh in the American mind (Nixon resigned in 1972), and starred Robert Redford and Dustin Hoffman, actors then at their commercial zenith.

Spotlight and *The Big Short* cost—in Hollywood terms—damn near nothing to make, starred no major marquee-value talent, and featured nothing but people talking to each other. Yet, combined, the two movies earned just about the same as *The Divergent Series: Insurgent* (2015), on about one-third the cost (excluding marketing).

Like the other myths we've looked at in this book, there's a time and place for "Show, Don't Tell" and where it works the way its proselytizers say it should. One of my all-time favorite detective flicks is *Bullitt* (1968), with a script by Alan R. Trustman and Harry Kleiner based on Robert L. Pike's novel, *Mute Witness*. Even though the best-remembered scene in the movie is its classic car chase through the streets of San Francisco, the scene I always look forward to seeing is where a pair of detectives (Steve McQueen and Don Gordon) are going through two steamer trunks; the luggage of a strangled woman with ties to a murdered government witness. According to Marshall Terrill's *Steve McQueen: Portrait of an American Rebel*, director Peter Yates stocked the trunks with clues without telling the actors what they'd find. In one of the best examples of "Show, Don't Tell," the audience watches the actors/cops sift through the clues and piece together the truth behind part of their case (165).

The short of it is, there's room in the screenwriter's toolbox for both: showing *and* telling.

A strong case for the peaceful co-existence of both concepts can be made through the first two films of writer/director J.C. Chandor: *Margin Call* (2011), nominated for a Best Original Screenplay Oscar; and the critically-acclaimed *All Is Lost* (2013).

Margin Call is the story of the financial collapse of 2007–2008 told through the prism of one brokerage firm's overnight discovery that their organization is on the verge of disaster. Set in the abstract world of money moving here and there and evaporating in the digital realm, *Margin Call* is a story that can *only* be told by telling since there is nothing to show; it relies completely on exposition.

All Is Lost is the polar opposite; a nearly wordless piece following Robert Redford's solo struggle for survival at sea after his sailboat sinks in the Indian Ocean. This is a purely visual tale—nothing but *showing*—eschewing the usual solo piece cheats i.e., voiceover narration and/or a character speaking thoughts aloud (think *Gravity,* 2013; *Cast Away,* 2000; *The Martian,* 2015). We *see* Redford puzzle out using a sextant, figuring out how to distill salt water for drinking, etc., just as we *see* his consternation, frustration, and, ultimately, his desperation. *We* bring the insight; not the writer. Consequently, the screenplay for *All Is Lost* is only 31 pages long (*All...*).

Two respected films, same writer/director, stories told in completely opposite yet equally effective (in fact, *powerfully* effective) modes.

I offer up, in summation, writer/director Ron Shelton's refutation of a younger generation of filmmakers' blind allegiance to "Show, don't tell." "(The) old canard that action defines character is only partly true," Shelton argued in an interview. "Hamlet wasn't doing a whole lot when he said, 'To be or not to be'" (Mesce, "Pyromaniacs...," 126).

The Film Evaluator: Youssef Kdiry

(Kdiry will tell you—in true, New Jerseyan fashion, without much prompting—that he fell in love with movies when he saw Jaws *as a small child. While going for his B.A. in film studies at Jersey City State College in the mid–1990s, Kdiry landed an internship at Home Box Office in their film evaluation department. After his internship, Kdiry continued freelancing for the department, which, in turn, led him to a fulltime gig there. In his decade-long stint with HBO, Kdiry easily viewed over a thousand titles per year, analyzing and assessing them for programming, scheduling, and marketing purposes. Kdiry's love for cinema was—and remains—so bottomless, that after a day watching movies for HBO, his way to relax was to go home, kick back, and watch still more movies on TV, that is if he wasn't going out to the nearest multiplex to catch a new release. After being downsized out of HBO at the end of 2004, one of his post-company occupations was launching the website MoonStar Film Reviews (www.moonstarfilmreviewswww) in 2006, and a blog version of MFR in 2012, meaning Kdiry still spends a lot of time sitting in the dark, watching all kinds of movies—from the ridiculous to the sublime—dance across the small and big screen.)*

As someone who has viewed literally thousands and thousands of movies in my lifetime (thus far), I can proudly state that I am an expert in the movie-viewing experience. Well, that and my multiple degrees in Film & TV Studies & Production should validate my credentials—as will $2.50 for a subway ride in New York City!

Many of those movies that passed before my peepers were done in the employ of cable network Home Box Office where, as a film evaluator, I had the pleasure of screening a plethora of movies for our various channels. Mind you, before that, when not catching movies at the theaters, yours truly would enjoy movies at home on TV. Those were the quaint days before the internet, cell phones that provided instant media gratification, and 1000-plus channels on cable.

Come to think of it, how did we ever survive as a society?

But I digress...

Besides consuming movies on regular TV during the late show—and even the late, late show with titles such as *Invisible Invaders* (1959), *Vanishing Point* (1971), and *The Devil's Rain* (1975) playing regularly—I would sneak into the basement at night while my family slumbered and enjoy the forbidden cinematic fruits that the nascent HBO film programming schema had to offer. Ah yes, movies like *Damnation Alley*, *Mr. Majestyk* (1974), *Porky's* (1981), and hundreds of other adult fare warped my young mind indeed.

Which brings me to the yearning I have for the great movies of yesteryear. Whether it is *Metropolis* (1926), *The Wizard Of Oz* (1939), *Casablanca* (1942), *Ben-Hur*, *Lawrence Of Arabia*, *All That Jazz* (1979), *Aliens* (1986), or even *Armageddon* (1998), the movies pre–Millennium had style, substance, and, more importantly, cinematic immortality. All of the aforementioned titles—and thousands more—are movies I can enjoy over and over again. Sadly, the same cannot be said with the current crop of movies in this new century.

We currently (and sadly) live in the "Mega-Tent Pole Movie" era, where every studio picture has to be a sequel, prequel, remake, redo, reboot, requel, blah-blah-blah, wash-rinse-repeat. Mind you, I was reared right around the time that *Jaws*—the first real "event" movie—premiered, so the high-concept concept of the tent pole movie that finds its beginnings in hits like the aforementioned fish movie, *Star Wars*, *The Terminator* (1984), *Die Hard* (1988), *Jurassic Park* (1993), and dozens of other films dwells in the cinematic DNA of the mass media collective. What grinds my gears is that everything today has to be a sequel, prequel—... You get the idea. Ugh.

Combining the synergy of movies, merchandising (thanks George Lucas!), theme parks and other auxiliary money streams (repackaging movies for modern viewing such as the internet and packaged media) coveted by the conglomerates who own the movie studios today, the moviegoing experience and programming schemas have become rote and cookie-cutter. I am not saying that we always need the gravitas of a Bob Rafelson (auteur of such New Hollywood classics such as *Five Easy Pieces* [1970] and *The King Of Marvin Gardens* [1972]), the rebellious streak of a Robert Altman (auteur of more New Hollywood classics *McCabe & Mrs. Miller* [1971] and *The Long Goodbye*), the anti-establishment bemusement of a Hal Ashby (auteur of even *more* New Hollywood classics such as *The Last Detail* [1973] and *Shampoo* [1975]), buoyed, of course, by the gonzo vitriol of the late, great Sam Peckinpah (auteur of kick-ass New Hollywood classics such as *The Wild Bunch*, and *Bring Me The Head of Alfredo Garcia* [1974]).

(Notice that I pontificate on the classic New Hollywood canon; films that came out right around the same time I did. See, I stated earlier that I loved the movies of yesteryear...)

The other filmmakers who grew from this fertile wellspring—Stanley Kubrick, Steven Spielberg, Martin Scorsese, Francis Ford Coppola, George Lucas, Ridley Scott, James Cameron, Brian De Palma, Oliver Stone, etc.—gave us some of the greatest movies of all time. But what is past may not be prologue, as the filmmakers of today, pressured by the studios and their conglomerate handlers (bean-counters as opposed to champions of Cinema), have to put out those sequels, prequels, etc., to bring fannies into the theaters of today. Notable exceptions are modern day *auteurs* such as Christopher Nolan, David Fincher, Quentin Tarantino, Alfonso Cuaron, Guillermo Del Toro, Alejandro G. Iñárritu, Michael Bay (for better or worse), and others who can still make quality pictures.

In fact, I can honestly state (in both a professional and personal capacity) that the best movie of the new Millennium thus far is Nolan's *The Dark Knight*, buoyed by excellent writing, editing, cinematography, and acting on the part of the late Heath Ledger as a terrifying Joker. The film is a clinic in what a masterpiece should look (and sound) like. We need more movies such as this one.

To be fair, going to the movies is still a quasi-religious experience for me as I do enjoy all types of movies. In fact, as of spring 2016, I saw a fantastic science-fiction thriller named *Midnight Special*, starring the talented Michael Shannon and directed by up-and-coming *auteur* Jeff Nichols. Again, a film that stands out. And I can proudly call it a "film," as it was shot on real 35mm film in the beautiful anamorphic Panavision format. You know; like movies used to be made. I could go into the downward trend of shooting feature movies on digital HD format, but that would require another book all on its own!

All told, it is like I always say: when in doubt and you need something to watch, pop in the brilliantly-crappy, philosophical roundelay known as *Road House* (1989)—the quintessential American film ... yeah, lensed in 35mm film via Panavision. They don't make movies like that one anymore, the topic of which I will cover in my own forthcoming book, *Road House: The Quintessential American Film.* Grab the popcorn and watch out for the flying chair.

Dead End: *Road Ends*

During the 1990s, I was scuffling around for screenwriting work in places other than the low-budget turf of Florida. I even had a few brushes with a possible shot at getting back into the majors.

My friend Steve Szilagyi hired me to adapt his 1992 novel, *Photographing Fairies*, into a screenplay, but when the property finally found a home, the buyers wanted to do their own screenplay and I was out.

Then there was a play of mine produced at a small professional theater company in New Jersey which generated enough good buzz that I was getting calls from the other side of the Hudson. Some were from the specialty divisions of major movie companies (the divisions charged with turning out art house–caliber films) like Sony and 20th Century Fox. I even got a call from Julia Roberts' production company. None of it came to anything. Roberts' company passed because "there isn't a part for Julia," and the specialty divisions, despite dealing with small films, thought my play was "too small," although it being a play, I've always wondered how big did they think it was going to be?

I also kept responding to other trade ads and that's how I linked up with Travis Rink.

Travis was on a bit of a hot streak, having written two movies back to back for Roger Corman's Concorde/New Horizons company. Although these were low-budget, direct-to-video features, that Travis had worked for Corman's company not only impressed the hell out of me, but left me a bit envious.

Corman was the legendary "King of the B's." He'd started out in the 1950s doing made-on-a-shoestring sci fi and horror flicks for American International Pictures with titles like *Attack of the Crab Monsters* (1957) and *Teenage Cave Man* (1958), then started developing a culty reputation with young audiences in the 1960s while also showing how much flair could be injected into his low-budget efforts with movies like *X: The Man with the X-Ray Eyes* (1963) and especially his string of colorful Edgar Allan Poe adaptations. Eventually, Corman would leave AIP to run his own shop, the most recent incarnation of which, at the time, was Concorde (Finler, *Directors...*, 194–195). I'd watched Corman's '50s flicks on television as a kid, gone to all of his Poe movies when I was old enough to toddle off to the neighborhood movie house with my buddies from the block, and studied him in college. He was one of my moviedom Mickey Mantles.

My being impressed with Travis' connection to Corman wasn't just hero worship once removed. As much as for his own work, Corman was equally legendary for providing a launch pad for an incredible number of young talents who would go on to their own stellar careers; people like Martin Scorsese, Francis Ford Coppola, Peter Bogdanovich, Jonathan Demme, James Cameron, Ron Howard (as a director), screenwriter Robert Towne (who would go on to win an Oscar for *Chinatown*), and—another Jersey boy—Jack Nicholson (Finler, *Directors...*, 195). My hope was Travis would follow in that long, lustrous line, and maybe I could ride his coattails on that trip up the ladder.

He was certainly off to a good start. Travis had headed out to L.A. from his native Poughkeepsie in the late 1980s to try to break into screenwriting. While out there, he'd gotten a number of short stories—mostly hard-boiled mysteries—published in men's magazines, got his first gig adapting a Western novel for a movie producer which landed him at an agency who started circulating some of his original material which is how he wound up in business with Concorde (Mesce, "On Corman's...," 146–147).

Eventually, Concorde would produce *Caroline at Midnight* (1994) and, just a few months later, *Unfaithful* (1994, which, with typical Corman showmanship, would be rechristened *The Heat of Passion II: Unfaithful* forcing a connection which didn't exist to an earlier Concorde release). *Caroline* did what a writer of low-budget stuff hoped it would do: got some buzz for standing out from the direct-to-video pack, for being better than you'd expect from that tier. It was the kind of career-building response I'd hoped to get from *Carjack.*

Travis had a couple of screenplays on which he'd felt he'd hit a wall. He was looking for a collaborator. We turned out to be a nicely complementary team. Except for that brief spate of creativity when I'd turned out those five screenplays, I generally don't generate much original material. It's why I had welcomed those script doctoring gigs George Barnes had fed me; someone else had already done what was, for me, the hard part of coming up with a plot. I got to do the fun part of making it work.

That was Travis's great strength; he was terrific at coming up with strong, often complex plots, establishing interesting characters and setting up their interrelationships. My job was to fine-tune the plot, play with the characters, and strengthen the dialogue. We worked through three screenplays like this, were very happy with the results, but couldn't find them a home. The connections Travis had formed through *Caroline* and *Unfaithful* weren't biting.

Around the end of 1994 or early 1995, Travis called me up to tell me he'd landed with a new agency, Innermedia, and recommended I pitch myself to them as well. The agency took me on, but it wasn't quite the boon either of us had been hoping for.

The backstory on this outfit was that it had been a one-man operation, but then that one man had died. His wife wanted to keep the agency running and brought in a guy named Ron Graham to take up the reins.

Ron was a sweet guy, and damned if he didn't try his hardest, but he was hardly a slick, Hollywood pro. Travis and I used to refer to him as "Columbo," after the bumbling police detective Peter Falk had played on TV. A typical conversation with Ron went like this:

"So, Ron, has there been any movement on that last piece I sent over?"

"Hm, oh, yeah, I'm pretty sure I heard something, I've got a message; where is that thing? (heavy rustle of papers) I know I had a note here some–. Oh, there it is! Wups, nope, that's for something else. What the hell did I do with that thing?"

We had, briefly, gotten a nibble on my sci fi piece *Lab 7,* but the interested company eventually passed for the oddest of reasons.

"I think you wrote it too well," Ron explained.

"What does that mean?"

"The first part of the script, before the monster shows up, you wrote that so well they thought it was going to be a different kind of movie. They were actually a bit disappointed when the monster came in."

"So if I write a monster movie, it has to be dumb?"

"Seems so."

Ron wasn't placing anything, and despite his Concorde credits nobody was biting at Travis's work, and I was pumping out work for Sam Lupowitz in Florida that was coming to nothing and for which I was only occasionally getting paid. Like my actor friend, I started thinking, It's not gonna happen, and that maybe it was time to walk away from the business. You can only beat your head against a wall so long before you realize the wall is winning.

Despite his shortcomings, Ron was nothing if not persistent, and persistence sometimes does the job. Around October/November of 1995, he called to tell me it looked like he'd placed one of my screenplays on a cold call (which, for those of you who don't know, almost never happens) to a small company called Spectacor. I thought, Well, I can always walk away tomorrow.

*   *   *

Spectacor was the production arm of distributor Promark Entertainment, putting four-five DTV and made-for-cable features in the $2–2.5 million budget range into Promark's distribution pipeline each year. The whole company was just three guys—the boss, the development guy, and an assistant—rambling around a mostly empty suite of offices on Sunset Boulevard. Every great once in a while, a Spectacor release would break from the pack. A few years before, they'd sold *Wedlock* (1991, aka *Deadlock*) to HBO, a futuristic sci fier about the prison of tomorrow where inmates are paired through electronic collars. Get too far from your partner—as in attempting a breakout—and the duo's heads are blown off. HBO had presented the movie as an "HBO Original Film," and, bizarrely, this bit of decapitation-filled schlock was, for years, HBO's highest-rated original movie, even above the channel's classier history-based pieces like *Murrow* (1986), *Mandela* (1987), and *The Josephine Baker Story* (1991). As such, *Wedlock* was also Spectacor's biggest bragging point (Mesce, "Guerilla...," 166).

The piece Spectacor was interested in was one of my five original specs; a script called *Road Ends*. I'd gotten the idea from a *Parade* article about the busting of a drug ring led by a Latina woman known as "The Butterfly." Feeling they needed a Latino to successfully ingratiate himself with The Butterfly and infiltrate her operation, the feds arm-twisted an immigrant from South America who'd gotten himself into some tax and immigration trouble to be an agent for them, promising they'd clear up his various legal problems as compensation. But once The Butterfly had been convicted, the feds reneged, and not only did their guy still have to deal with his legal headaches, but now he had to worry about revenge from the bad guys as well.

I made the immigrant—I christened him Maceda—a Cuban exile, brought to Florida by his refugee father when he was a kid. Just like his real-life counterpart, Maceda's minor legal problems are used as leverage to get him to become a trusted friend of drug boss Tommy Orosco, and, also like in the real case, once Orosco is convicted, Maceda is abandoned. But I added a twist; Orosco's conviction is overturned and now he has to be re-tried. The feds, having screwed Maceda over, now need him again.

But Maceda has gone on the run. He knows the feds will be coming for him, but he also knows Orosco wants to make sure he never testifies as well as take revenge for Maceda's betrayal. To draw both sides away from his family and allow them to escape, Maceda lams out for the Florida keys, to a now-dying town next to the shuttered Coast Guard station where he'd come into the country. This is as far as the southbound highway goes. That idea of running out of ground—and the title—came to me during a vacation in south Jersey and a visit to Sunset Beach near the southernmost tip of New Jersey. The road abruptly ends at a guardrail overlooking the beach, and there's a warning sign there: Road Ends.

While the basis was there for a strong crime drama, that's not what I wrote. I wanted a piece that would *sell,* so I grafted this plot onto a guy-on-the-run action thriller with regular set-pieces where the guns came out. I remembered something I'd heard about the build of *Bonnie and Clyde;* that each gunfight was constructed to be more intense than the one before—not necessarily bigger, but with a greater dynamism. One gunfight takes place at night, a gunfight in the dark having a visual pop daylight shoot-outs don't have. The following gunfight is punctuated by a posse turning their guns on one of the duo's getaway cars and shooting it to pieces. Like I said: not bigger, but each more intense than the one before, and I designed the same kind of build into *Road Ends,* each battle having its own signature.

Spectacor optioned the screenplay and I spent several months working with their development guy, Abraham Gordon. Abraham had moved to L.A. from his native Wisconsin in the late 1970s to break into the movies as an actor, but the work was spotty, and often in low-budget junk like *Carnosaur 2* (1995) where he played a cop eaten by some kind of big reptile. One of his acting buddies had taught him accounting skills as a way of keeping himself fed when roles were scarce, which is how he wound up at Spectacor doing their books (Mesce, "Guerilla…," 165). Abraham started picking up some of the scripts of movies Spectacor had in the pipeline and was appalled. "They were *awful!*," he once told me, and managed to wangle himself a job as their head of development (166).

Abraham and I hit it off from the start: we'd seen the same movies, liked the same stuff, could easily connect through the same reference points. He believed *Road Ends* had the possibility of being another break-out flick for Spectacor, having the right balance between a strong story and characters, and the requisite bouts of heavy gunplay which would make the piece work for their markets. Abraham had a great gift for knowing how to engineer a screenplay for Spectacor's budget limitations, and also how to sculpt a well-designed arc. Our working relationship was so fun and easy that it quickly evolved into a friendship.

It was good he had that kind of ability because we had a problem. *Road Ends* wasn't afflicted with the usual second act sag. In fact, the script had a smooth escalation through the second act, building to a nicely apocalyptic finale in the third act. The problem was where you usually don't have it; right at the top in act one.

The main issue was that a big hunk of that strong plot which had hooked Abraham was backstory. My screenplay started with a cop surveillance team staked out at Maceda's home, then when they see Maceda's family leave the house and they try to pursue, they find themselves locked in the back of their surveillance van. Later, the main cop in the piece—Gene Gere—shows up and we find the house is empty except for two bodies left in the basement. And then Gere meets with his boss for a briefing and the pieces start getting put together for us: the two dead guys were Orosco goons, Maceda had killed them, taken the clothes of one so the surveillance crew wouldn't know it was Maceda making a break. Maceda lams out drawing attention away from his family while they head off in another direction. And then Gere's boss explains how Maceda is needed for Orosco's retrial.

It's a lot of information with a lot of names not attached to faces getting thrown around. It was confusing and inert.

I had tried to give the opening some pop by opening it with Maceda on the road at night ambushing a pair of Orosco's hitmen on his tail. He changes cars with the dead men, stuffing their bodies into his old car which he lights on fire causing it to explode. Abraham always told me that was a good move: "You *have* to have a car blowing up. You need the explosion for the trailer."

It was a zesty curtain-raiser, but then the plot slows and sags. Abraham and I went through several drafts trimming all that exposition as much as we could: what did we really *need?* How little could we get by with?

"We need another action scene," Abraham finally concluded. "And it has to come earlier." The screenplay was out of balance: the escalating gunfights didn't start until well into the second act, which made the first act come off even draggier. We came up with a scene to close out the first act where Gere has gone to an auto glass repair shop to question one of Maceda's relatives and bumps into some of Orosco's shooters on the same mission. I thought of an auto glass shop because a friend of mine owned one, and I thought all that bullet-shattered glass would give the scene its own signature.

We never quite licked the first act problem (lesson learned: keep your backstories simple), but the script did get tighter, and the first act pace did pick up.

I thought we'd pretty much had the screenplay wrapped when I got a call from Abraham. He sounded off somehow, ill at ease, and when he got to the point, I understood why: "Can you get Maceda in bed with the girl (Kat, the female lead character)?"

"What?"

"You know; a sex scene between Maceda and Kat."

"Maceda's supposed to be a good guy. He's going through all this to keep his family safe. He cares that much about his family, and then he sleeps with this girl? He's not gonna seem so much of a good guy. And she's supposed to have a thing for the police chief."

"Yeah, yeah, I know, you're right, you're right." A pause. "What about if she sleeps with the chief?"

"Through the whole movie, these two have a maybe-they-will, maybe-they-won't thing going. She sleeps with him, we lose that suspense."

"Yeah, yeah, you're right, I know, I agree." Another pause. "Can you get Kat naked? Maybe coming out of the shower or something like that?"

Up until now, everything Abraham had asked me to do had been about making the screenplay stronger and tighter. This didn't seem like him at all. "What's going on?"

Abraham sighed. "Our marketing guy says if you get the girl naked, it'll add fifteen percent to the overseas sales."

"Jesus."

"Yeah. Look. Just put something in there. Don't worry; if we get a big enough name, she won't do it, and we'll have to take it out."

So, Kat comes naked out of the shower.

With that last, marketable element, we thought we had a winner.

Abraham's boss disagreed. He pulled the plug.

Abraham was as sick about this as I was. He had, bless 'im, a lot of faith

Road Ends was better than the average DTV feature, predicted another HBO sale, maybe even a small theatrical release. He would've liked having his name on it as a producer.

While we'd been working on the script, Abraham had been showing the screenplay to directors and had gotten Rick King interested.

Rick had learned filmmaking under the legendary documentarian Richard Leacock at MIT. He self-financed his first feature, *Off the Wall* (1977) with $30,000 he'd made from his job in an automobile factory. It was good enough to earn him his first trip to the Sundance Film Festival (Mesce, "Guerilla...," 170). His second film—*Hard Choices* (1985)—brought him back to Sundance and finally landed him in Hollywood. Rick came close to a career breakthrough developing the original *Point Break* (1991), but the project eventually went to director Kathryn Bigelow. He had another shot at the majors when he optioned Jim McGlynn's Nicholl Fellowship-winning screenplay for *Traveller* (1997), but couldn't place the project (it was eventually produced by Bill Paxton, who also starred) (173).

Then, as Rick explained to me in an interview several years ago: "When you get to the point of having a family, a mortgage, that becomes a major consideration ... (I) moved into taking whatever work I could, but sure I could invest it with something" (Mesce, "Guerilla...," 173).

He helmed a number of DTV and TV made-fors, including several for Promark/Spectacor which is how Abraham knew him. Still hoping *Road Ends* could be a little special, Abraham thought Rick was the right guy to accent the script's dramatic strengths.

Rick, in turn, showed the screenplay to actor Chris Sarandon, with whom he'd made the Holocaust drama *Forced March* (1989), with the idea of Sarandon playing Maceda.

Despite Rick's track record with Spectacor, and Sarandon's cachet as an Oscar-nominated actor (for 1976's *Dog Day Afternoon*) with a sizable body of respected work, Abraham's boss still wouldn't go ahead with the project. That's when Abraham showed me just how decent a guy he was. He talked Spectacor into releasing the property to Rick and Chris as a "goodwill gesture" toward two people the company would like to work with again. There was no gain in this for Abraham; from now on, it was a King and Sarandon project. So why'd he do it?

"I just thought it was a movie that deserved to be made," he told me. They don't make many like that in the movie business. At least I haven't met many of them.

Rick and Chris eventually brought *Road Ends* to PM Entertainment, a DTV company grinding out low-budget mixes of blood and boobs. At the time, their big brag was they'd signed a deal with Anna Nicole Smith for a string of softcore pics to be made for $800,000 each; a typical PM budget (Mesce, "Guerilla...," 173–174).

I'm not exactly sure if it was a case of Rick and Chris talking PM into stepping up their game, or PM was already considering such a move when my guys came through the door, but the company was interested. Another cast member had been added and that clinched the deal: Dennis Hopper.

Hopper's name carried weight; it would help sell the movie, and even though he bounced back and forth between supporting roles in big movies and bigger parts in an almost steady stream of low-budget stuff, there was a cachet of quality attached to his name.

Initially, I was flattered Hopper wanted to do the movie, but working at HBO, I'd seen, on our schedules, he'd also run through a lot of low-end sludge.

"You have to look at it this way," Rick said to me, "You're right; he makes a lot of movies. But he picked *yours*. There's stuff out there that'd pay him better, but he wanted to make yours."

Which gave me a nice, warm glow.

PM was willing to do the movie if Hopper signed on, but Hopper would only sign on if shooting could take place during a hole in his schedule beginning in just a few weeks and lasting only about a week, *and* if he was paid up front. Rick promised him the dates, PM fronted the money, Hopper signed on and we had a deal to make *Road Ends* for $1.6 million (less $600,000 for Hopper) (Mesce, "Guerilla...," 174).

During the time Rick and Chris were trying to find a home for *Road Ends,* I was continuing to work with them honing the script; tightening where we could, especially during the still problematic first act. After a couple of drafts I had to call them and tell them, "I'm out."

That didn't make them happy. We'd been working well together; it was probably one of the happiest, smoothest jobs I've been on, but I was burning out. I'd been over the material so many times I couldn't "feel" it anymore. It was just typing on a page. Maybe it was good, maybe it sucked, but I could no longer tell.

"Look, guys, I already went through a couple of drafts with Abraham, and I'm just sick of looking at this thing. It's starting to feel like the only thing I've ever written. It's starting to feel like the only thing I ever *will* write! I can't do it anymore."

The call ended a bit sourly, but a few days later, Rick called back on behalf of himself and Chris.

"Naturally, we were disappointed you wanted to leave. It's your script, we wanted you to be the guy to finish it. But we get it. We weren't aware of how much work you'd put into this before we came on. It's ok; don't worry about it."

And then Rick did one of the classiest things I've ever experienced in this business. There was a clause in my contract that if I remained the sole writer, I'd receive a bonus. If another writer came on, no bonus. I knew Rick would do enough work on the screenplay to warrant sharing the writing credit, but he wouldn't have it. "It'll just be your name."

I told him I didn't have a problem sharing the credit; he'd be earning it.

"It's ok. Look, my name's gonna be all over this thing anyway (as producer and director). I don't need another credit. You did a lot of work, you earned it."

A few days later, I got a call from Ron Graham telling me they were also going to give me an "associate producer" credit.

"But I didn't do anything! I was just a writer!"

"They wanted to do something for you. Look, it's not like they're giving you any more money with it, so just take it."

For such a small budget, Rick was able to put together an exceptionally strong cast. Besides Chris and Hopper, he got Mariel Hemingway for Kat (with Chris and Hopper, this meant we had three Oscar-nominated actors in our little movie), and Peter Coyote for Gene Gere to fill out the principles. The supporting cast included Tony-winning actress Joanna Gleason, Geoffrey Thorne who had a recurring role on the hit television series *In the Heat of the Night,* and my personal favorite, Bert Remsen (more about Bert later).

As Abraham had predicted, Mariel Hemingway had decided her show-it-all-on-the-big-screen days were over. The naked-out-of-the-shower scene became a more reflective Kat-in-a-bathrobe-in-the-bathroom scene.

The shoot was a bit of a kamikaze production. It was a short schedule; 15 days, I think. And to get Hopper during his open window meant beginning shooting while Chris was still on another film and Rick was still working on the script. Chris came available just as Hopper was coming to the end of his term giving them just enough time to shoot the scenes they had together before Hopper took off for his next gig.

Rick had had to do a lot of rewriting to accommodate the tight budget, but also conditions set down by PM. Shooting in Florida was out. The movie had to be shot close by in California, around Piru, a location PM used regularly. That meant no road ending at the ocean in the Florida Keys, but the less definitive image of the road ending at a lake. There'd be no shuttered Coast Guard base but an orange packing plant. The shoot-outs were going to be scaled down with a lot of hit teams becoming lone wolf assassins (although Rick felt the scale-down helped the film, elevating the dramatic elements by bringing down the bang-bang elements). He would continue to rewrite through the production as he tailored the script for the locations available.

Rick was also obligated to use PM's house staff, also a cost-saving measure, but Rick would later tell me that was fine; it was a smooth-running crew, knowing how to move fast yet still deliver solid work.

As hectic a shoot as it was, it went off smoothly and finished on time and on budget. After the film was done with post-production, Rick sent me a VHS.

I didn't then, nor do I now have any illusions about what we were doing. This wasn't *The French Connection* we were making. But Rick had delivered a punchy little B, something akin to those tough little *noirs* RKO used to make in the 1940s-1950s.

The movie still had problems. Rick was expert at compressing scenes. He eliminated the early briefing scene by retailoring it to happen at Maceda's house (that also saved the cost of another location). But even though that picked up the pace a bit, that first act still never quite came off as tight and energetic as we would've liked. But at least it's out of the way early, and about 15-minutes in or so, the movie hits its stride.

Still, I felt the movie could've used a slight trim, and I talked to Rick about that. He would've liked to trim it as well, by a few minutes, but PM Entertainment insisted on a running time of 96 minutes; no more, no less. It had something to do with one of their overseas markets requiring that specific length.

But other than those issues—and I thought them rather minor—the movie worked. It had a nice flow, Rick letting the movie breathe and the characters gain heft during the dramatic scenes. Rick would let the pace for those scenes ease up, take on a more conversational rhythm. A particular favorite of mine was a scene Chris and Hemingway had by a creek. She's fishing, they both chat about their backgrounds, and cinematographer Bruce Douglas Johnson gave the scene a lovely late afternoon glow which fit with the idea of the two characters ruing a more innocent lost past, missteps they were still paying for, and trying to figure out their respective third acts.

Rick had added a series of lines from the Gene Gere character referencing his ex-wife. They were bitterly funny: "My ex-wife loved jelly doughnuts. She liked to stab them with a fork and watch them bleed." The lines were so vivid and on-point, I couldn't believe Rick had made them up out of nothing. When I called to talk about the movie after screening it, I said, "I didn't know you were divorced."

"I'm not," he chuckled. "Those all came from Peter."

I had also been worried Dennis Hopper might be too old for the part of the chief. I'd written him as someone in his late 20s–early 30s, somebody locked in a job no one else wanted and who had no other options. Kat has left town, seen the outside world, and come home. The chief has never left. At the time of filming, Hopper was pushing 60, although he could pass younger, but not 30 years younger. I'd also been worried because Hopper's usual image was as a cackling villain. I'd asked Rick during the filming how Hopper was coming off.

"Dennis is in nice-guy mode," he said.

And that was how he came off in the finished film. There was still something boyish about him giving the character a sense of an unsophisticated, small town type of guy, and it played nicely.

Through all the drafts I'd done with Abraham, and then with Rick and Chris (six or seven all together, I think), besides the first act sag, another persistent problem was we couldn't come up with a "button"; that last line and/or image giving a movie its ideal closing note. It's Humphrey Bogart and Claude Rains walking off into the fog together at the end of *Casablanca* (1942) as Bogart says, "Louie, I think this is the beginning of a beautiful friendship." It's Joe E. Brown at the end of *Some Like It Hot* (1959) who reacts to his fiancée's confession that she's really Jack Lemmon in drag with a blithe, "Nobody's perfect!" It's cop Popeye Doyle in *The French Connection* disappearing into a derelict building in pursuit of the French drug kingpin he's been chasing the whole movie, and then the sound of a gunshot; Doyle shooting at shadows, consumed by his obsession. It's Charlton Heston angrily writhing in the surf, bellowing out, "Goddamn you all to hell!" as he kneels at the foot of a half-buried Statue of Liberty, realizing the *Planet of the Apes* is the post-nuke holocaust remains of Earth. Every draft of *Road Ends* had a different button, and we weren't happy with any of them.

After the climactic gunfight in a closed orange-packing plant, Kat and a wounded chief finally connect. They walk away from the camera, heading out of the plant, and Rick let them adlib the whole way out. Maybe because it was spontaneous, it had a charm and a warmth none of us could manufacture. Considering the nature of everything that had come before, it was surprisingly and refreshingly sweet.

Now came the hard part: selling the movie.

*   *   *

When Spectacor had sold *Wedlock* to HBO, it was about more than earning bragging rights. The sale pulled *Wedlock* out of the DTV slush pile, elevated it, and in the process, allowed Spectacor to boost its asking price for distribution rights in other markets. If they'd gotten a theatrical release—even a tiny one—that would've elevated the title even more and its distribution price along with it, and almost guaranteed a cable sale as well giving the company another shot of additional revenue. Without those sales, *Wedlock* would've been just another generic DTV title ending up on the ninety-nine cent rental shelf at the neighborhood video store.

Since I was working at HBO and knew Bob Conte, whose responsibilities included screening finished films for the company, I took *Road Ends* to him. HBO offered two possibilities: the top end was their picking up the film to present as an HBO original movie (most of the company's original films were produced for the company, but they sometimes supplemented them with a pick-up like *Wedlock*). Next-best was their "HBO Premiere" slot. As a way of trying to boost their feature offerings beyond their studio deals, once a month the channel would premiere either a feature film which hadn't been theatrically released or had only had a limited theatrical distribution; or a high-end DTV feature they felt had enough entertainment and production value to stand shoulder-to-shoulder with most of their second tier movie offerings.

Bob called me after the relevant HBO scheduling and programming people had screened the movie. "It *looks* like a movie," he said.

He made it sound like a compliment, but I couldn't see what was complimentary about it. That was like me asking somebody how they liked my new car and they say, "Well, it's got four wheels."

But then Bob explained. A lot of the low-budget stuff the company screened for possible Premieres *looked* like low-budget stuff; shoddy, trying to squeeze too much movie out of too little money, C-list actors, etc. *Road Ends* didn't look like that. It had a polish and completeness a lot of DTV Premiere candidates didn't have. Not that the tight budget didn't occasionally show.

"Are these the only five people who live in that town?" Bob asked.

I know what he meant. There hadn't been much money for extras to fill in the background and there were times the locale did seem awfully depopulated. I think Rick King did a hell of a job on the money he had to work with, but I think of what he could've done with another million which is what he would've had if Spectacor hadn't backed out.

HBO passed. Bob never explained why. Not that an explanation would've made us feel any better.

PM screened *Road Ends* at that year's Cannes Film Festival. For the uninformed, as well as being a high-class competition, Cannes also functions as one of the biggest international film markets of the year. Producers bring movies large and small, epic and intimate, artistic and exploitative to the festival to screen them and hopefully get some distribution deals. We didn't get a nibble.

George Barnes had been at Cannes that year and called me when he got back to the States. "Hey, I saw your movie while I was over there! I really liked it!"

"How did it play?"

"The crowd stayed through the whole thing."

Like Bob Conte's it-looks-like-a-movie comment, George made this sound like a good thing but I was hard put to see what was so grand in hearing an audience managed to make it through to the end.

"You don't understand," George said. "The people shopping for movies at this thing don't *watch* a movie. They run from one to the other, they stick their head in the theater, they go, 'Ok, it's in color, it's got sound, the actors are pretty,' and that's all they need to see, then they run to the next one. When they came to yours, they *stayed.* They wanted to see the whole movie."

"If they liked it so much, how come nobody wanted to buy it?"

George had a theory. "The people who usually buy PM movies can't use it. And the people who might've wanted it didn't come to see it because it was a PM movie and they thought it was going to be their usual junk."

Hearing people who didn't want to buy the movie liked it was hardly consolation. After Cannes, I conferred with Rick King by phone, asking what our next move was. "What about taking it to Showtime?" I asked.

Rick hesitated. It wasn't that he was being snobby about going to HBO's much smaller competitor. "I'm worried about what happens to us if they pass on it." Having struck out at Cannes, if both HBO and Showtime also rejected the film, there was a good chance *Road Ends* would be tainted, labeled a dud. He wanted to try something else first.

He managed to get the movie invited to be screened at several smaller film festivals around the country: Mill Valley, Sacramento, San Jose, Breckenridge. The critical reaction was mixed. One guy who saw the movie at San Jose panned it saying, "Just about every gun-related movie cliché was in evidence" (Cummins). On the other hand, Jeffrey Lyons, the nationally known print and television film reviewer who hosted that year's Breckenridge, thought so highly of it he told Rick that if he ever got a theatrical release for the movie he'd provide a positive blurb. As for the audiences, Rick told me they always seemed to enjoy it. That it didn't sweep reviewers unanimously off their feet may have hurt my artistic vanity, but it was clear we had a movie which worked for a paying public. We just couldn't get past the distribution gatekeepers; no offers came out of the festival screenings.

Chris Sarandon told to tell me he had a possibility, maybe even a shot at a limited theatrical release. He was going to screen the movie for this guy and some of his people in New York; why didn't I sit in and see what *Road Ends* looked like on a big screen?

My friends, it *does* make a difference. I don't care what you say about your big screen TV, if a movie is working at all, there's an electric, enveloping sense that goes with seeing it on a movie screen and sharing that experience with a crowd of people. I still winced at the first act problems, but after that, I thought, "Ya know, this is a decent flick."

After the screening, I waited outside the auditorium while Chris conferred with the guests. When he came out to me to deliver the verdict, it was clear on his face we'd struck out again.

"Did he say what he didn't like?" I asked.

Chris' face soured. "He said it wasn't nasty enough."

So, apparently, trying to class the movie up by tamping down the amount of violence hadn't worked for us.

By now, Rick, Chris, and PM had been trying to sell *Road Ends* for several months. We'd struck out at HBO, at Cannes, on the festival circuit, and now with this New York guy. We were running out of moves, and it looked like we might have to risk offering it to Showtime.

Then, like a coach calling for a second string benchwarmer to get off his ass and get in the game, Rick called to tell me Cinemax wanted the movie.

Cinemax was HBO's sister channel. It was, so we used to call it inside the company, a movie junkie's channel. Where HBO offered a mix of mainstream theatricals and original programming, Cinemax, at that time, was 90 to 95 percent movies, all kinds of movies: big, little, mainstream, art house, recent releases and oldies, the familiar and the cultish. Like its big sister, Cinemax also had a Premiere slot, but being a more movie-heavy channel, they had four of them each month; one a week. A hole had opened in one of their monthly schedules, they needed a movie, and one of their people had remembered *Road Ends* from when it had been screened at HBO. They thought it would make a good fit.

It wasn't an HBO buy, but we were still under the HBO umbrella (kinda/sorta). Even though Showtime, as HBO's main competitor (at the time) was often thought of as the No. 2 pay–TV service, in a number of markets, Cinemax was actually the second largest service in terms of subscribers. If we couldn't get on HBO, this was a next-best placement.

I don't remember what one of the Cinemax Premieres was in our month, but the other two were *The Apostle* (1997)—a critically acclaimed limited theatrical release that had earned an Oscar nod for its star, Robert Duvall; and *City of Industry* (1997)—a tough little neo-*noir*, also a limited theatrical release, starring Harvey Keitel and a pre–*X-Men* Famke Janssen. Both movies had bigger budgets than ours, bigger stars, and more visibility thanks to their small runs in movie theaters. They also got a bigger push in Cinemax's on-air promotions than we did.

So my expectations were low when I called the guy heading up Cinemax at the time after our weekend debut. I was already wincing when I asked him how we did.

"Your numbers went up over the course of the running time," meaning our viewing ratings.

"That doesn't make sense." I had assumed either the numbers would hold steady if people who tuned in liked what they saw, or they would drop as they got tired of watching and punched out. But that they went *up?*

"You don't understand how people watch Cinemax," he explained. "It's not like HBO. HBO viewers pick their movie and sit down to watch. Ours tend to cruise through the channels. If they see something on Cinemax they think is interesting, they'll stick around until they're bored, then keep cruising. What your numbers suggest is that when they came into your movie, they stayed until the end."

In those days, Cinemax ran 1,200 to 1,400 movie titles a year. At the end of the year, *Road Ends* came in at #23 or #24. So, despite the movie's faults, and the mixed reviews, and the distributors and exhibitors who passed on it, we knew the movie worked. Yeah, there were things we could've done better, especially if we'd had a bit more money, but it *worked.* It just would've been nice to see it work in theaters.

But maybe there was another reason we'd had so much trouble trying to sell that damned thing.

* * *

What we weren't aware of at the time was that even as *Road Ends* was shooting, the direct-to-video market was dying. The culprit: DVD. Studios had priced their VHS tapes too high for individual purchases, often over $90 for major titles. Consequently, the VHS business became a rental business. Looking at all that rental revenue they *didn't* get, studios re-thought their strategy with the introduction of the DVD, pricing disks as a "sell-through" product, often under $30 for even top-end offerings. DVD purchases soared and video stores began to die off, and with them, their huge appetite for shelf-filling DTV features. (Mesce, "Appendix C...," 265).

There was still room for some original DTDVD product, but not the kind of cheapie pulp outfits like Spectacor pumped out. The major studios themselves were jumping in, often making low-budget sequels to some of their high-profile hits for the DVD market, the way Warner Premiere (Warner Bros.' DTDVD arm) did with *The Dukes of Hazzard: The Beginning* (2007), their DTDVD sequel to their 2005 midrange hit, *The Dukes of Hazzard* (Mesce, "Appendix C...," 263).

Outfits like Spectacor and PM couldn't compete against offerings like that. Not only did major studio DTDVD offerings have bigger budgets than most DTV features, but they had studio marketing muscle behind them as well. Warners could hype their *Dukes* sequel with the same promotional machinery which had pushed the 2005 original. Spectacor and the like were outgunned at every level (Mesce, "Guerilla...," 175).

"PM would've been really smart four years earlier," Rick King would later tell me. Recalling going over to their offices during *Road Ends,* he said, "The place was *busy!* There were people running everywhere, all these people carrying cans of film.... They were for real, this wasn't some fly-by-night outfit" (Mesce, "Guerilla...," 174). Yet just a few years later and they were gone.

They weren't alone. According to the Internet Movie Data Base, Spectacor hasn't produced a film since 1999. Promark's last release was in 2003. I guess we were lucky just to have gotten the film made.

Road Ends would not be my last screenplay gig, not even the last project I worked on that made it into production. As a writer, script doctor, or some kind of consultant, I've been attached to almost two dozen projects, of which six have made it onto film. *Road Ends* is the only one on which I have a screenwriting credit, and if that's how my score remains, well, I can live with that. Is it a great movie? No. But it's a good movie and I like it.

Sometime after *Road Ends* started showing up on Cinemax (and later, even HBO) and then home video, I received a royalty check as the writer on the film. I didn't remember seeing anything about royalties in my contract, so it was a nice surprise ... although a *little* surprise. I don't exactly know what the royalties are for: television licensing agreements, home video sales ... but I get one each year. The breakdowns are specific about where the payments are coming from that go into the check: a few dollars from The Netherlands, a few from Italy, a couple of bucks from Spain. My last royalty check totaled $37.64.

Monetarily, it's not much. Hell, I spend more than that on gas each week. Still... Twenty years after *Road Ends* wrapped shooting, there are still people somewhere in the world that think it's a movie worth watching. Not many, maybe, but they're there. Even as I'm laughing about the royalty amounts, I still feel pretty good about that. In this business, you take your victories, small as some of them are, where you can find them.

*   *   *

In the process of writing a tribute to British character actor Michael Gough upon his passing in 2011, I penned something of a salute to all supporting players:

> Stars bring a character to life on the screen; but behind them is another kind of actor that brings life to that character's world. They are the seasoning which turns a good meal into a great meal.... Call them what you will: supporting players, character actors, familiar faces, second bananas ... [Mesce, "Michael Gough...," 119].

When Rick King told me he'd gotten Bert Remsen for a supporting part in *Road Ends,* he seemed surprised I knew the name, but then I'd been a fan of these cinematic utility players for years: people like George Kennedy, Claude Akins, Jessie Royce Landis, Jack Elam, L.Q. Jones, Charles Durning, Thelma Ritter, Woody Strode, Willis Bouchey, Joe Turkel, and on and on. They might have only one scene, maybe just a few lines, and yet they sometimes provided one of the most remembered elements from a movie, sometimes even in all moviedom. Ask somebody to quote a famous line from *The Graduate,* and odds are what you'll get back is Walter Brooke, in his one, short scene, giving some succinct advice to young college grad Dustin Hoffman: "Plastics."

I'd been watching Bert's face pop up in movies and on television most of my life, and he'd been a particular favorite of Robert Altman. And now this guy was in *my* movie!

After I'd seen the completed picture, I sent some of the actors thank you notes for their work. I sent one to Bert saying how happy I was that he was part of my movie; that I felt he was my one brush with a generation of great characters actors, naming some of my favorites including Strother

Martin (another supporting player who supplied another all-time classic line in *Cool Hand Luke* [1967]: "What we got here, is failure to communicate!").

Bert called me as soon as he got my note. He was open, friendly, sweet-natured and delightfully chatty. He called not just to thank me for my note: "It's funny you mentioned Strother Martin. I was a friend of Strother's! In fact, I was probably one of the last people to see him before he died!"

Bert, Martin, Royal Dano (another iconic familiar face), and a fourth actor whose name I can't recall, had had dinner together one night; a Mt. Rushmore of great character actors. Martin had flown home the next day from wherever they were at, and then a day or two later suffered a fatal heart attack on August 1, 1980.

Bert was one of those people that you start yakking with and soon feel like you're talking to an old friend. We talked about movies we liked, and found we shared an affinity for Westerns.

"That's what I liked about *Road Ends*," he said. "I always thought of it as a Western." He enjoyed working with Rick King so much he said, "If you and Rick ever get something else going, just call me and I'm there!"

We hoped we'd get to meet face-to-face someday, and vowed to keep in touch. I sent him a card that Christmas, got a note in return ... and then nothing. I thought, perhaps as warm and cuddly as it had felt on the phone with Bert, maybe this had been a fleeting show business bromance. But the more I thought about it, remembering that call, I felt Bert had seemed too authentic a person for that. On a hunch, I Googled him.

I found out Bert Remsen had died in his sleep April 27, 1999, at age 74 ... a good friend I'd never met.

But that, as they say, is show biz.

The Programmer: Andrew Goldman

(Andy Goldman was yet another HBO programming wiz I interviewed around 2010. With his encyclopedic knowledge of film and TV, Dave Baldwin—his boss—considered Goldman his "'go-to' guy when I have questions about what's going on in popular culture." That's probably

After a short stint with Showtime, Andy Goldman moved to Home Box Office where he spent over 30 years, attaining the position of Vice President, HBO/Cinemax Program Planning and Scheduling. (Since leaving HBO in 2015, Goldman has been working with TVtibi, overseeing acquisition and programming strategy for a platform aiming for a global reach.)

One point coming up again and again with Goldman on the subject of what's salient and common among today's big budget offerings is that of character: how it's defined, how it's portrayed, its importance to the overall story. Or, rather, the lack thereof on those same counts.

"These days, we learn about character through CGI," says Goldman. "How many movies are there today where you actually spend time learning the tics of a character?" Having not long before caught a rerun of the 2001 *Planet of the Apes* remake on one of his company's channels, he gives the example of the 1968 original, pointing out how much screen time viewers spend with the lead character of Taylor (Charlton Heston) before the main plot kicks in.

"Heston has several soliloquies that perfectly represent a feeling of the time—a sense of disillusionment with the human race. Those scenes also carry a more universal discontent that still feels relevant today. It's maybe a good half-hour or more before the hunt in the cornfield where we see the apes for the first time. It gives us time to know Taylor, and you know something? He's not a very nice guy!" Goldman ticks off Taylor's abrasive elements: arrogance, condescension, misanthropy, a haughty disdain for the rest of humankind; he's a bundle of foibles. That kind of moral complexity, Goldman feels, was a trademark of movies of the time. "The hero did not have to be a stalwart. Taylor is actually something of a prick, but we identify with his discontents."

Goldman then looks at the *Planet of the Apes* remake pointing out how, instead of that breathing space at the head of the original, the action starts almost immediately. "It can't be more than ten minutes into the movie before (lead) Mark Wahlberg is off into space, he crashes, and not long after that he's running from the apes. (As a character) there's nothing to him!"

There was an ethos of time-taking in storytelling in the best movies of the 1960s/1970s, says Goldman. "We used to watch a character breathe.

We used to watch characters take their time assessing *other* characters. You snuck into a character's life. It was a bleeding-over (into commercial films) of the *cinéma vérité* process of documentaries of the 1960s and 1970s. Pauses are good; that's when you get to know characters."

The Man Who Would Be King (1975), John Huston's adaptation of Rudyard Kipling's adventure novel, serves as another example. "That movie is *all* about character," says Goldman. "Huston knew how to do that. It's kind of an upper crust *Treasure of the Sierra Madre* (1948, also written and directed by Huston). There's a lot of elliptical conversation that doesn't explain everything but indicates a history between the two leads (Sean Connery and Michael Caine)." The movie gives the sense, Goldman continues, of the two men having had a distinctive life before the movie begins; a long-lasting, well-lived-in comradeship.

"Compare that to something like *Black Hawk Down* (2001) where, because the action is so constant and starts so early, there's little introduction to any of the people in the story. The characters are so indistinguishable the movie gives me a headache."

Another example of that "hidden life" giving resonance and depth to characters is *The Professionals* (1966), written and directed by Richard Brooks; a Mexican Revolution-era tale of four mercenaries (Lee Marvin, Burt Lancaster, Robert Ryan, Woody Strode) hired by millionaire Ralph Bellamy to rescue his wife (Claudia Cardinale) from a Mexican bandit and sometime revolutionary (Jack Palance). Marvin and Lancaster, we learn, had ridden together with Palance earlier in the Revolution only to drop out of the rebel cause in disillusionment. It is that sense of disappointment and failed altruism which gives *The Professionals* an unusual-for-the-genre melancholic undertone. Yet, that mournful subtext is integral to the film.

"It's the reason you believe in these characters; you believe they have a history. It's not the main plot," Goldman emphasizes, "but it's main to the characters. It's what makes you believe that they do what they do."

The movie gives Goldman reason to pinball to another difference between the thrillers of thirty/forty-odd years ago and those of today: their restraint. Over the course of *The Professionals,* the protagonists "hardly pull their guns!"

Along with some minor moments of suspense, there are only three major action sequences throughout the film's 117-minute running time: well into the film, after the foursome hired by Bellamy are on their way into Mexico, they are attacked by a gang of *banditos* in an episode that is explosive, violent, but quickly over; the central set piece of the movie is the successful attempt to break Cardinale out of Palance's rebel camp; and the climax where Lancaster stays behind to buy time for the others by delaying Palance and his fellow pursuers.

More than an action climax (those used to the spectacular finishes of most contemporary thrillers would consider it surprisingly small-scale), the fight between Lancaster and Palance & Co., is the *dramatic* climax of the film. Composed as a hit-and-retreat series of brief spurts of action and lulls, the sequence is punctuated by several verbal exchanges between Lancaster and Palance. The conversations between the one-time comrades-in-arms are a parry-and-thrust duel between opposing philosophies: one of self-interest bred of cynicism and disillusionment; the other, the tattered, faded pennant of a bruised but still extant faith. When Lancaster brings up how the ideals of the Revolution went bad in the hands of politicians, Palance chides him for "wanting perfection or nothing."

> **Palance:** La Revolucion is like a great love affair. In the beginning, she is a goddess. A holy cause. But every love affair has a terrible enemy.
>
> **Lancaster:** Time.
>
> **Palance:** We see her as she is. La Revolucion is not a goddess but a whore. She was never pure, never saintly, never perfect. We run away, find another lover, another cause. Quick, sordid affairs. Lust, but no love. Passion, but no compassion. Without love, without a cause, we are ... *nothing!* We stay because we believe. We leave because we are disillusioned. We come back because we are lost. We die because we are committed.

Another example of how the thriller has changed since their 1960s/1970s creative heyday can be found by comparing generally similar films made a generation apart: 1974's *Juggernaut*, with that archetype of the contemporary thriller, 1994's *Speed*.

In *Juggernaut*, an extortionist has placed several bombs on a transatlantic ocean liner threatening to sink the vessel if his monetary demand is not meant. The passengers are trapped on the ship; the bombs will go off before they can reach another port or another ship reaches them, and the sea is too rough to send them off in lifeboats. A bomb disposal team led by Richard Harris risks a dangerous airdrop, and is brought aboard in an attempt to disarm the bombs while police back in England try to run down the extortionist.

In *Speed*, a member of the Los Angeles Police Department's bomb squad (Keanu Reeves) finds himself trapped on a bus with its passengers and a bomb set to go off if the bus's speed drops below 50 mph. While

Reeves, with Sandra Bullock at the wheel, navigate the traffic shoals of the L.A. freeway system, police try to track down the extortionist.

Juggernaut is a "mental cat-and-mouse game" between chief bomb disposal expert Harris and the—for most of the movie—anonymous bomber. It is, literally, a mental duel to the death pitting Harris' dexterity and skill against the imagination of the bomb designer. The bomber—"Juggernaut"—actually becomes a character long before we meet him, sketched in by the "style" of his bomb design: a combination of false leads, booby traps, and practical jokes. Harris is no steely-eyed hero. At first brash and confident, then shaken when one device detonates killing a friend on his team, then finally recomposing himself for a final do-or-die assault on the bomb.

But where *Juggernaut* opts for the "internal" intensity of its mind-on-mind challenge, *Speed* is pure viscera: a parade of increasingly incredulous stunts built around keeping the bus up to speed (perhaps the most ludicrous being getting the aged GM behemoth going fast enough to leap a missing bridge span). The steely one-note Reeves never does disarm the bomb, or make much of an attempt at it. Instead, the bus is driven to the airport where the passengers are picked off the vehicle, and the abandoned bus rolls on to smash into a jumbo jet (despite the fact the airport was specifically selected to give the bus running room) for the purpose of providing the movie with a climax as spectacular as it is gratuitous.

Speed, says Goldman, has all the major trademarks of the modern thriller; what he calls "shorthand characterization," and the false suspense element.

The former, he says, is usually represented by giving the hero a "chip on his shoulder"; some previous error or mistaken judgment against him. Goldman says this creates an automatic tie with a culture of victimization. "Today, everybody's a victim. It's the Dr. Phil-ization of society." As a dramatic device, however, it diminishes the 1970s' notion of a larger canvas. "Real life isn't that easy. Movies shouldn't be that easy, either. Harry Callahan (in *Dirty Harry*) and Popeye Doyle (in *The French Connection*) weren't trying to work out some personal problem. They were just trying to do what they thought was right." The cheap shortcut characterizations of today make the movie thriller world a place of small concerns.

This false suspense element Goldman illustrates by measuring the 1971 screen adaptation of Michael Crichton's best-selling sci fi novel *The Andromeda Strain* against the vaguely similar 1995 *Outbreak*.

Crichton's novel was styled as a *faux* report of a biological disaster. An Air Force satellite has brought back an incredibly lethal microorganism which wipes out a small town in the American southwest. The satellite is transported to a secret government lab where a team of scientists attempt to identify, analyze, and contain the "bug." Displaying many of the same hallmarks marking Crichton's television co-creation, *E.R.*, both his novel and Nelson Gidding's screen adaptation respect the intellectual integrity of the story and its characters, most of whom are scientists, doctors, and technicians (contrary to that example William Price Fox pointed out to my screenwriting class in *Collision Course: Truman vs. MacArthur*). The assumption behind the storytelling is that while an audience may not understand everything they see and hear regarding highly arcane bits of microbiology and theorizing about alien biology, they will grasp enough to mentally put the larger picture together. Thus, like the doctors of *E.R* (or other medicine-immersed dramas like the series *House*), *Andromeda*'s scientists and technicians speak to each other in the jargon and terminology of real scientists and technicians, giving the story an air of authenticity. The enemy in *Andromeda* is something invisible to the naked eye; the only weapons our heroes have at their disposal are their intelligence and scientific expertise.

Outbreak's screenplay by Laurence Dworet and Robert Roy Pool, on the other hand, is a veritable catalog of the dramatic devices so many contemporary thrillers use to mug an audience rather than intrigue it.

In contrast to the four, level-headed science/medical professionals in *Andromeda* motivated by the big-enough motive of saving humanity from an alien infection, and of whose personal life we learn almost nothing, Dustin Hoffman is the colorful day-saver in *Outbreak*. In true "shorthand characterization" fashion, Hoffman's Army doctor is one of those maverick-do-it-his-own-way types unafraid to mouth off to his superiors (yet somehow managing to keep his rank and status) who labors under the shadow of a previous misstep. Part of the "false suspense" of the latter film is to personalize the threat of the Ebola variant confronting Hoffman by first having one of his good friends die of the disease, and then having his ex-wife (typical movie couple: he impetuous and boyish in his enthusiasms, she adult and restrained, and they still love each other despite their inability to live together under the same roof) becomes infected, pushing the movie into race-against-time mode.

Feeling the audience needs a villain and a microbe doesn't quite qualify, *Outbreak* also features a sneering Donald Sutherland as a military officer who orders the incineration of an infected town under the guise of containing the outbreak but actually to conceal some military bio-weapon hanky-panky.

While the *Andromeda* science team use their intellect to puzzle out their bug, there's very little science or medicine in *Outbreak*. Hoffman leaps from a hovering helicopter to a ship at sea, commandeers a television studio at gunpoint, survives an aerial helicopter chase and dogfight, and finally faces off with the plane en route to bomb the infected town. "Who knew you could cure a disease with a helicopter chase?" says Goldman.

Goldman renders a generalized verdict on the modern studio blockbuster: "Very few of these movies are for adults." Adult thrillers still do get made, occasionally, and Goldman points to *Insomnia* and *L.A. Confidential* as major studio efforts to make movies that are "more emotional and with more moral grays in them than most films. *L.A. Confidential* is a movie where you have to pay attention; you can't miss a moment."

While one can bemoan the rarity of such grown-up movie treats, the inhibitions the major studios have against making too many of them are understandable. There is a cost factor to contend with. While these films may not be as expensive as the typical CGI/pyrotechnic-riddled action opus, any kind of movie at the major studio level is an expensive proposition. That fiscal commitment has to be weighed against the limiting factors of the adult audience.

Even a wonderfully reviewed adult-oriented film like *Insomnia* topped out its box office at a little under $70 million. Oscar-nominated *L.A. Confidential* grossed even less, yet with its production and marketing costs "probably wound up costing Warner about $100 million." *Road to Perdition* (2002), says Goldman, only made it over the $100 million mark on the marquee muscle of Tom Hanks in the starring role, and even then "the last few weeks it took to go over ($100 million) were a slow crawl."

It's not a recent problem, Goldman says, citing the performance of 1993's *Falling Down,* featuring Michael Douglas as a defense contractor employee who loses his job and goes on a rampage. "It was a success but it topped off early," reports Goldman. "Only grown-ups could appreciate the sense of dislocation and the post–Cold War context of the story that puts the main character out of his job."

There are good new thrillers, Goldman maintains, movies that "respect the past but have an eye on the future. They don't just add bells and whistles to do it, but look to use them appropriately to create more texture." The cost vs. box office potential paradigm for indies makes efforts like *The Usual Suspects* a reasonable exercise. The cost/return formulas for the majors, however, nudges them toward targeting a young audience which, in turn, puts the big studios on a quest for sensational hooks, novelties, derivatives, and repeatable franchises. "Today," Goldman judges, "it's not about the next new thing; it's about the next *any* thing."

This makes so many of today's big budget adventures, in Goldman's words, "disposable." The pictures don't offer a vision. The writers are not "real writers," but crafting a framework for stunts and special effects; a framework which may get re-written by a dozen other writers if not more. Regarding some of the acclaimed original programming which appeared on HBO's channels, Goldman says of *The Sopranos* and *Six Feet Under*, "They were as strong as they were because we let the show-runners stay with their visions. We didn't keep making them tweak shows for the market."

Goldman considers what he's been saying and sighs. He realizes that the essential component of the classic thrillers of four decades ago—and that's so rare these days—is a pretentious-sounding thing for such commercial offerings. Nonetheless he concludes, "What's missing is art."

Myth #6:
Dr. Phil-izing Characters

This memory comes to me from, I believe, the first season of *Saturday Night Live*, back in 1975. John Belushi was doing a skit with guest host Robert Klein. They played a pair of bug exterminators poking around a dingy basement, with Belushi—doing his Rod Steiger (look him up, kids)—as the wise old veteran, and Klein the rookie. At one point, Klein asks Belushi about his obsessive hatred of bugs. "I had a brother," Belushi-as-Steiger replies, "his name was Billy..." And the audience started laughing.

It wasn't that the line was funny. Like a lot of parodies, the humor was in recognizing the cliché that was being spoofed (see *Airplane, Scary Movie*, etc.). The cliché in question was that point in so many movies in which a character gets a bit dreamy-eyed as they remember some person and/or event that turns out to be the motivating key to their character.

Written well and integrated smoothly into the story, these histories become critical gears in the machinery of a plot. They can add a shade to a character we haven't seen (*In Cold Blood,* 1967), make near-psychotic obsessions painfully understandable (*Moby Dick,* 1956), make paralyzed inaction pitiable (*Ordinary People,* 1980). Want to see some other great examples? Humphrey Bogart's apathetic, war-scarred vet in *Key Largo* (1948); Norman Bates' (Anthony Perkins) mother-driven serial killer in the aptly titled *Psycho* (1960); William Peterson's FBI profiler in *Manhunter* (1986), psychologically traumatized from getting inside serial killer Hannibal Lektor's head, and then unable to get out of it; shark hunter Quint's (Robert Shaw) tale of surviving marauding sharks after his cruiser was sunk in World War II in *Jaws*; misanthropic astronaut Taylor's (Charlton Heston) take on the worthlessness of life on Earth as a justification for the one-way space trip that lands him on the *Planet of the Apes*; P.L. Travers (Emma Thompson) creating the character of Mary Poppins to save a fictionalized version of the whimsical (if self-destructive) father she couldn't save in real life in *Saving Mr. Banks* (2013). And so on.

But when this kind of thing *isn't* done well, the device becomes a cheap, kick-in-the-crotch bid to gain immediate sympathy for a character, usually one heading for a pretty dismal end. It's the screenwriter's attempt to do in one scene what he/she failed to do over the other 115 minutes of storytelling: make us feel for a character.

In a war movie, that character is the guy who has a little speech about all the great things he's going to do after the war when he gets home—the girl he's going to marry, the kids he's going to have, the family he'll be returning to, etc. When you hear that speech, cross that guy's name off the company roster because he's as good as dead. In a cop movie, he's the cop with a nice little bit about what he's going to do when he retires. Dead. The gunfighter who talks about hanging up his guns, the gangster who talks about going straight, the race car driver who says this is his last season: dead, dead, dead. Those little soliloquies of theirs are supposed to be enough to get you to feel bad about the passing of a character you otherwise couldn't have cared less about (and since these set pieces are usually so heavy handedly manipulative and provide the movie's sole emotional investment in those characters, you probably *still* couldn't care less when their inevitable demise comes to pass).

Just as painfully manipulative is the reverie and/or flashback that has to do with some traumatic event—a screw-up, a missed opportunity (think *Cliffhanger* [1993], *Outbreak* [1995])—which continues to haunt the protagonist. Dogged by guilt, a sense of incompletion, of failed duty, of unfair blame (or some combination of same), he/she now has a chance to (yet another beaten-to-death cliché) "make things right." And when they do make things right (and they *always* do), we're supposed to feel flush with satisfaction that the karmic scales have now been, at long last, balanced, and/or penance and atonement made.

Does the scenario sound familiar? Does it sound *painfully* familiar?

Unlike the other myths we've dealt with in this series, this is a long-standing penchant in movie storytelling (which is what made it ripe for lampooning as far back as that 1975 installment of *Saturday Night Live*). As long as there have been movies, there have been bad movies, and this is something a lot of bad movies do. It's the kind of thing that makes bad movies bad.

But it's part of this series of screenwriting myths because over the same period in which the other myths we've looked at have bloomed— since the 1980s—this kind of gimmick has somehow been elevated from a lazy cheat to a dramatic necessity. It's part of a larger trend of "constructing" a character rather than conceiving one.

Ok, this is going to get a little semantical here, but bear with me. When I say "construct," I mean putting together an assemblage of tics and traits not because they're believable or even remotely credible, but because someone—the writer, the star, the director, the producer, the marketing chief, the audience research staff, maybe all of them—thinks they're cool. Characters do and feel things not because any normal human being would do and feel them, but because someone (the writer, star, etc.) wants them to.

I know I've picked on this movie quite a bit in the past, but let me kick it around some more: *Lethal Weapon* (1987, script by Shane Black) and its lead character, Mel Gibson's Los Angeles police detective Riggs.

Riggs is a veteran cop who has unraveled since the death of his wife. He lives like a frat boy with his dog, swilling beer and wandering naked around his beachside trailer, occasionally so despairing he considers putting a specially prepared bullet through his head. A departmental psychiatrist has tagged him as probably suicidal, his outrageous conduct during his introductory scene—a drug bust—testifies that he is manifestly unreliable (as well as a bit nuts) and a danger as much to himself as others. And yet he's still on the job, armed and on the street (more incredible; they team this walking jug of nitroglycerin with a cop—Danny Glover—on the eve of retirement).

So no one thinks I'm the Grinch here, I'm the first one to say this flick is a fun watch, although mostly (in my view) because of a wonderful Odd Couple kind of chemistry between Gibson and Glover.

But it's still a dumb movie. Shane Black was in his mid–20s when he wrote it, and that's how the movie plays; like a young guy's macho fantasy, almost a pre-videogame movie version of *Grand Theft Auto*. Now, in contrast, let's compare it to some other Maverick Cop movies carrying a bit more substance.

Clint Eastwood's Harry Callahan in *Dirty Harry* (1971) is also a widower, lonely, has nothing but his job; not unlike Riggs. And writers Harry Julian Fink, R.M. Fink, and Dean Reisner also indulge a bit in cop fantasy themselves: Callahan carries a monstrous .44 magnum pistol, and, like Riggs, he's—of course—a dead shot. But, for the most part, the movie keeps itself more-or-less life-sized, and perhaps the most affecting example of this is how Callahan deals with his wife's death. In a conversation with his wounded partner's wife, the woman asks how Callahan's wife handles the stress of being married to a cop.

"She never did, really," and then he admits his wife is dead, killed in a car crash when another driver crossed the center line. "There was no reason for it, really."

No histrionics, no *Sturm und Drang*, no breast beating, no tortured revelation. A simple, colorless statement made all the more melancholy by its matter-of-factness. Like Riggs, the job is all Callahan has, but instead of babbling to his partner that the only thing keeping him from blowing his brains out is his job (*Lethal Weapon*), when Callahan is asked by the woman why he stays with the job, he calmly says, "I don't know. I really don't."

We get it, we connect the dots. Callahan is in the same drifting boat as Riggs. The differences are A) he's a grown-up about it, and B) he doesn't feel compelled to have to spell it out.

Dirty Harry director Don Siegel was a master of that kind of storytelling minimalism and had a fervent belief in the tactic's ability to engage the audience in a way spoon-feeding them emotional content didn't. He offers an even better example of this in *Escape from Alcatraz* (1979, with Richard Tuggle adapting J. Bruce Campbell's book), working with Eastwood again. According to Siegel's memoir *A Siegel Film*, when *Alcatraz* was placed at Paramount, he was called in for a script meeting at which he was handed four pages of notes from the studio's "creative group," most of which called for adding material to the screenplay that would tell the audience "all about Morris's (Eastwood) criminal history, what kind of person he was and, especially, why he had chosen a life of crime."

Siegel's response was "the more you describe, analyze and *explain* a character, the less real he becomes. The trick is to *suggest*, to try to leave holes, problems, questions that the viewer's imagination will fill in a much more satisfying way than we could ever do" (Siegel, 439–440).

Want to see that at work in the movie? There's a scene where Eastwood is sitting in the exercise yard next to another con who mentions that it's his birthday. When he asks Eastwood about his own birthday, Eastwood replies that he doesn't know when it is.

"What kind of childhood did you have?" the con asks.

"Short."

Siegel's right; that tells us *everything*. Further details and specifics would not only give it *less* weight, but would do something even worse; kill its poetry.

Let's step up to one of the all-time classic cop movies, *The French Connection* (1971), with Ernest Tidyman adapting Robin Moore's account of the true life case. The movie isn't quite a true story, but a dramatization of the biggest heroin bust in U.S. law enforcement history, and as such, does have its undeniably Hollywoody elements (some shootings and a car chase that were definitely not part of the real case). For all that, however, *Connection* is considered one of the most realistic cop films ever made. And what do we know about the main character of the movie: narcotics detective Popeye Doyle (Gene Hackman)?

Not a damned thing.

There's nothing to explain his rough-and-tumble tactics that would give any ACLU lawyer a heart attack, nor his obsession with bringing down Frog 1 (Fernando Rey), the prime mover in a big-dollar drug smuggling operation. There is no break in the action where someone asks Hackman why he's so nuts about chasing down dope dealers, and he stares dreamily off into the distance and says, in a faraway voice, "I had a brother. His name was Billy..."

He doesn't say anything like that because the movie doesn't need it. Most movies don't. Even the ones that have it.

I had the opportunity some years ago to interview Sonny Grosso, one of the real life French Connection cops—in the movie, Roy Scheider's character is based on Grosso—and who would go on to become a television and film producer when he left the NYPD. I asked him if he thought *The French Connection* could be made today. "Maybe," he said, "But Popeye'd [the Hackman character] have to be way better looking. And they'd give him a girlfriend" (Mesce, "A Conversation...," 49).

This kind of opacity was acceptable at the time, but today, it's off the table. Production execs, either out of distrust of the audience, or having been to too many screenwriting seminars, have plugged into what Andy Goldman labels "shorthand characterization."

Now, major characters *have* to make a near-immediate impression, *have* to have an arc with regularly spaced "reveals" leading up to that I-had-a-brother-his-name-was-Billy moment. I remember a screenwriter telling about meeting with a producer for a story meeting, and when he got to the part midway through the screenplay when one of the characters dies, the producer mused, "But what did he *learn?*"

* * *

In my files I have a 2002 entry from Wiley Miller's comic strip *Non Sequitur* entitled, "The Magic of Hollywood." Seven look-alike movie execs are sitting around a conference table while the honcho at the head of the table says, "A motion has been put forth that we should seek to create rather than imitate. All in favor of killing this silly notion, nod in mindless agreement...."

I'll give studio execs the benefit of the doubt and say it didn't happen this way (probably). But the growing fealty to the kind of rules, templates, systems, philosophies, etc., that have been breeding like flies over the last 30–35 years has had the same net effect. In his 1996 *Entertainment Weekly* piece, "Who Killed the Hollywood Screenplay?" Benjamin Svetkey moaned: "Story lines veer in nonsensical directions, dialogue is dim or dopey, characters have the heft of balsa wood.... The rock-bed basics of dramatic writing ... seem to have been forgotten or abandoned by today's commercial filmmakers" (34).

And those traits have since had 20 years to become even further embedded in the movie-making process. All that dopiness might be palatable—well, understandable—if it paid off at the box office. After all, superficially the mindset makes a sad sort of sense; if you want a movie to be a hit, write it like other hits.

Except that's not how things work.

In 2015, over 700 films were released theatrically in the United States. Yeah, that's a pretty huge number, but remember; that includes *everything*—foreign films, artsy-fartsy stuff that maybe played in a handful of art house theaters in two or three cities, documentaries run on a single screen so they'd qualify for awards consideration. Total box office for 2015: $11.1 billion dollars, up 4 percent from 2014, in large measure because of one movie—*Star Wars: The Force Awakens* (which, by year's end, had pulled in $899 million domestic).

But now let's break out some numbers. The lowest-earning movie to crack the $100 million line was *Creed*, at $108.7 million: #29 in box office for the year. Those 29 top-earning titles alone accounted for over *half* of the year's total box office: $6.8 billion. Once you get past #29, box office tallies begin to drop off precipitously. Six hundred and ten releases earned less than $30 million; 565 earned less than $10 million. And while a lot of those low-ranked flicks were small-budgeted art house indies, a few major studio bombs are floating around down there as well, like the Johnny Depp disaster *Mortdecai* (a little over $7 million in box office against a budget of $60 million).

Still, even if most major studio releases are in, say, the top 100 earners or so, here's some other numbers to keep in mind. According to a 2011 AP story by Ryan Nakashima, the average budget for a studio film at the time was $78 million, excluding marketing costs which, on average, easily push costs north of $100 million (although there's no updated stats I can find, trust me: those numbers haven't gone down since then). The rule of thumb in Hollywood accounting is that to reach break-even, a movie typically needs to earn two to three times its budget.

In other words, despite all the energy, money, rewrites and script doctoring to make sure movies closely clone successful predecessors, most studio movies flop at the box office. DVD sales are collapsing, downloads and streaming don't generate the kinds of revenue that can compensate, and if it weren't for some expanding foreign markets (like China), red ink would be spilling down studio office hallways like the blood from the elevators at the Overlook Hotel in Stanley Kubrick's *The Shining*.

So if the numbers say this kind of thinking doesn't work, why doesn't the system change?

Fear.

Remember William Goldman's proclamation in *Adventures in the Screen Trade* that, "NOBODY KNOWS ANYTHING"? In the years since Goldman's book, along has come McKee and Syd Field and a host of other how-to-write-a-perfect-script gurus, and Hollywood has gulped that Kool-Aid down like a parched man crawling across the Kalahari Desert.

They believe this stuff because they *want* to believe it, they *need* to believe it, because—as Goldman also wrote—"Studio executives ... share one thing in common with baseball managers: They wake up every morning of the world with the knowledge that sooner or later they're going to get fired (39)." The formulas and templates and all that stuff are almost a religious faith; a belief that success *can* be bottled, and consequently stave off that inevitable day when a Human Resource specialist sets some storage boxes on their desk and asks them to have their stuff cleared out by 5 o'clock.

Yeah, the stuff they pump out has a bland sameness to it as a consequence ... and that's the point. And it's not a new point, either. Five-time Emmy-winning producer/writer/director Bill Persky once explained to me how all the Hollywood bullshit that kills creativity and innovation exists as much to protect the powers-that-be not so much *against* failure, but for when it inevitably comes:

> you can say, "Well, the marketing guys said it would do well," and you can say the research showed it was a good bet, and you can point to all these other people who had a hand in it—"We had the right cast" and so on—then you hope it looks like it's not so much your fault if it bombs [Mesce, *Overkill...*, 207].

In a way, I hope that cynicism is the case, because truly believing these just-follow-the-directions methodologies can produce creatively solid (or even commercially viable) work is ... well, it's just stupid.

I'm not saying that out of a writer's vanity. It's common sense. I know I've tossed around words like "poetry" and (I can see studio execs holding up crosses and throwing holy water at me over this one) "art," but even at its most mercenary, crassly commercial level, movie-making still involves a measure of creativity even if it's only as functional as how to get a story from point A to point B. The writer has to come up with *something* to do that. But saying there's a way to write a movie as good as *The Revenant* or *The Big Short* or *Room* (2015) or *The Martian* (2015) by simply cloning elements from them, or by following a book about what all those movies have in common, is comparing writing a movie to assembling a piece of Ikea furniture.

Forget about art; does that even make any *sense?* If you think so, hang around Studio Row; I'm sure somebody'll be losing their job any day now, and you can step right into their place.

The Screenwriter: Nicholas Pileggi

(After a 30-year career as a journalist, particularly noted for his reporting on organized crime, Pileggi notched his first screenwriting credit collaborating with Martin Scorsese on the adaptation of his 1986 book Wiseguy *which became the film* Goodfellas *[1990]. His many subsequent film and TV credits include—working with Scorsese again—*Casino *[1995], and* City Hall *[1996].)*

I'm the last person to write about screenwriting. *Goodfellas* was my first script and I wrote it with Martin Scorsese. Both our names are on it. You want to know how to write a good script? Write it with Marty Scorsese.

The Button

Sometime in the late 1990s, Travis Rink called to tell me he was dealing with an outfit called World International Television—a production cooperative made up of outfits in a number of countries—interested in one of the screenplays we'd worked on together, a crime story called *Pinball*. WIN was asking for changes ... but not quite asking for them.

It's an old producer's stratagem; "I like it, but it's not quite right for us. But you know, if the penguin was a whale, well, we might give that a second look." The idea here is not to formally option the material, or to make an upfront request for specific changes which would imply a commitment, but still get the material into a shape where the producer will finally put money on the table. If the writer is hungry enough, he/she will make the changes—in effect, a free rewrite or rewrites—in the hopes the producer will, in the end, say, "Yes, I'll take it."

WIN had run Travis through two or three passes this way. Just as frustrating as working for nothing was what Travis saw happening to the material. In trying to satisfy WIN's vague "suggestions," each pass sanded down more and more the distinctive edges which had, paradoxically, been what had attracted WIN to the piece to begin with (or so they said).

That's another old industry paradigm: being drawn to material which feels fresh, unique, has its own voice, and then panicking that it's *too* unique and having the writer hammer it into something generic; something *safe*.

WIN was asking/not asking for Travis to make another pass and he wanted to talk to me about what to do. The options sucked:

1) Keep working with WIN, and, if he could make them happy, it could mean a paycheck, but it would also mean a forgettable piece that wouldn't do us any good professionally;

2) Walk away hoping that one day we'd find a better home for *Pinball* and see it made in a way which might make people in the industry say, "Hm, that's an interesting little flick; I wonder who these Rink and Mesce guys are?"

Travis decided to walk away and I seconded the move. We never did find a home for *Pinball,* and sometimes, when money's tight, I do wonder if we shouldn't have just grabbed the paycheck and lived with having a crappy movie on our respective resumes (or, in my case, *another* crappy movie).

Just a few years later, I found myself in a similar circumstance with my sci fi piece, *Lab 7.* Since the days when George Barnes had optioned it, I'd gone back to the piece more than once to punch it up. Among the alterations I'd made, I'd set it back in the desert, and I changed the lead character—the commander of the lab's security detail—to a woman. After Sarah Connor in *The Terminator* movies and Ripley in the *Alien* flicks, I thought the change might make it more marketable.

The changes must've worked because the screenplay won in a writing competition connected to an agency. I don't know if the agency was new or just the guys I was dealing with, but in a conference call with three of them it was obvious they were all young and eager ... and filled with "helpful" suggestions.

They wanted to represent the script, but only if I did a rewrite. As they worked their way through their suggestions, it was a replay of Travis's experience with WIN. *Lab 7* was hardly a groundbreaker, and a sci fi buff with a sharp sensibility could read it and tell what monster movies I'd watched as a kid. Still, I thought I'd given it enough style to where it felt less like a rehash and maybe more like a fun revisiting.

Evidently, that was too novel an approach (flashback a few years to Ron Graham telling me I'd written *Lab 7* too smart). Like WIN, this agency trio wanted me to tamp down some elements and add others so *Lab 7* would look like a dozen other movies. The capper was when one of them said, "And you need to write a scene where the woman is face to face with the monster. I mean, it's right up in her face!"

"Wait a minute. That's from *Alien!*"

"Yeah!"

"It didn't make it into the final cut, but it was in all the trailers!"

"Yeah!"

"It was even on the posters!"

"Yeah!"

"Everybody's gonna know where we got it!"

Which didn't seem to bother him.

I sometimes refer to "stealing" from movies I've seen, but when I say that, I don't mean *steal* steal. I look at the narrative architecture of *Winchester '73* and I say, "Oh, yeah, I can use that in *Carjack!*" *Road Ends* has a vaguely similar build to *High Noon* (1952), the female lead in *Lab 7* plugged into a then recent trend in strong women characters anchoring action movies. Familiar ... but different. I look for useful tools in other movies, but I still want to give my pieces something that's distinctly *me*. This is about more than creative vanity or not wanting to get sued. This is practical strategy. If I turn out material that's only schlocky retreads of better pictures, and is about as distinctive as one Q-Tip from another, then where's the value in hiring me over some other hack?

I again pointed out to this guy—and putting aside how awkward it would be to twist the plot around to accomplish what he wanted—that everybody would see this as direct *steal* stealing from *Alien.*

"I know," he said, "but I *love* that image!"

I walked away.

*   *   *

In a WGA interview widely quoted in the screenwriting blogosphere, Billy Ray, whose credits include *The Hunger Games* (2012) and his Oscar-nominated screenplay for *Captain Phillips* (2013), described the screenwriter's job thusly: "95 percent of what we do is problem-solving. It's really not waiting for a moment of artistic inspiration.... It's just grinding" (Rubin).

William Goldman, even at the top of his game when he was writing *Adventures in the Screen Trade,* described screenwriting as "shitwork"— "work that when it is well done is unnoticed." Screenwriting, he said, was, in terms of creative accomplishment, "a rather soulless endeavor" (78).

The only people who think screenwriting has any glamour to it at all are people who've never written professionally for the screen. Read movie reviews: actors get mentioned, directors get mentioned, rarely does anyone mention the screenwriter. The only moment of glitz and attention for screenwriters is if they're among the fortunate few who pick up an award now and then and get to walk the red carpet and make a quickie speech on TV. Short of that, you're invisible. Worse, among the creative team on a movie, screenwriters are the most disposable (remember *The Flintstones'* army of writers?).

Look, when you write a screenplay, you're not writing a movie. You're writing a plan for a movie, a blueprint. For some actors and directors, it may be no more than a strong suggestion for a movie. You provide a platform for *other* creative people to exercise *their* creativity, creativity that's tangible, that the audience can see and hear: dazzling performances, beautiful camerawork, a stirring music score. Your screenplay isn't a movie until all of those people do their jobs, and when they do—even though it's built on the foundation you laid—your contribution becomes invisible.

I've sometimes tried to give my writing students an idea of the screenwriter's role by telling them to picture a long conference table. You've created a screenplay, a studio has picked it up, and now you're in a story conference. At one end of the table is the producer (or producers), the director, the star (or stars), one or two "creative executives" from the studio, and a representative of the studio's marketing department. At the other end of the table sits you, the writer. The only person at that table who doesn't have a say about what goes into that screenplay is the person who wrote it. You'll write what they want you to write or you'll get shown the door, because once they gave you money for your work—this piece you may have sweated over for months on your own—it's theirs to do with as they will. And they will. If you stay, you'll write to suit an actor (even a woefully miscast one), a producer's or director's whims, you'll write to fit locations that have no resemblance to what you wrote and may even be completely inappropriate, you'll write to fit a budget, you'll write in response to any number of demands of which only very few might have anything to do with making a better movie.

With all that in mind, the how-to-write-a-screenplay books and seminars make an awful lot of sense. If that's all screenwriting is—shitwork, problem-solving—then, yeah, why *can't* you assemble a screenplay the way you'd assemble a model airplane? By following a set of directions?

Still...

Even with all that being true, there's not only room for something more than mere assemblage, but, if you're going to be anything more than a disposable hack, it's required. It's a *necessity*.

Herman J. Mankiewicz and Orson Welles decided to tell *Citizen Kane* not by anchoring the movie on the central character, but through the eyes of the different people who knew him at different times in his life; it's a mosaic pushing the viewer to make judgments about Charles Foster Kane. Good guy? Bad guy? Some of both?

Daniel Mainwaring's screenplay for the 1956 *Invasion of the Body Snatchers* turned a humble little B sci fier into a classic about dehumanization (Johnson, 168).

William Goldman infused *Butch Cassidy and the Sundance Kid* with a sharp wit—what Goldman called "smart-assness"—which made a Western, the oldest established American film genre, something it had never been before: cool and hip (Goldman, *Adventures...*, 199).

That final image of *Planet of the Apes*—one of the all-time great visuals in American cinema—isn't in Pierre Boulle's source novel, but was dreamed up by Rod Serling, one of the two writers on the project (Sander, 204).

In adapting his 1984 play *Glengarry Glen Ross* (1992) for the screen, David Mamet created a scene not in the play; a brilliant prologue which primes the movie's dramatic pump with a "get-out-there-and-sell!" speech, possibly the best-remembered scene from the movie.

It's not until the end of Christopher McQuarrie's Oscar-winning screenplay for *The Usual Suspects* that we learn we've been watching an elegantly constructed pile of lies based on the most innocuous bits of detritus in a littered police detective's office.

The Oscar-winning Charles Randolph/Adam McKay screenplay for *The Big Short* does everything screenwriting common wisdom tells you not to do; it's an ensemble piece with no main character, several barely connected parallel plotlines, no particularly sympathetic characters, and the material is so arcane—how a number of exploitative investors took advantage of the financial crash of 2007—the movie has to periodically stop so the audience can be lectured on the elements leading up to the crash.

I'm inclined to agree with my friend Steve Szilagyi in that screenwriting isn't really writing; not in any literary sense. As he says, there's all that white space on the script page. An author has to do what a screenwriter can rely on a cast and crew to do. A particular film might attain the status of art, but a screenplay? Afraid not.

And, frankly, the opportunity to go beyond the norm, beyond the expected and safe is limited. If you're working on the umpteenth by-the-number superhero franchise installment, or pumping out weekly scripts for TV Land's latest bit of original sitcom generica, there's not much chance for you to shine. (An aside: I'm not pooh-poohing this kind of work. You get a paying gig, no matter what it is, God bless you because creative gratification doesn't pay the mortgage or your kid's college tuition; remember, I've got *The Versace Murder* on my c.v.)

But as the examples above show—and there are dozens, *hundreds* more over the history of American cinema—there is a place for, oh, call it inspiration, imagination, creative leaps. And that, my friends, requires something that can't be learned. It calls for talent.

Screenplays may be no more than a form of carpentry, but the difference between the forgettable and the memorable is the difference between the competent carpenter and the craftsman, that difference being the ability to use the same learnable skills as the carpenter in an unlearnable way.

*   *   *

There's another unlearnable element to good screenwriting, and it's even harder to come by than talent. Napoleon supposedly once said of one of his officers, "I know he's a good general, but is he lucky?"

Luck. The movie business's dirty little secret.

Said director Robert Aldrich, "if you must make a choice between luck and talent, you have to opt for luck. It's nice to have some of both, or a lot of both, but if you can't, luck is the answer. Nowhere else more so than in this business" (Silver, 16).

Look, you can write a brilliant and beautiful screenplay, but so what if you don't have the means to get it in front of people who can turn it into a movie, let alone get it in front of the *right* people who can turn it into a *good* movie?

Let's say you sell your brilliant and beautiful piece of material. Any number of things can kill that project at any stage: an attached actor with a bankable name pulls out, gets sick, gets hurt; the studio has a bad year and has to trim back their production slate; there's a management turnover at the studio and every piece of material associated with the previous management—including your script—gets shelved; everybody associated with the project thinks it's terrific, but then the studio's marketing department says, "It's a hard sell," and that's the project-killing veto.

Ok, let's say your brilliant and beautiful piece of material actually gets produced. There's still any number of steps along the road that can derail it: the lead actor was miscast; the director had absolutely no touch for the material; it was released the same weekend the new Marvel all-star superhero flick came out and nobody even knew your movie was out there; the reviewers didn't get it; the marketing for the movie brought the wrong crowd into theaters and they bad-mouthed it on their way out; good as the movie is, maybe its appeal was too limited, or the right audience never found it; the studio got cold feet and never released it. Whatever the reasons, your movie flopped.

And the odds are it will. Over 700 movies were released in 2015. Of them, 520 made less than $2 million. A number of larger earners also stiffed, but it's reasonable to assume that even the smallest-budgeted flicks with a gross under $2 million were duds. Some were bad, some were good, and the same could be said of the biggest hits of the year. You don't necessarily fail because the work was bad, or go home with a bag of money because it was good. Sometimes ... but not necessarily. It's not enough just to do good work.

Singer/actor Frank Sinatra—who, like Aldrich, also had his share of career ups and downs—paid tribute to the one-two punch any creative individual needs to survive, because whether you're a singer, composer, writer, sculptor, painter, or perhaps humblest of them all, a screenwriter, creative arenas are among the most competitive with more hungry wannabes than there are seats at the table. Said the man who often sat at the head of that table: "Luck is fine, and you have to have luck to get the opportunity. But after that, you've got to have talent and know how to use it" (Sullivan, *Sinatra...*, 49).

Luck and talent; talent and luck. You can't get them out of a book. Not even this one.

Bibliography

All Is Lost. LA Screenwriter (Dec. 13, 2013): http://la-screenwriter.com/2013/12/13/all-is-lost-script/.

Agel, Jerome, ed. *The Making of Kubrick's 2001.* New York: New American Library, 1970.

Bach, Steven. *Final Cut: Dreams and Disaster in the Making of* Heaven's Gate. New York: Plume, 1985.

Baldwin, Dave, Andrew Goldman, and Robert Conte. Interviews. Originally part of a single piece titled, "HBO's Three Wise Men on Why Movies Stink—Or Do They?" which appeared in the web magazine *Sand on Sight* on December 4, 2010.

Balio, Tino, ed. *The American Film Industry.* Madison: University of Wisconsin Press, 1976.

Bart, Peter. *The Gross: The Hits, The Flops—The Summer that Ate Hollywood.* NEW YORK: St. Martin's, 1999.

Batiuk, Tom. *Funky Winkerbean. The Star-Ledger* (April 17, 2016): J5.

Baxter, John. *Science Fiction in the Cinema.* 2nd ptg. New York: Warner, 1974.

The Bellboy. http://www.tcm.com/tcmdb/title/68415/The-Bellboy/.

Biskind, Peter. *Down and Dirty Pictures: Miramax, Sundance, and the Rise of Independent Film.* New York: Simon & Schuster, 2004.

_____. *Easy Riders, Raging Bulls: How the Sex-and-Drugs-and-Rock-'n'-Roll Generation Saved Hollywood.* New York: Touchstone, 1998.

Bloom, David. "Black List 2014 Gets Star Treatment in 10th Anniversary Announcement Monday." Deadline Presents AwardsLine (Dec. 14, 2014): http://deadline.com/2014/12/black-list-2014-announcement-schedule-1201324672/.

Blottner, Gene. *Columbia Pictures Movie Series, 1926–1955: The Harry Cohn Years.* Jefferson, NC: McFarland, 2012.

Borden, Mark. "1 Minute Read: Most Creative People 2010—#21. Josh Sapan, CEO Rainbow Media." http://www.fastcompany.com/3018735/most-creative-people-2010/21-josh-sapan, May 22, 2010.

Brady, John. *The Craft of the Screenwriter.* New York: Touchstone, 1981.

Breznican, Anthony. "Winner Take All." *Entertainment Weekly* (March 11, 2016): 26–32.

Brownlow, Kevin. *The Parade's Gone By...* Berkeley/Los Angeles: University of California Press, 1968.

Calamandrei, Camilla. "Prisoners in Paradise." http://www.prisonersinparadise.com/history.html.

Canby, Vincent. "Beatty's *Reds,* with Diane Keaton." *The New York Times* (Dec. 4, 1981): http://www.nytimes.com/movie/review?res=9406E4DC103BF937A35751C1A967948260&scp=1&sq=Reds%2520Vincent%2520Canby&st=cse.

Chute, David. "Scarface." *Film Comment* (February 1984): 66–70.

Collis, Clark. "The Nice Guys." *Entertainment Weekly* (April 22/29, 2016): 42–44.

Conte, Robert *see* Baldwin, Dave.

Couturie, Bill (d). *Boffo! Tinseltown's Bombs and Blockbusters.* HBO Films, 2006.

Cummins, Michael Warner. "Road Ends." Michaelvox.com (Jan. 31, 1998): http://www.michaelvox.com/film/r/r9701.html.

Dempsey, Michael. "The Return of *Jaws*." *American Film* (June 1978): 28+.

"Estes Kefauver (1903–1963)." *American Experience: Las Vegas—An Unconventional History.* http://www.pbs.org/wgbh/amex/lasvegas/peopleevents/p_kefauver.html (July 11, 2005): p. 9.

Everson, William K. *The Bad Guys: A Pictorial History of the Movie Villain.* New York: Citadel Press, 1964.

Fabrikant, Geraldine. "The Media Business; Golan Quits Cannon Group to Form His Own Company." *The New York Times* (March 1, 1989): http://www.nytimes.com/1989/03/01/business/the-media-business-golan-quits-cannon-group-to-form-his-own-company.html?scp=2&sq=Cannon%20Films&st=cse.

Field, Syd. *Screenplay: The Foundations of Screenwriting.* New York: Dell, 1982.

Fierman, Daniel. "*Harry Potter* and the Challenge of Sequels." *Entertainment Weekly* (Nov. 22, 2002): 24–31.

Fine, Marshall. *Bloody Sam: The Life and Films of Sam Peckinpah.* New York: Donald I. Fine, 1991.

Finler, Joel W. *The Hollywood Story.* New York: Crown, 1988.

_____. *The Movie Directors Story.* New York: Crown, 1985.

Goldman, Andrew *see* Baldwin, Dave.

Goldman, William. *Which Lie Did I Tell? More Adventures in the Screen Trade.* New York: Random, 2000.

_____. *Adventures in the Screen Trade: A Personal View of Hollywood Screenwriting.* New York: Warner, 1983.

Harlan, Jan (d). *Stanley Kubrick: A Life in Pictures.* Warner Bros.: 2001.

Harmetz, Aljean. "Arts & Leisure." *The New York Times* (Jan. 10, 1988): 1+.

Henry, Lawrence. "History *vs.* Hollywood: *A Beautiful Mind*." *The American Spectator* (July 31, 2002): http://spectator.org/52949_history-vs-hollywood-beautiful-mind/.

Higham, Charles, and Joel Greenberg. *The Celluloid Muse: Hollywood Directors Speak.* New York: Signet, 1972.

Humphries, Patrick. *The Films of Alfred Hitchcock.* London: Bison Books, 1986.

Huston, John. *An Open Book.* New York: Ballantine, 1980.

Irvine, Martha. "Connected 'round the Clock." Associated Press, rptd. in *The Star-Ledger* (Dec. 25, 2004): 24.

Johnson, William. Ed. *Focus On: The Science Fiction Film.* Englewood Cliffs, NJ: Prentice-Hall, 1972.

Kael, Pauline. "Raising Kane," *The New Yorker*, 1971, rptd. in *The Citizen Kane Book.* New York: Bantam ed., 1974: 2–124.

Kaufman, Amy. "James Cameron Promises Four More *Avatar* Movies." *The Los Angeles Times* (April 16, 2016), rptd. *The Star Ledger*: 13.

Keefer, Louis E. *Italian Prisoners of War in America 1942–1946.* New York: Praeger, 1992.

King, Susan. "Bill Persky, That Guy from *That Girl*." *Los Angeles Times* (January 1, 2013): http://articles.latimes.com/2013/jan/01/entertainment/la-et-st-bill-persky-20130102.

Knauer, Kelly, ed. *TIME: American Legends—Our Nation's Most Fascinating Heroes, Icons, and Leaders.* Special Edition. New York: Time Books, 2001.

Knelman, Martin. "John Kemeny, Forgotten Giant of Canadian Film, Dies at 87." *The Toronto Star* (Nov. 27, 2012): http://www.thestar.com/entertainment/movies/2012/11/27/john_kemeny_forgotten_giant_of_canadian_film_dies_at_87.html.

"Leonard, Sheldon." The Museum of Broadcasting. http://www.museum.tv/eotv/leonardshel.htm.

McDonnell, Ann. "...Happily Ever After." *American Film* (Jan.–Feb. 1987): 42+.

Mesce, Bill, Jr. "Appendix C: HBO Home Entertainment's Henry McGee." *Sound on Sight* (Oct. 25, 2010): Rptd. *Inside the Rise of HBO: A Personal History of the Company That Transformed Television.* Jefferson, NC: McFarland, 2015.

_____. *Artists on the Art of Survival: Observations on Frustration, Perspiration, and Inspiration for the Young Artist.* Lanham, MD: Hamilton, 2004.

_____. "Bubbas, Chop-Sockies, Splatters and Sleaze—Oh My!" *Sound on Sight* (Jan. 23, 2011): Rptd. *Reel Change...*: 127–134: Albany, GA: BearManor, 2014.

_____. "A Conversation with Producer (and Legendar Copy) Sonny Grosso." *Sound on Sight* (Feb. 20, 2011). Rptd. *Reel Change...*: 44–49. Albany, GA: Bear-Manor, 2014.

_____. "Guerilla Filmmaking." *Sound on Sight* (April 10, 2011). Rptd. *Reel Change...*: 163–181: Albany, GA: Bear-Manor, 2014.

_____. "HBO's Three Wise Men On Why Movies Stink—Or Do They?" *Sound on Sight* (Dec. 4, 2010), rptd. at PopOptiq http://www.popoptiq.com/hbos-three-wise-men-on-why-movies-stink-or-do-they/.

_____. *Inside the Rise of HBO: A Personal History of the Company That Transformed Television.* Jefferson, NC: McFarland, 2015.

_____. "Michael Gough (1916–2011): Oh, Yeah! *That Guy!*" *Sound on Sight* (March 18, 2011). Rptd. *Idols, Icons, and Illusions: The Movies We Love—and Love to Hate—And the People Who Made Them:* 119–120.

_____. "Neo-Noiriste: John Dahl." *Sound on Sight* (Nov. 10, 2010). Rptd. *Reel Change: The Changing Nature of Hollywood, Hollywood Movies, and the People Who Go to See Them:* 182–189. Albany, GA: BearManor, 2014.

_____. *No Rule That Isn't a Dare: How Writers Connect with Readers.* Florham Park, NJ: Serving House Books, 2016.

_____. "On Corman's Front Line: Travis Rink." *Sound on Sight* (Sept. 22, 2010). Rptd. *Reel Change: The Changing Nature of Hollywood, Hollywood Movies, and the People Who Go to See Them:* 146–153. Albany, GA: BearManor, 2014.

_____. *Overkill: The Rise and Fall of Thriller Cinema.* Jefferson, NC: McFarland, 2007.

_____. "Pyromaniacs: Hollywood's Bad Boys." *Sound on Sight* (May 15, 2011). Rptd. *Reel Change...*: 119–126.

_____. "The World's First Screenwriter: Aristotle." *Sound on Sight* (Dec. 8, 2010). Rptd. *Reel Change...*: 351–353. Albany, GA: BearManor, 2014.

_____. "Writers on Writing: A Writer's Reboot." *The Write Place at the Write Time* (winter/spring 2014). Rptd. *No Rule That Isn't a Dare: How Writers Connect with Readers.* Florham Park, NJ: Serving House Books, 2016.

Meslow, Scott. "How Hollywood Chooses Scripts: The Insider List That Led to *Abduction.*" *The Atlantic* (Sept. 23, 2011). http://www.theatlantic.com/entertainment/archive/2011/09/how-hollywood-chooses-scripts-the-insider-list-that-led-to-abduction/245541/.

Michel, Lincoln. "The One Underlying Substance of All Story Structure Models: Bullshit." Electric Lit, http://electricliterature.com/the-one-underlying-substance-of-all-story-structure-models-bullshit/: Jan. 7, 2016.

Muller, Jurgen (ed.), Jorn Hetebrugge. *Movies of the 70s.* Koln, Germany: Taschen, 2003.

Nelson, John. "I Saw What I Said I Saw: Witnesses to Birds and Crimes." *The Missouri Review* (Winter 2015): 36–52.

Nordern, Eric. "*Playboy* Interview: Stanley Kubrick." *Playboy,* Sept. 1968. Rptd. in *The Making of Kubrick's* 2001. New York: New American Library, 1970: 328–354.

Palley, Marcia. "*Double* Trouble." *Film Comment* (October 1984): 12–17.

Peel, Eva. "Plotting 101." Hollywoodlitsales News, www.Hollywoodlitsales.com, Newsletter Vol. 4 #19: Oct. 7, 2003.

Persky, Bill. *My Life Is a Situation Comedy.* Weston, CT: Mandevilla Press, 2012.

Puzo, Mario. "How I Went To the Festival But Missed All the Movies." *The New York Times* (June 5, 1977): D1.

Ratledge, Ingela. "Little Big Screen." *What's Next: A Conde Nast Special Edition,* vol. 1, #1. 2016: 93.

Rubin, Ari (interviewer). "Episode 10: Billy Ray; and Richard Stayton the editor of *Written by.*" 3rd & Fairfax: The WGAW Podcasts (Oct. 22, 2015): http://www.wga.org/3rdandfairfax/.

Sander, Gordon E. *Serling: The Rise and Twilight of Television's Last Angry Man.* New York: Dutton, 1992.

Schager, Nick. "All Things Being Sequels." *What's Next: A Conde Nast Special Edition,* vol. 1, #1. 2016: 92–93.

Siegel, Don. *A Siegel Film.* Paperback ed. London: Faber and Faber, 1996.

Silke, Jim. "Dialogue on Film: Robert Aldrich." *American Film* (November 1978): 51–62. Rptd. in *Robert Aldrich Interviews*. Eds. Eugene L. Miller, Jr., Edwin T. Arnold. Jackson: University of Mississippi Press, 2004: 143–158.

Silver, Alain. "Mr. *Film Noir* Stays at the Table." *Film Comment* (Spring 1972): 14–23.

Smith, Gavin. "Dream Project." *Film Comment* (November 2002): 28–31.

Stafford, Jo. "Pathways to Making Meaning: Inroads to Interpretation of the Nature of Evil in *Heart of Darkness*." Yale National Initiative. http://teachers.yale.edu/curriculum/viewer/initiative_13.02.02_u.

Stelter, Brian. "Few TV Shows Survive a Ruthless Proving Ground." *The New York Times* (May 13, 2012): http://www.nytimes.com/2012/05/14/business/media/few-tv-shows-survive-a-ruthless-proving-ground.html?_r=0.

Stern, Marlow. "The Making of *Boyhood*: Richard Linklater's 12-Year Journey to Create an American Masterpiece." *The Daily Beast* (July 10, 2014): http://www.thedailybeast.com/articles/2014/07/10/the-making-of-boyhood-richard-linklater-s-12-year-journey-to-create-an-american-masterpiece.html.

Stock, Kyle. "Hollywood Is a Cartoon-Making Machine, But Will All Make Money?" *Bloomberg* rptd. in *The Star-Ledger* (March 17, 2016): 21.

Sullivan, Kevin P. "The Next *Dazed and Confused*." *Entertainment Weekly* (April 1/8, 2016): 90–91.

Sullivan, Robert. *Sinatra at 100*. New York: LIFE Books, 2015.

Svetkey, Benjamin, et al. "Who Killed the Hollywood Screenplay?" *Entertainment Weekly* (Oct. 4, 1996): 32+.

Terrill, Marshall. *Steve McQueen: Portrait of an American Rebel*. New York: Donald I. Fine, 1993.

Thomson, David. "The Decade When Movies Mattered." *Movieline* (Aug. 1993): 43+.

Weber, Bruce. "Elliott Kastner, Who Produced Literary Films, Dies at 80." *The New York Times* (July 2, 2010): http://www.nytimes.com/2010/07/02/movies/02kastner.html.

"Wells, H.G." *SFE: The Encyclopedia of Science Fiction*. http://www.sf-encyclopedia.com/entry/wells_h_g (Feb. 13, 2016).

Whitty, Stephen. "Return of the Man-Child." *The Star-Ledger* (March 22, 2016): 23.

Index